PSALMS 101–150

Brazos Theological Commentary on the Bible

Series Editors

R. R. Reno, General Editor
First Things
New York, New York

Robert W. Jenson (1930–2017)
Center of Theological Inquiry
Princeton, New Jersey

Robert Louis Wilken
University of Virginia
Charlottesville, Virginia

Ephraim Radner
Wycliffe College
Toronto, Ontario

Michael Root
Catholic University of America
Washington, DC

George Sumner
Episcopal Diocese of Dallas
Dallas, Texas

PSALMS 101–150

JASON BYASSEE

BrazosPress

a division of Baker Publishing Group
Grand Rapids, Michigan

Published by Brazos Press
a division of Baker Publishing Group
PO Box 6287, Grand Rapids, MI 49516-6287
www.brazospress.com

Printed in the United States of America

Library of Congress Cataloging-in-Publication Data
Names: Byassee, Jason, author.
Title: Psalms 101–150 / Jason Byassee.
Description: Grand Rapids : Brazos Press, 2018. | Series: Brazos theological commentary on the Bible | Includes bibliographical references and index.
Identifiers: LCCN 2017055341 | ISBN 9781587433528 (cloth : alk. paper)
Subjects: LCSH: Bible. Psalms, CI-CL—Commentaries.
Classification: LCC BS1430.53 .B93 2018 | DDC 223/.207—dc23
LC record available at https://lccn.loc.gov/2017055341

18   19   20   21   22   23   24   7   6   5   4   3   2   1

For James Howell

preacher, mentor, friend

CONTENTS

SERIES PREFACE

Near the beginning of his treatise against gnostic interpretations of the Bible, *Against Heresies*, Irenaeus observes that scripture is like a great mosaic depicting a handsome king. It is as if we were owners of a villa in Gaul who had ordered a mosaic from Rome. It arrives, and the beautifully colored tiles need to be taken out of their packaging and put into proper order according to the plan of the artist. The difficulty, of course, is that scripture provides us with the individual pieces, but the order and sequence of various elements are not obvious. The Bible does not come with instructions that would allow interpreters to simply place verses, episodes, images, and parables in order as a worker might follow a schematic drawing in assembling the pieces to depict the handsome king. The mosaic must be puzzled out. This is precisely the work of scriptural interpretation.

Origen has his own image to express the difficulty of working out the proper approach to reading the Bible. When preparing to offer a commentary on the Psalms he tells of a tradition handed down to him by his Hebrew teacher:

> The Hebrew said that the whole divinely inspired scripture may be likened, because of its obscurity, to many locked rooms in our house. By each room is placed a key, but not the one that corresponds to it, so that the keys are scattered about beside the rooms, none of them matching the room by which it is placed. It is a difficult task to find the keys and match them to the rooms that they can open. We therefore know the scriptures that are obscure only by taking the points of departure

for understanding them from another place because they have their interpretive principle scattered among them.[1]

As is the case for Irenaeus, scriptural interpretation is not purely local. The key in Genesis may best fit the door of Isaiah, which in turn opens up the meaning of Matthew. The mosaic must be put together with an eye toward the overall plan.

Irenaeus, Origen, and the great cloud of premodern biblical interpreters assumed that puzzling out the mosaic of scripture must be a communal project. The Bible is vast, heterogeneous, full of confusing passages and obscure words, and difficult to understand. Only a fool would imagine that he or she could work out solutions alone. The way forward must rely upon a tradition of reading that Irenaeus reports has been passed on as the rule or canon of truth that functions as a confession of faith. "Anyone," he says, "who keeps unchangeable in himself the rule of truth received through baptism will recognize the names and sayings and parables of the scriptures."[2] Modern scholars debate the content of the rule on which Irenaeus relies and commends, not the least because the terms and formulations Irenaeus himself uses shift and slide. Nonetheless, Irenaeus assumes that there is a body of apostolic doctrine sustained by a tradition of teaching in the church. This doctrine provides the clarifying principles that guide exegetical judgment toward a coherent overall reading of scripture as a unified witness. Doctrine, then, is the schematic drawing that will allow the reader to organize the vast heterogeneity of the words, images, and stories of the Bible into a readable, coherent whole. It is the rule that guides us toward the proper matching of keys to doors.

If self-consciousness about the role of history in shaping human consciousness makes modern historical-critical study critical, then what makes modern study of the Bible modern is the consensus that classical Christian doctrine distorts interpretive understanding. Benjamin Jowett, the influential nineteenth-century English classical scholar, is representative. In his programmatic essay "On the Interpretation of Scripture," he exhorts the biblical reader to disengage from doctrine and break its hold over the interpretive imagination. "The simple words of that book," writes Jowett of the modern reader, "he tries to preserve absolutely pure from the refinements or distinctions of later times." The modern interpreter wishes to "clear away the remains of dogmas, systems, controversies, which are encrusted

---

1. Fragment from the preface to *Commentary on Psalms 1–25*, preserved in the *Philokalia*, trans. Joseph W. Trigg (London: Routledge, 1998), 70–71.

2. *Against Heresies* 9.4.

upon" the words of scripture. The disciplines of close philological analysis "would enable us to separate the elements of doctrine and tradition with which the meaning of scripture is encumbered in our own day."[3] The lens of understanding must be wiped clear of the hazy and distorting film of doctrine.

Postmodernity, in turn, has encouraged us to criticize the critics. Jowett imagined that when he wiped away doctrine he would encounter the biblical text in its purity and uncover what he called "the original spirit and intention of the authors."[4] We are not now so sanguine, and the postmodern mind thinks interpretive frameworks inevitable. Nonetheless, we tend to remain modern in at least one sense. We read Athanasius and think of him stage-managing the diversity of scripture to support his positions against the Arians. We read Bernard of Clairvaux and assume that his monastic ideals structure his reading of the Song of Songs. In the wake of the Reformation, we can see how the doctrinal divisions of the time shaped biblical interpretation. Luther famously described the Epistle of James as a "strawy letter," for, as he said, "it has nothing of the nature of the Gospel about it."[5] In these and many other instances, often written in the heat of ecclesiastical controversy or out of the passion of ascetic commitment, we tend to think Jowett correct: doctrine is a distorting film on the lens of understanding.

However, is what we commonly think actually the case? Are readers naturally perceptive? Do we have an unblemished, reliable aptitude for the divine? Have we no need for disciplines of vision? Do our attention and judgment need to be trained, especially as we seek to read scripture as the living word of God? According to Augustine, we all struggle to journey toward God, who is our rest and peace. Yet our vision is darkened and the fetters of worldly habit corrupt our judgment. We need training and instruction in order to cleanse our minds so that we might find our way toward God.[6] To this end, "the whole temporal dispensation was made by divine Providence for our salvation."[7] The covenant with Israel, the coming of Christ, the gathering of the nations into the church—all these things are gathered up into the rule of faith, and they guide the vision and form of the soul toward the end of fellowship with God. In Augustine's view, the reading of scripture both contributes to and benefits from this divine pedagogy. With countless variations in both exegetical conclusions and theological frameworks, the same pedagogy

3. Benjamin Jowett, "On the Interpretation of Scripture," in *Essays and Reviews* (London: Parker, 1860), 338–39.

4. Jowett, "On the Interpretation of Scripture," 340.

5. *Luther's Works*, vol. 35, ed. E. Theodore Bachmann (Philadelphia: Fortress, 1959), 362.

6. *On Christian Doctrine* 1.10.

7. *On Christian Doctrine* 1.35.

of a doctrinally ruled reading of scripture characterizes the broad sweep of the Christian tradition from Gregory the Great through Bernard and Bonaventure, continuing across Reformation differences in both John Calvin and Cornelius Lapide, Patrick Henry and Bishop Bossuet, and on to more recent figures such as Karl Barth and Hans Urs von Balthasar.

Is doctrine, then, not a moldering scrim of antique prejudice obscuring the Bible, but instead a clarifying agent, an enduring tradition of theological judgments that amplifies the living voice of scripture? And what of the scholarly dispassion advocated by Jowett? Is a noncommitted reading—an interpretation unprejudiced—the way toward objectivity, or does it simply invite the languid intellectual apathy that stands aside to make room for the false truism and easy answers of the age?

This series of biblical commentaries was born out of the conviction that dogma clarifies rather than obscures. The Brazos Theological Commentary on the Bible advances upon the assumption that the Nicene tradition, in all its diversity and controversy, provides the proper basis for the interpretation of the Bible as Christian scripture. God the Father Almighty, who sends his only begotten Son to die for us and for our salvation and who raises the crucified Son in the power of the Holy Spirit so that the baptized may be joined in one body—faith in *this* God with *this* vocation of love for the world is the lens through which to view the heterogeneity and particularity of the biblical texts. Doctrine, then, is not a moldering scrim of antique prejudice obscuring the meaning of the Bible. It is a crucial aspect of the divine pedagogy, a clarifying agent for our minds fogged by self-deceptions, a challenge to our languid intellectual apathy that will too often rest in false truisms and the easy spiritual nostrums of the present age rather than search more deeply and widely for the dispersed keys to the many doors of scripture.

For this reason, the commentators in this series have not been chosen because of their historical or philological expertise. In the main, they are not biblical scholars in the conventional, modern sense of the term. Instead, the commentators were chosen because of their knowledge of and expertise in using the Christian doctrinal tradition. They are qualified by virtue of the doctrinal formation of their mental habits, for it is the conceit of this series of biblical commentaries that theological training in the Nicene tradition prepares one for biblical interpretation, and thus it is to theologians and not biblical scholars that we have turned. "War is too important," it has been said, "to leave to the generals."

We do hope, however, that readers do not draw the wrong impression. The Nicene tradition does not provide a set formula for the solution of exegetical problems.

The great tradition of Christian doctrine was not transcribed, bound in folio, and issued in an official, critical edition. We have the Niceno-Constantinopolitan Creed, used for centuries in many traditions of Christian worship. We have ancient baptismal affirmations of faith. The Chalcedonian definition and the creeds and canons of other church councils have their places in official church documents. Yet the rule of faith cannot be limited to a specific set of words, sentences, and creeds. It is instead a pervasive habit of thought, the animating culture of the church in its intellectual aspect. As Augustine observed, commenting on Jer. 31:33, "The creed is learned by listening; it is written, not on stone tablets nor on any material, but on the heart."[8] This is why Irenaeus is able to appeal to the rule of faith more than a century before the first ecumenical council, and this is why we need not itemize the contents of the Nicene tradition in order to appeal to its potency and role in the work of interpretation.

Because doctrine is intrinsically fluid on the margins and most powerful as a habit of mind rather than a list of propositions, this commentary series cannot settle difficult questions of method and content at the outset. The editors of the series impose no particular method of doctrinal interpretation. We cannot say in advance how doctrine helps the Christian reader assemble the mosaic of scripture. We have no clear answer to the question of whether exegesis guided by doctrine is antithetical to or compatible with the now-old modern methods of historical-critical inquiry. Truth—historical, mathematical, or doctrinal—knows no contradiction. But method is a discipline of vision and judgment, and we cannot know in advance what aspects of historical-critical inquiry are functions of modernism that shape the soul to be at odds with Christian discipline. Still further, the editors do not hold the commentators to any particular hermeneutical theory that specifies how to define the plain sense of scripture—or the role this plain sense should play in interpretation. Here the commentary series is tentative and exploratory.

Can we proceed in any other way? European and North American intellectual culture has been de-Christianized. The effect has not been a cessation of Christian activity. Theological work continues. Sermons are preached. Biblical scholars produce monographs. Church leaders have meetings. But each dimension of a formerly unified Christian practice now tends to function independently. It is as if a weakened army has been fragmented, and various corps have retreated to isolated fortresses in order to survive. Theology has lost its competence in exegesis.

8. *Sermon* 212.2.

Scripture scholars function with minimal theological training. Each decade finds new theories of preaching to cover the nakedness of seminary training that provides theology without exegesis and exegesis without theology.

Not the least of the causes of the fragmentation of Christian intellectual practice has been the divisions of the church. Since the Reformation, the role of the rule of faith in interpretation has been obscured by polemics and counterpolemics about *sola scriptura* and the necessity of a magisterial teaching authority. The Brazos Theological Commentary on the Bible series is deliberately ecumenical in scope because the editors are convinced that early church fathers were correct: church doctrine does not compete with scripture in a limited economy of epistemic authority. We wish to encourage unashamedly dogmatic interpretation of scripture, confident that the concrete consequences of such a reading will cast far more light on the great divisive questions of the Reformation than either reengaging in old theological polemics or chasing the fantasy of a pure exegesis that will somehow adjudicate between competing theological positions. You shall know the truth of doctrine by its interpretive fruits, and therefore in hopes of contributing to the unity of the church, we have deliberately chosen a wide range of theologians whose commitment to doctrine will allow readers to see real interpretive consequences rather than the shadow boxing of theological concepts.

The Brazos Theological Commentary on the Bible endorses a textual ecumenism that parallels our diversity of ecclesial backgrounds. We do not impose the thankfully modest inclusive-language agenda of the New Revised Standard Version, nor do we insist upon the glories of the Authorized Version, nor do we require our commentators to create a new translation. In our communal worship, in our private devotions, and in our theological scholarship, we use a range of scriptural translations. Precisely as scripture—a living, functioning text in the present life of faith—the Bible is not semantically fixed. Only a modernist, literalist hermeneutic could imagine that this modest fluidity is a liability. Philological precision and stability is a consequence of, not a basis for, exegesis. Judgments about the meaning of a text fix its literal sense, not the other way around. As a result, readers should expect an eclectic use of biblical translations, both across the different volumes of the series and within individual commentaries.

We cannot speak for contemporary biblical scholars, but as theologians we know that we have long been trained to defend our fortresses of theological concepts and formulations. And we have forgotten the skills of interpretation. Like stroke victims, we must rehabilitate our exegetical imaginations, and there are likely to be different strategies of recovery. Readers should expect this reconstructive—not reactionary—series to provide them with experiments in postcritical doctrinal interpretation, not commentaries written according to the settled principles of a well-functioning tradition. Some commentators will follow classical typological and allegorical readings from the premodern tradition; others will draw on contemporary historical study. Some will comment verse by verse; others will highlight passages, even single words that trigger theological analysis of scripture. No reading strategies are proscribed, no interpretive methods foresworn. The central premise in this commentary series is that doctrine provides structure and cogency to scriptural interpretation. We trust in this premise with the hope that the Nicene tradition can guide us, however imperfectly, diversely, and haltingly, toward a reading of scripture in which the right keys open the right doors.

R. R. Reno

ACKNOWLEDGMENTS

I'm so grateful to have gotten to spend years with Psalms 101–150 for the sake of the Brazos Theological Commentary on Scripture. I owe thanks to Rusty Reno for the invitation to write, to Dave Nelson for his editorial help at Brazos, and to Eric Salo for his editing work. I'm honored beyond what I can say to be part of a series with such extraordinary authors. It is grace to have this volume included in that number.

I began writing this commentary while pastoring Boone United Methodist Church in the Appalachian Mountains of North Carolina, and completed it while teaching preaching at the Vancouver School of Theology (VST). I am grateful to friends, parishioners, and colleagues in both places for their input in writing and editing. Davis Hankins of Appalachian State; Pat Dutcher-Walls, Laura Duhan Kaplan, and Harry Maier of VST; and Shawn Flynn, then of St. Mark's College and now of St. Joseph's College at the University of Alberta, all read chapters and made helpful suggestions and saved me from (some of my) mistakes.

James Howell read so many chapters so well that I just kept sending them to him. I first started learning from James as a college freshman at Davidson and intend to keep on learning from him as long as I can. He was a good enough friend to say hard things that I needed to hear ("You're rushing in this section!" "Quit the academic pretension!" "Say something for us preachers!"). James, under the great Roland Murphy at Duke, did his own dissertation on Psalm 90 in the history of Israel's and the church's interpretation. I learned some of the love for the psalms in the history of God's people from James, through him from Father Murphy, and through them back, back, back.... A key contention of this work is that the communion of the saints includes the author and the reader of scripture. There are always more interpreters and more hearers than we can see or imagine—and we get to join in their long-standing conversation about the meaning of the scriptures in our life together. I am grateful to James for including me in this ongoing raucous argument. This book is dedicated to him with so much gratitude.

I learned much about the psalms from the monks of Mepkin Abbey. I started going for retreats in that perfectly named hamlet in South Carolina, Monck's Corner (named for some guy named Monck, not for the monks), while in seminary. I watched the monks chant from their Psalters seven times a day, obeying the psalmist's directive with outrageous enthusiasm: "Seven times a day I praise you for your righteous ordinances" (Ps. 119:164). Some of the older monks didn't have to open their Psalters—they knew, as the ancient church would say, "the whole David." Yet those physical books, handwritten by the nuns from another monastery, were instructive. Inside their front covers was a quote from St. Augustine about how the psalms are prayed by Christ. This is obvious enough: in key moments of Jesus's life and ministry the psalms are on his lips, as they would be on any Jew's. But Augustine goes on—they are prayed by *the whole Christ*, head and members, as Paul says. Sometimes Jesus Christ speaks as his head in the psalms, referring to his own life and ministry. Sometimes he speaks in us, his members, who are bound to him by baptism and being transfigured by him from sinners into saints. Sometimes Christ expresses his suffering for us, even his "sins" (really *our* sins absorbed by him) as a result of being joined to us in the incarnation. Other times he expresses his triumph, naming his resurrection, ascension, and eventual gathering of all his people into his body. I couldn't believe how beautiful the notion was, how deep and magical and mysterious. I'm still trying to fathom it. I do some of that fathoming in this book. And so I should thank the monks of Mepkin Abbey. In a later delightful turn, I got to introduce the Methodists of Boone to the monks of Mepkin and watch them approximate the one body of Christ together.

I started to study the psalms in conjunction with the history of the church under Robert Wilken, who let me audit his course at the University of Virginia when I was flailing in graduate school at Duke. I remember how odd it all seemed—how could any reader claim to know what a text meant before he or she even started reading, even if that meaning was Jesus Christ? Wilken has been one of the crucial scholars reintroducing the church and the academy that serves it to the strange, counterintuitive, and wonderful way of reading the psalms that the church pursued for millennia, like Israel before us. I don't contend we have to read every line in an explicitly christological way—Steve Chapman at Duke taught me Brevard Childs well enough to avoid that—since the Old Testament often refers to Christ without mentioning him. Nevertheless, christological exegesis is so beautiful the church has often deployed it liberally, maximally, and with delight. Wilken turned to me at one point in class and suggested I write my dissertation on Augustine's commentary on the psalms, just then appearing in English. I did, and that became my book *Praise Seeking Understanding.* One of the editors of that volume, Peter Ochs, got me involved with Scriptural Reasoning and its remarkable practice of having Jews, Christians, and Muslims read our respective scriptures together. I have continued with christological exegesis partly because I think that gives us Christians something worthwhile and genuinely different to say in such conversations—and of course the fruit of our readings has to be a blessing to our interlocutors, to their communities, and to the world.

In this book I try to expand the list of interpreters from whom I learn beyond Augustine, though he is still at the center. The edges include other patristic, Jewish, Reformed, and modern interpreters. I am a little harder on historical criticism in my earlier book than I now wish I were. There is no reason to be above learning from absolutely anyone. The ultimate arbiter of meaning, however, is not the historian's best reconstruction of what the original author intended, though that can be valuable to contemplate. It is rather what God is saying to the church now, as God transforms us into the blessing to the world that God intends. Right now God is working to knit the universe back together. The church has often been a counter-witness to God's work of repair, especially in much of our relationship to our Jewish forebears and neighbors. The way to do better, I contend, is not to read the text as though Jesus does not matter to us Christians. I don't detect in Jewish interlocutors any resentment toward Christians for reading like Christians. The way to do better is to read Israel's scripture in a way that honors Israel. I try hard to do that here but don't doubt I have failed more than once in this and in many other ways. I trust the God of Israel is as merciful as our stories and psalms say he is.

The real determination of the validity of an exegetical approach is the character of the people it produces. I hope this book helps the church contemplate God's unendingly gracious character in such a way as to become full of grace ourselves, as we constantly pass it on to others. If this work helps toward that end, it will not have been a fool's errand. But that result, like all other results, is in the hands of the one to whom all praise and honor are due.

ABBREVIATIONS

Old Testament

Gen.	Genesis	Song of Sol.	Song of Solomon
Exod.	Exodus	Isa.	Isaiah
Lev.	Leviticus	Jer.	Jeremiah
Num.	Numbers	Lam.	Lamentations
Deut.	Deuteronomy	Ezek.	Ezekiel
Josh.	Joshua	Dan.	Daniel
Judg.	Judges	Hosea	Hosea
Ruth	Ruth	Joel	Joel
1–2 Sam.	1–2 Samuel	Amos	Amos
1–2 Kings	1–2 Kings	Obad.	Obadiah
1–2 Chron.	1–2 Chronicles	Jon.	Jonah
Ezra	Ezra	Mic.	Micah
Neh.	Nehemiah	Nah.	Nahum
Esther	Esther	Hab.	Habakkuk
Job	Job	Zeph.	Zephaniah
Ps. (Pss.)	Psalm (Psalms)	Hag.	Haggai
Prov.	Proverbs	Zech.	Zechariah
Eccles.	Ecclesiastes	Mal.	Malachi

Deuterocanonical/Apocryphal

Wis.	Wisdom of Solomon	2 Macc.	2 Maccabees
Sir.	Sirach		

New Testament

Matt.	Matthew	1–2 Thess.	1–2 Thessalonians
Mark	Mark	1–2 Tim.	1–2 Timothy
Luke	Luke	Titus	Titus
John	John	Philem.	Philemon
Acts	Acts	Heb.	Hebrews
Rom.	Romans	James	James
1–2 Cor.	1–2 Corinthians	1–2 Pet.	1–2 Peter
Gal.	Galatians	1–3 John	1–3 John
Eph.	Ephesians	Jude	Jude
Phil.	Philippians	Rev.	Revelation
Col.	Colossians		

INTRODUCTION

I wrote this commentary in the same way that I preach. Scripture exists only for the formation of a people in faith and love, and scholarly work is meant to support that formation. As a Christian preacher, I read scripture in an effort to discover Christ, and having discovered him, I then try to present him anew to his people. This is a fraught task. Often Jesus hides himself, or I think I've discovered him but then manage to lose him as I try to pivot from reading to preaching. More often, Christian interpreters would say, he discovers us, despite our best intentions and worst failures. But I wrote this commentary on the assumption that its readers would, like me, have a Bible open to the pertinent psalm and would be hunting for Jesus there, with hopes of presenting him to other people for their edification and the world's blessing.

That's a lot of assumptions! And it is different than the way I was taught scripture or, I wager, the way you were taught scripture. I was taught to listen to the Old Testament (or the Hebrew Bible or any number of other aliases folks keep proposing) on "its own terms," in "its own voice," a number of metaphors meant to say we read it without reference to Jesus.[1] Perhaps later, say, in a preaching class, we might learn how to relate this text to Jesus (but usually not there either—where did teachers of preaching learn how to interpret scripture?).[2] This end run around

1. Stephen Fowl points out the way modern scholars tend to resort to metaphors like these and rarely unpack them when defending anti-christological interpretation. Fowl, *Engaging Scripture: A Model for Theological Interpretation* (Eugene, OR: Wipf & Stock, 2008), 185.
2. Nicholas Lash's image is unforgettable: we speak as though interpretation is a relay race, with the biblical scholars on the first leg. The problem is the baton never actually gets passed. Lash, *Theology on the Way to Emmaus* (London: SCM, 1986), 79.

christological interpretation is understandable and defensible even on Christian grounds (Ellen Charry gives a beautiful defense in her volume on the first third of the Psalter in this series).[3] And sometimes that works out just fine; the psalms are a rich feast—folks can get fed without too much worry over what utensils we use. But other times it produces oddities, even absurdities. How is it that Christian interpreters of the psalms end up saying that we shouldn't interpret the psalms the way the New Testament does? As every opening Bible class hammers home on the first day, the collection of books we call the "Old Testament" was the only Bible that the first Christians knew. So they found the Messiah in Pss. 2 and 110, Jesus prayed the twenty-second and thirty-first psalms from his cross, and Jesus told his disciples that the psalms were written about him and must be fulfilled (Luke 24:44). What argument do we have against reading these psalms christologically? That the New Testament is *wrong* as it depicts Jesus teaching how to read Israel's Psalter? What if, on the contrary, *Jesus is actually teaching us how to read?* These New Testament passages aren't, then, awkward misunderstandings born of understandable piety but not to be repeated; they are rather signs for how Jesus wants his people to read his scriptures.

I offer here what we might call a "christologically maximalist" interpretation of the psalms. I offer a longer defense of this way of reading elsewhere,[4] but for now we might address a few common and legitimate objections. First, why bother reading the Old Testament with reference to Jesus? Why not just read the New Testament? The answer is that it is delightful to find Jesus where we had not expected to find him. The motion of christological exegesis is from befuddlement ("this passage makes no sense") to slow illumination ("wait, I think I see the contours of God in Christ even here") to delight ("wow, the Lord was in this place and we didn't know it!"). This is the same motion of every sermon, of every soul, of every particle of the created universe: We expect initially that we are on our own, without meaning, and lost. We find that, in fact, God has already come close, even here. And then with delight we wish to preach about this, evangelize with it, do social justice with it, and most importantly, offer praise to God for it. The disciplines of discerning Christ in the Old Testament and discerning Christ throughout creation are braided together. Once we lose one, we lose the other— and the Old Testament becomes a foreign and forbidden place for Christians;

---

3. Ellen Charry, *Psalms 1–50*, Brazos Theological Commentary on the Bible (Grand Rapids: Brazos, 2015), xix, xxi.

4. Jason Byassee, *Praise Seeking Understanding: Reading the Psalms with Augustine* (Grand Rapids: Eerdmans, 2007), esp. chaps. 2–3.

creation becomes simply a commodity that can be bought, sold, chopped up, and ruined. No. Both are made by God and are being used by God to renew all things.

The second common objection is whether this way of reading is supersessionist and lops off Israel's pride of place as God's beloved. The answer there is yes, it often has been and done precisely that. And no, it never should have and never should again. I try here to read in as philo-Jewish a way as possible. There is no necessary reason for allegory to be anti-Jewish, or for readings that bless Israel to be only the non-allegorical kind. The pervasiveness of this critique is a particularly long-lasting trope of the Reformation, the Enlightenment, and modernity: to let someone read supraliterally will mean bad things will happen. You might find Mary in 2 Chronicles somewhere (the Reformation) or you'll do something unreasonable like discern the Trinity or the church where they logically cannot be (the Enlightenment) or you'll do violence to the original and necessarily not-Christian nature of the text (modernity). The shrillness of the opposition lets you know immediately that the arguments are suspect. The way to read without doing violence to Israel is to read without doing violence to Israel. The answer to curses is blessings. I try to read here in a way that is maximally catholic and maximally Jewish—as universal and as particular as possible. I do this because the psalms do this. They insist that Israel is the apple of God's eye and that through Israel God means to bless God's entire creation. The answer to the church's massive and nearly[5] unforgivable failure to read in ways that bless Israel is to do it better, not to abandon the effort. I assume the church will go on reading the Bible for worship. Wouldn't it be beneficial if we had resources with which to read our own Bibles, the Old and New Testaments, in ways that honor the text and honor our neighbors—especially our older siblings in faith? Whether I've succeeded here is up to others, but not merely to scholars. The fruit of biblical interpretation is the life of the worshiping community. If the church can read this commentary and become more faithful in its love for Israel and for the planet and most importantly for God, then it was worth the time. If not, hopefully God will be merciful.

I feel grateful and delighted to have gotten to interpret this last third of the Psalter, 101–150, minus an extensive treatment of 119, which Reinhard Hütter will write in a separate volume. I get some of the most important psalms of all: 118, absolutely crucial for the church's life and preaching and worship and self-understanding; 121, key in Christians' piety; 137 with its troublesome blessings; the crescendo of praise in 145–150. This section of the Psalter covers Israel's

---

5. I am inclined to excise the "nearly." But God's mercy is unfathomable. And Israel has resources for forgiveness that constantly surprise and delight.

---

attempts to return from exile and so offers wisdom crucial for the church's understanding of the gathering-in of the Gentiles. I get the ascent psalms, 120–134, with their tutoring of our praises as it instructs pilgrims walking up Mount Zion. I get meaty historical psalms among the first ten or so and then the final section of psalms attributed to David in 139–144. And I only get 100,000 words in this manuscript to work with. This seemed entirely too many before I started, now entirely too few. It works out to roughly 140 words per verse—pleasingly brief.[6] I remember before starting seminary asking my mentor, to whom this book is dedicated, whether we would have a course on every book of the Bible. It seemed rational to me—how could I preach on something I hadn't studied? He managed to repress a laugh at my mathematical inattention. No, he said, but we teach you how to interpret different sorts of scripture. So it is with Jesus and his Psalter—he teaches us how to read. I try here to read in as christological a manner as I can. Sometimes I will fail—the results won't fit with the words on the page, the theology of the church, the blessing of Israel, or the world. Then, by all means, leave my interpretation behind. But sometimes, I hope, my work might succeed in fitting beautifully with the words, the tradition, and the needs of God's people today.

I comment here in conversation with ancient interpreters (Augustine above all but not only), homiletical interpreters (like the great C. H. Spurgeon), and contemporary historical critics (some with greater faith friendliness and some with slightly less). Ancient interpreters would give anything for just some of the technical skills we can now take for granted in manuscript reconciliation, translation, and knowledge of historical background—they often complain about the limitations they face in each area. Yet their interpretations often succeed precisely where modern ones fail: they're interesting. Modern interpreters, with access to much correct information, are often boring. The difference is in whether one interprets the text with reference to God. Ancients do that. The ancients often fail, Lord knows, and not just for technical deficiencies beyond their ability but also for moral or theological reasons. Yet they often succeed in the thing that matters most—they bring delight in God to their hearers.

The church is in, among other things, a multigenerational argument over how to read scripture for the sake of a faithful life together. I do not propose by any

6. I gave some thought to spending more words on psalms that appear in the Revised Common Lectionary for the sake of preachers more likely to need help there than on psalms not so assigned. I decided against it, partly because there are resources for those already (e.g., Van Harn and Strawn 2009). But I also assume we should be preaching the breadth of scripture beyond the already wide bounds of the lectionary. A psalm is scripture—the word of God—even if the church neglects it.

means these are the only conversation partners valid for such a debate. They are just the ones I used with my limited time and ability. The goal in this raucous conversation is love of God and the blessing of the world.[7] May the one who is enthroned on the praises of Israel make it so.

7. Herbert McCabe, *God, Christ, and Us*, ed. Brian Davies (London: Continuum, 2005), 115.

PSALM 101

We see in Psalm 101 a glimpse of the way Christ reigns. What do we who participate in that reign, serving this king (101:6), stand to learn here about the peculiar nature of his kingdom?

Historians tell us that this psalm has some elements of a wisdom psalm and some of a royal psalm. Like the very first psalm, this one also sets out two ways: one of life, with promise of great reward, and the other of death, with just as sure destruction. The psalm comes from the mouth of a king, not only in the superscription's attribution to David, but also in the promises about the specific ways to rule. It is no surprise for Christians that wisdom and royalty are present in the same psalm, since Christ our King is Wisdom incarnate.

But if Christ is the "I" in this psalm, why then does it offer a choice between good and ill? What does Christ have to "study" and learn about the "way that is blameless" (101:2)? Why does Christ need to promise not to put before his eyes "anything that is base" (101:3)? What need does the sovereign Lord of the universe have for *others* to minister to him (101:6)? Even more troubling, why does he pledge to slay every morning "all the wicked in the land" (101:8)?

In his incarnation, the Son of God *did* learn and grow, and therefore must also have studied and struggled. "Although he was a Son, he learned obedience through what he suffered," Heb. 5:8 suggests, and the Gospel of Luke describes Jesus's growth "in wisdom and in years, and in divine and human favor" (Luke 2:52). Jesus did undergo temptation. His holiness was hard-earned and required the sorts of promise-keeping demonstrated in Ps. 101 and promise-making that all others must learn to imitate. Our head—Jesus—*currently* reigns. His members—all of us—have yet to join fully in his holy way of ruling. With this psalm we pledge to do so.

It seems immodest to say the church reigns. Yet we do—and so we must promise to do so virtuously. The long list of interior dispositions here is our way of being among a kingdom of priests. Our interior struggles may seem small to us, but the psalm suggests they take place on a grand historical stage. Our efforts to keep our eyes pure, our heads bowed, our mouths from slander are part of our participation in Christ's reign over the cosmos now. One day that reign will be universally acknowledged, when every knee shall bow (Phil. 2:5–11). John Howard Yoder, in an appropriately named essay "To Serve Our God and Rule the World," argued that as Christians we can be against militarism but not against triumphalism.[1] Why? The scriptures themselves are triumphalist. We are a kingdom of priests serving our God forever. No wonder the stakes are high in keeping our hearts dedicated solely to God.

This is not just an eschatological claim. Everyone has some power, however small, in this present world. The question is whether that power will be exercised well, for the sake of human flourishing, or selfishly, for aggrandizement of self and belittlement of others. James Mays tells the story of a ruler in the seventeenth century, a Duke Ernest the Pious of Saxe-Gotha, who would send this psalm to one of his underlings if that one failed to rule properly. It was said when such a one would act afoul that "he will surely receive the Duke's psalm to read" (Mays 1994: 322).[2] The psalm affirms something modern politics have generally denied: the state of the leader's soul matters for the way she or he performs the work of authority. We all have a stake in the faithfulness of those "over" us, for which we pray. And, as those who exercise responsibility over others, we had better tend the gardens of our own souls before we lift a finger in authority.

Psalm 101 opens with a promise to sing of "loyalty" and "justice." The English words lack some of the texture of a good, chewy Hebrew word. "Loyalty" is a translation of *hesed*, with its broader implications of covenant righteousness and dogged commitment to Israel. The refrain of Psalms 118 and 136 that "his *hesed* endures forever" is sometimes translated as "steadfast love" (NRSV), or "mercy" elsewhere, as in the King James. "Justice" is a translation of *mishpat*, again a richer word in Hebrew. Here is a vein of great biblical depth: the prophets demand

---

1. John Howard Yoder, "To Serve Our God and Rule the World," in *The Royal Priesthood: Essays Ecclesiastical and Ecumenical*, ed. Michael Cartwright (Grand Rapids: Eerdmans, 1994), 128–40.

2. If there is one commentary I will lean on more than any other in this book, this is it—informed by historical criticism but beholden primarily to the faith of the church and its preaching ministry.

justice from God's people. We are to "seek justice, rescue the oppressed, defend the orphan, plead for the widow," as Isa. 1:17 demands. It is *mishpat* that is to roll down like waters, words from Amos 5:24 that the civil rights movement made famous over again, and *mishpat* that the prophet Micah insists God expects from us (Mic. 6:8). Cassiodorus said of his Latin version of the two words that open this psalm, "Here the totality is told briefly but fully, for in these two words all the Lord's works and the building up of the entire church are clearly told" (*Expositions of the Psalms* 100.1, in Wesselschmidt 2007: 206).

St. Augustine and his Reformation student Martin Luther both find a glimpse of the gospel in the twinning of judgment and mercy. Mercy and justice are only together in the communion of the saints. In hell, justice reigns alone. Luther concludes, "If we know ourselves, we easily sing of judgment; but if we know God we easily sing of mercy."[3] Augustine imagines the pairing of justice and grace as a glimpse of two successive temporal eras. Now we are under an era of grace. An era of justice or judgment is coming (Augustine 2003: 29–30). It is important to note that Christians often imagine now as a time of grace compared to the old covenant's *past* time of justice. Yet Augustine says something different. Now is still the time of mercy, but judgment is coming, before which all human beings should tremble.

In the meantime, "I will study the way that is blameless. When shall I attain it?" (101:2). It would seem odd that Christ would pledge to study and even long to know when he will reach blamelessness. Sinners long for an absent holiness, but Christ himself is the source of holiness. So why this lament? Augustine imagines Christ, the whole Christ, head and members this way: "He is still dying in you, as you have already risen in him" (2003: 33). We are all the members of Christ on earth. He dies with and for and in us. We are joined to our head, who is already at the right hand of the Father. In him, we too have risen. This nimble body of Christ stretches across the cosmos and the eons. It "explains" Christ's ongoing suffering among us and our certain victory in him. This kind of plaintive cry by Christ on our behalf is a glimpse of the mystery of salvation, in which God gives us all his glory in Christ and receives in exchange all our need. In us, Christ too longs for holiness. In him, even we find it. This prayer gives meaning to our efforts at study. We long for wisdom and holiness. In Christ we will find both.

Augustine (2003: 33–36) finds in this longing for holiness a key to not reading the psalm as a rationale for distancing oneself from those who are less holy. If

---

3. Martin Luther, *Lectures on the Psalms II*, trans. Herbert J. A. Bauman, ed. Hilton C. Oswald, vol. 11 of *Luther's Works* (St. Louis: Concordia, 1976), 283.

God distanced himself from the unholy, God would have no followers left! The longing for holiness is good. Yet Jesus eats with sinners and refuses to separate himself from humanity. With this psalm we can pray for the removal of blame. And knowing what we know of the compromised nature of all human community, we can be patient with the sinners still in our midst, who teach us patience and grace. For Christ is the only blameless one.

The psalmist seeks blamelessness throughout. Mays describes blamelessness as "coherence" and "consistency" with "some fundamental value" (1994: 321). A similar passage comes in Ps. 18:20–30, where the psalmist acclaims, "With the blameless you show yourself blameless" (18:25). The opposite of such blamelessness is a twisted and incoherent heart. This psalm is concerned with character, human nature in its deepest depths, the right ordering of which allows us to minister to God himself. Without a blameless character, we serve only ourselves—which is chaos indeed (Mays 1994: 322).

The psalm ends jarringly, with a promise to slay evildoers every morning. Interpreters as early as Origen notice this oddity and insist that no Christian reader can take the promise literally (*Against Celsus* 7.19, in Wesselschmidt 2007: 208). Not even the most bloodthirsty ruler has executions every morning! We might say that such a promise shows God's impatience with lies, pride, and deceit. God cuts such things off every single day. Luther reads the reference tropologically: morning is the new start God brings daily, without the stain of the day before. Morning is a glimpse of the resurrection to come. Luther suggests the liars and deceivers are like the babies of Ps. 139, the whining desires and resentments that have to be nipped in the bud or they will ruin us spiritually.

More positively, we might say this promise from God gives hope. We should all long to be sheared of lies. But we cannot do it ourselves. God can, and promises to do so one morning, perhaps tomorrow, perhaps on resurrection day, when all things shall be made new.

One overzealous NRSV study Bible notation worries about this verse. Though its meaning is "probably" not literal, "religious fanatics have taken it literally and do so still" (Harrelson 2003: 843). Sure enough. But the answer to "wrong" readings is *better* ones. Morning is the time of God's new mercy, of Christ's resurrection, of the dawn of the kingdom, when untruth shall end. This king promises to bring that day by his might. Those who love truth, including true biblical interpretation, will long for that kingdom to come soon.

The college town where I served a church has a vibrant set of campus ministries. Perhaps it's because we're still a remnant of Christendom. North Carolinians who go to that state school usually grew up in a church. You can ask a stranger here *where*, not *whether*, they go to church. The school also hitched its wagon to the horse of the green economy early on. Sustainable development and energy programs are important on campus, and environmental activism is held in high regard. These two cultures—campus ministry and environmentalist zeal—exist uneasily alongside one another. In the campus ministry with which I'm most familiar, disciple-making and ecological sensitivity seem to compete for space. Students who are convinced that all people should shun Styrofoam and eat organic and local food feel that the church is the problem for our endangered ecology. Students more interested in being and making disciples feel that ecology is a side issue and can become its own form of snobbery ("You make your own clothes? Well, I never ride in a car!").

Psalm 101 speaks to this impasse—one likely to grow as contentiousness over climate change worsens. The psalmist—in our reading Jesus—praises *both* God's covenant-bound love and God's other-oriented mercy, both God's *hesed* and God's *mishpat*. There is not a moment of pause between them, and one requires the other. In our world, we can become fascinated with one at the expense of the other, as though righteousness ("Let's save the planet!") disqualifies mercy ("Let's tell others about Jesus!") or vice versa. But for the Bible, these two cannot be uncoupled from one another without disastrous results. Discipleship means we love the world that God loved into being, took flesh in, and died to save. Love for God's world also means we proclaim his gospel to all creatures. May the God of the scriptures sew back together these two that we have often ripped apart.

PSALM 102

At the beginning of his commentary on Ps. 102, St. Augustine teases his listeners. Who on earth could this first line refer to? Who is the "one afflicted," praying here, as our NRSV translates the superscription? Who is the "one poor man" to whom Augustine's Latin text refers? "I have not identified the poor man yet," he preaches (Augustine 2003: 45). Several pages (or minutes for his listeners) later, he claims success: "Give me credit for having discovered at last who this poor suppliant is" (Augustine 2003: 48). We know he is teasing. He knows we know. His congregation knows, as every reader of his Psalms commentary knows, who the afflicted, praying, poor person is. It is Jesus, the whole Christ, head and members, including us today. For Augustine, Christ not only teaches us how to pray the psalms, though he does that. He also joins us to God in his body. He takes on our affliction, misery, and sin and gives us, in exchange, his divine favor, grace, and sonship. That's not a bad trade. And it's illustrated yet again in this psalm. Whatever else we may think of Augustine's approach to the psalms, his invitational posture is clear: "Let us hear ourselves in these words," he suggests.

Augustine shows what a psalm is. It is not just a private prayer. It is canonized scripture. It is God's own way of praying, passed down by God's people. Individuals pray psalms, to be sure; congregations recite them; generations treasure them. But most importantly, God speaks in the psalms and teaches us how to speak back to God.

For us Gentile Christians, our way into this scripture is Jesus, through whom we are grafted into Israel against our nature (Rom. 11:17–24). How can we pray this psalm with anything other than *our* own mouths, in *our* own heads, as part of the body of Christ, who teaches us a scripture not naturally our own? Christian interpreters who are reserved about christological exegesis still occasionally make reference to the triune God at the end of their treatments—perhaps with a New Testament reference. The ancient church teaches us to *assume* Christ from the beginning, and then to see how these words refer to that steady referent.

Psalm 102 refers to God with remarkable intimacy, referring to two parts of God's very head. Interpreters throughout time have been quick (and right) to say these are metaphors. God does not have ears or a face any more than God sits on a physical throne with an actual beard or hands. I like Karl Barth's response to this eschewal of anthropomorphism: maybe we should say instead that *only* God has a face, ears, or hands: "Only God has hands—not paws like ours."[1] One modern commentator describes the psalmist's posture as a plea for "attentive, intense listening" (Hossfeld and Zenger 2011: 23). We can imagine here a grandchild in his grandmother's lap, physically turning her face to him, grabbing her ear, not letting her ignore him any longer. The psalmist is adamant, intimate, and physical in all prayers.

Christians have often seen in these anthropomorphisms in the psalms a hint of the Word made flesh. Scripture is not merely pretending God has physical features; it is preparing the way for a God in a manger, on a cross, in triumph. Martin Luther speaks of this appeal to see God's face as a reference to three advents. The first was when the Lord showed his face in the flesh. The second is a spiritual advent, by faith, in human hearts, "without which the first advent is of no avail."[2] The third will come when we see Christ face-to-face. The church prays for the latter two advents, since the first has already happened. Luther adds another meaning for God's "face" here in Ps. 102:2: it refers to the Spirit, rather than the letter, of scripture (2 Cor. 3:6). Those who see God's face see scripture in its fullness and vice versa; those who do not see God's face see only dead letters.

Psalm 102 is a lament psalm, as modern scholars classify these things. The church agrees, having made the psalm one of seven traditional psalms of penitence, specified for the church's worship on days of mourning. Once, I read it aloud to a small gathering of committed laypeople. They paused. "Depressing," one said. "Why don't we pray like that?" another asked. The psalms teach us how God wants us to pray. But we often take our cues poorly.

1. Karl Barth, *The Faith of the Church*, trans. Gabriel Vahanian (Eugene, OR: Wipf & Stock, 2006), 47 (a short commentary on the Apostles' Creed). He develops this theme further in *Church Dogmatics* II/1, trans. G. W. Bromiley (Edinburgh: T&T Clark, 1957), 225–29.
2. Martin Luther, *Lectures on the Psalms II*, trans. Herbert J. A. Bauman, ed. Hilton C. Oswald, vol. 11 of *Luther's Works* (St. Louis: Concordia, 1976), 296.

In its historical setting, the psalm may have been a lament over demolished Jerusalem, now in dust and ash, with scavenger birds free to roam and God's promises for Zion's deliverance undone. It may also have been an individual lament for someone close to death. The psalm moves back and forth from personal to national lament. Ancient Jews' identities were bound up with their national, corporate peoplehood, recognized by God, neighbors, and enemies, in a way that modern people's identities often are not. Christians may ask here who is a single entity whose identity incorporates all of God's people, including Gentiles, strangers, and a generation yet unborn (102:15, 18).

The psalm's classification is unusual in its turn from deep lament to powerful hope. Yet the psalmist stakes a claim on hope with precious little present evidence for it. Some psalms point backward to God's previous mighty deeds as reason for hope of future deliverance. This one points forward. The psalmist commands, Write this down! (102:18). He makes a prediction now that will come true in its fullness in a way that no one would believe if written record were not kept from the moment of deepest despair.

The psalmist refers to two banquets of misery: "I am too wasted to eat my bread," he protests in 102:4, and in 102:9 laments, "I eat ashes like bread, and mingle tears with my drink." It's been said that Jesus eats his way through the Gospels. Church people do few things together more often than eat and drink. There was a day when the church also fasted corporately. It seems strange to hear of loss of appetite, the sour bread of ash, and the drink of tears—especially if we have lost the discipline of fasting altogether. What do we make of this aversion to food, beyond the obvious poetic power? The patristic writer Theodoret of Cyrus (393–458) writes, "The word of God is our soul's bread." This is why Christ commands us to pray for our daily bread, so we can eat his word and be nourished. Without it we waste away: "The flower of virtue no longer has the strength to bloom" if we fail to eat (*Commentary on the Psalms* 102.3, in Wesselschmidt 2007: 209). Augustine repeats this admonition to eat the Lord's word lest we vanish. But he adds an incarnational twist: the true Bread has come from heaven, so we can eat and be satisfied (Augustine 2003: 51). Martin Luther is more willing than either of his patristic forebears to let multiple conflicting meanings sit alongside one another. He reiterates the patristic readings first. Then he suggests the psalmist may be presenting a moral example—to eat bread may mean to do whatever one pleases. Not to eat, then, is to discipline the body toward a commendable leanness rather than self-indulgent girth. "Thus we have two meanings in opposition, and either one is true and good," he concludes.[3] It is not that any reading is as good as any other. But there is here a flexibility in interpreting scripture for the sake of the church's health.

The birds in this psalm bear more than ornithological import. The NRSV translates the Hebrew as "owl," "little owl," and "lonely bird," whereas the ancient Septuagint and generations of Christian interpreters saw a pelican, an owl, or a sparrow. Other modern interpreters suggest the bird intended may be a jackdaw or crow. One point of commonality is that the birds referred to are all unclean in Jewish dietary practice. They are also solitary birds. The Jerusalem depicted here is so desolate that solitary birds can nest in its ruins and not be disturbed— no human is rebuilding a thing. For most modern interpreters, that is enough. For Augustine and those in his tradition, it is not. The "I" reference is rich and elusive and important. Who is speaking in this psalm? The specifics in scripture matter—the tangible particularities contain treasures designed to further our salvation. Augustine argues often that one needs secular knowledge to interpret the Bible well. What do we learn about these birds, then?

Augustine has never seen a pelican. They do not live in his part of North Africa. But he learns from the Romans by way of Jerome that mother pelicans peck their young to death in the nest. Then the mother wounds herself, pouring blood out on her young, who then revive. Augustine, for one, is a skeptic: "You must listen with discernment, so that if the report is true, you may find that it fits in with the known truth, but if false, it may not persist" (2003: 53). But if it *is* true, what a wonderful image for Christ, who kills and makes alive (so Deut. 32:39), who has a motherly love for the chicks (Matt. 23:37). If even Paul has a motherly love for his churches (Gal. 4:26), how much more must Jesus? Ever after Augustine's pelican image, that bird has been a marker for Christ in Christian imagination. Thomas Aquinas wrote hymns to Christ as "our pelican divine." Altar tables are supported on pelicans' heads as their foundation, signaling the one sacrificed there. I taught this tradition at Garrett-Evangelical Theological Seminary outside Chicago and noticed the students snickering. Apparently, the building we were in had a sculpture above each entryway of a mother pelican in wing over a nest above tiny beaks. When I was about to propose to my wife, the wine was drunk, the ring bought, the lady waiting by my side on the beach, and I was terrified. What did I see but a flock of pelicans. Either that is a coincidence, in which case I wish you a boring life,[4] or it is Christ, reminding me of his sacrificial and resurrecting love.

---

3. Luther, *Lectures on the Psalms II*, 298.
4. I remember this as a homiletical aside in a sermon of Barbara Brown Taylor's.

One piece of creation is marked in the imagination by the one who makes and redeems it. And that bit of creation reminds of Christ in a way that all creation, viewed aright, should and one day indisputably will do.

That's a pretty tenuous reading of the psalm, one based on a disputed manuscript not even in scripture's original language.[5] It is also based on a zoological account so legendary that ancient figures themselves were skeptical. It can be put to poor uses: the license plate and state flag of Louisiana display a pelican not only because of the state's native brown pelicans but also because the French state blended that Christ symbol into a sign of its own colonial power. We human beings can use anything for ill. Yet the symbol shows how the ancient church read. It works partly because it is a seldom-seen bird in scripture and in Augustine's world. True zoological accounts should be substituted for false ones, no doubt; Augustine himself insists on it.[6] Yet for all that prevarication, is it not a beautiful tradition, one that could enrich the way the church adores Christ in scripture and creation?

Think now of Jesus learning these psalms from Mary, digesting them on his own, trying to live a life forged by them. The Gospel writers depict him foretelling Jerusalem's destruction in AD 70. As he imagined the destruction of God's city and temple, he likely thought of this psalm, with its smoking ruins and its solitary birds delighting in their unmolested habitation. In Jesus's day, King Herod affixed a Roman eagle on the outer precinct of the temple, client-king that he was. Jesus, seeing this with his own eyes, praying this prayer, imagined a day when the bold bird of prey would be reduced to a skittish nocturne in a smoky citadel.[7]

"*You* have lifted me up and thrown me aside," 102:10 says. The praying one, in despair, sees God as the *agent* of his desolation. No reason is given for this wrath from God, but it determines everything in this lament. St. Augustine thinks here of original sin—no individual contribution to the sorry state of humanity is mentioned, yet the speaker is guilty anyway. Mays describes the psalmist here as one who "finds hope for existence under the wrath of God" (1994: 325). Even traditions (like my Wesleyan one) that deemphasize God's role in terrible events do well to regain this biblical theme of God's wrath. Psalm 102 names wrath here, not to assign blame, but to name God's saving presence amidst human catastrophe.

5. Though the Septuagint was the one most read by the New Testament writers and patristic authors before Jerome.

6. Augustine argues that love is the telos of exegesis, so one who misreads the words but reads in a way that builds up love should be corrected like one who takes a shortcut to the right destination. Augustine, *On Christian Doctrine* 1, trans. D. W. Robertson (Upper Saddle River, NJ: Prentice Hall, 1958), 31.

7. I'm grateful to James Howell for his extensive editing help with this entire manuscript and especially for the formulation of this paragraph.

Early Wesleyan societies gathered as those who wished to flee "from the wrath that is coming" (1 Thess. 1:10). They did not even have to profess faith in God right away. But they did want to align their lives for what was coming.

The psalm pivots suddenly at 102:12: "But you, O LORD, are enthroned forever; your name endures to all generations." Some scholars observe a superscription in the middle of the psalm, setting the direction for its second half (Hossfeld and Zenger 2011: 24). That is true literarily. Theologically, a turn toward God's action takes place here. Mays expresses the hope well that God "can overrule even their failure" (1994: 327). And ours. Augustine finds himself in a polemic with an imagined interlocutor who is critical of biblical faith. The interlocutor accuses Christians of undermining public morality. If people can be forgiven anything, why should they ever act virtuously? Augustine turns the claim upside down. If people *cannot* be forgiven anything, why should they ever act virtuously? Permanent record of sin is a reason for moral despair. The Bible's pivot, "But you, O LORD," over against our human ruin, is what Christians mean by "grace," and it is our best news for the world.

Devastation would seem a strange state from which to make a bold promise. But the psalmist asks for pen and ink and scribe: "Let this be recorded for a generation to come" (102:18; Alter 2007: 355). Write this down, or no one will believe the wonders that are about to happen. There are two promises that will be fulfilled. One, Zion will be restored. What is now dust and ash will be resurrected to the grandeur of divine rule from Jerusalem. Two, even the Gentiles will be drawn to Israel's beauty. Nations, kings, all peoples will come and learn from Israel how to say "hallelujah." Write this down, or when it happens you won't believe it was foretold in advance.

St. Augustine sees this two-part promise of God's coming action in the poetic line from 102:14: "For your servants hold its stones dear, and have pity on its dust." The stones, to his mind, are the Jews, the bedrock of God's people, now tossed in all directions in diaspora. They will be rebuilt. Augustine sees the Gentiles in the mention of "dust." Gentiles, the ungodly, are "like dust," Ps. 1:4 proclaims. *We* are the ones who crucified Christ; *we* are the ones in 102:8 who curse our physician and put him to death. Even so, from his cross he prays for forgiveness for us. Augustine sees so clearly what many Christians (including, in his later tradition, Luther) do not: any blame falls on us, not the Jews; any grace comes from the one we kill. God makes from this dust and these stones a new humanity, as God once did in Eden: "There arose from this dust a new humanity, freshly formed and beautiful" (Augustine 2003: 60). The church is this new creation. Christian interpreters see in this psalm's promise of Gentiles worshiping Israel's God a glimpse of the church: nations fear, kings worship (102:15), a generation yet unborn rises up in praise (102:18), peoples gather not to fight Zion but to worship its God (102:22), the children of God's servants—God's people by faith—rise up and give praise. These promises of future worship by Gentiles resonate throughout the prophets Isaiah and Zechariah. They are the language with which St. Paul tried to understand Gentiles worshiping Israel's God but most of Israel-according-to-the-flesh not doing so. These promises are the language of the church. Why have we so long neglected them? God enfleshed has appeared, "down," with us (102:16, 19). In Christ's ministry, God has poured out grace on groaning captives (Luke 4:18, quoting Isa. 58 and 61). Nations gather in response. The psalm uses the past tense: gathered. The church—that's us, and all whom God is gathering—sees why.[8] The prophet uses the future tense to announce what God will bring. The psalms praise in the past tense to show just how reliable God's promises are—they are as unchangeable as the past.

Yet the psalmist laments a shortened life, breaking the train of thought that ends with triumphant promise. Lament over shortness of life is common in Israel's scripture and in many people's religion and philosophy (Limburg 2000: 345). We are promised forgiveness, but we are not promised tomorrow, Augustine glosses (2003: 56–57). Luther suggests that for the wicked, death is always a surprise (1976: 315). The implication is clear: for those who trust God, every moment is a gift met with gratitude, and every next moment might bring death.

The final bit of Ps. 102 has resonated in Christian thinking about eschatology, time, and eternity. St. Augustine calls it one of the clearest descriptions of the end of the world in the entire Bible (*City of God* 20.24, in Wesselschmidt 2007: 211, 214–15). His claim renders all the more striking the fact that the psalm does not even appear in the Revised Common Lectionary! The book of Hebrews applies these verses about God's eternity *to Christ*: "Of the Son he [God] says . . . 'In the beginning, Lord, you founded the earth, and the heavens are the work of your hands'" (Heb. 1:8, 10). This great promise in Hebrews, that "Jesus Christ is the same yesterday and today and forever" (Heb. 13:8), may be forged on the anvil of Ps. 102:27, "you are the same, and your years have no end." If the Bible itself tells us to read Ps. 102:25–27 with reference to Christ's eternal reign, why wouldn't we do so? And if we do so, what do we learn?

St. Ambrose sees here the surprising reversal of the evidence before our eyes. The created cosmos *looks* permanent. It is not. We fragile creatures, frail as we are,

---

8. I am drawing here on Richard B. Hays, *Echoes of Scripture in the Letters of Paul* (New Haven: Yale University Press, 1989), esp. chap. 3.

subject to death at any moment, *look* temporary. We are not. We will not all die; we will all be raised. Indeed, in just a half step past Ambrose's rhetoric, all creation will be renewed. Christ himself promises that heaven and earth will pass away, but not his word (Matt. 24:35). We must understand that the whole visible and invisible order, every star and molecule, will pass away, in order to grasp Christ's own promise, "See, I am making all things new" (Rev. 21:5) (*The Prayer of Job and David* 1.7.24–25, in Wesselschmidt 2007: 213–14). Cyril of Jerusalem adds an important coda. This world's impermanence does not imply its unimportance. It will die, as will we all. But what does God do with dead things? God resurrects them: "So we should look for a resurrection of the heavens" (*Catechetical Lectures* 15.3, in Wesselschmidt 2007: 214).

Early church theologians are often attacked for denying the goodness of the body and creation. Sometimes the shoe fits. Here the psalm sounds the temporariness of creation, but the ancient interpreters insist on its resurrection-demanding importance to God. Fulgentius of Ruspe, a North African bishop in the late fifth and early sixth centuries, proclaims that the Holy Trinity is "the only one by nature unchangeable." St. Athanasius amens him with a glance at Mal. 3:6, "For I the LORD do not change" (*Discourses against the Arians* 1.10.36, in Wesselschmidt 2007: 216). This raises obvious questions: God seems to have done quite a lot of changing in Ps. 102! He has been riled up to act, he has looked down, he has come down, he has rebuilt Jerusalem, he draws Gentiles and Jews alike into adoration. The patristic readers know all of this. Yet they stand by their assertion: God is not actually changing. When God acts, he shows forth who he eternally is. If the God who makes good on his promises is not who God eternally and forever is, then we should not trust a word he says or build our lives on him. Thankfully, God is who he says he is. God will restore Zion, gather the Gentiles, and roll creation up like a garment in order to remake it anew, dazzling, as God intends, with all people included in the praise of the one who thought it all up and makes it all resplendent with his presence. The psalm proclaims it—write this down!

PSALM 103

One of the most important modern observations about the Bible is that the social identity of the reader(s) matters a great deal in interpretation. Who "we" are, doing the reading, is a key ingredient in determining what scripture "means." For example, imagine Ps. 103:2 prayed by students from an elite private college gathered at a professor's home. The professor has modeled his house on Italian Renaissance mansions and filled it with art from the period. The meal is exquisite, served on fine china, with enough silver at each place to render the guests nervous about which utensil to use when. The host wears a "casual" dinner jacket. He bows his bald head and in a soft voice prays, "Bless the Lord, O my soul, and forget not all his benefits." Amen, cue the feast.

Or try this setting: a family of five settles in for a meal in a hut in rural Indonesia. The single mother has done well for this meal by securing an egg to mix in to the children's noodles. Perhaps if her small business works out, funded by a microloan, she can add vegetables one day. For now, the egg will keep the four children relatively full, as long as she refrains from eating. But she will not refrain from praying, "Bless the Lord, O my soul, and forget not all his benefits."

Sounds different, doesn't it?

Psalm 103 is craftily knit together with the ones preceding and following it. Like Ps. 101 it names itself as a psalm of David, and like Ps. 102 it laments suffering, counts on God's intervention, contrasts the brevity of human life with God's expansive eternity, and uses dirt as a particularly apt image. Like Ps. 104 following, Ps. 103 concentrates on a divine saving intervention, glories in the bounty of creation, and uses grass as a fitting comparison to human longevity. One interpreter sees a trinitarian pattern, with Ps. 103 describing the work of

God the Savior and Ps. 104 describing economies of the Father in creation and of the Spirit in sanctifying (Limburg 2000: 350). Each psalm from 101 to 104 has a vast, cosmic sweep, making meaning from the dirt and grass under our feet and the pit (the grave? hell? both?) that the one praying seeks to avoid to the angels surrounding the throne of heaven.

Psalm 103 has been particularly treasured among Christians. It is a psalm of the staggering grace that God alone can bring about. Commentators name it an all-time favorite, in the company of such treasures as Pss. 23 and 121. In some ways, it cuts against the grain of much of the biblical narrative. "He does not deal with us according to our sins," the psalmist exults in 103:10, "nor repay us according to our iniquities." Really? God does not? Is this not the judge who will weigh our misdeeds at the end of time? The one who retaliates against children's children for the sins of their parents (Exod. 34:7)? Who cannot stand iniquity and must punish it? No. "As far as the east is from the west, so far he removes our transgressions from us" (Ps. 103:12). God does not punish the sinner as we might expect from those other verses; rather, God puts a crown on the sinner's head (103:4). This is because God "knows how we were made; he remembers that we are dust" (103:14). This is the one who breathed life into dirt in the first place, watching it breathe with parental pride. God knows we're frail, fragile. What can you expect but a little waywardness from people made like that? We're gone in an instant, like a day's flower, like chaff blown away. And so God becomes like us—dirt, grass, dust—to save us.

Some psalms read well enough on their own. Interpretation can just get in the way.

This one opens with an admonition to the one doing the praying. "O my soul" may run the risk of suggesting an interior space, sealed off from the body, the neighbor, the community. Nothing could be farther from the Hebrew notion expressed here. A more etymological translation would be "Bless the LORD, O my throat" (Kraus 1993: 291). The spirit within a human being expresses itself through the throat, in every breath and in every word. So too, the Spirit of God expresses words and psalms of praise through the redeemed.[1] Let all that is within me—my very guts—praise God's name. The vital organs without which there is no life are those called upon to praise. The person's soul or throat or very self is who she is. Just as YHWH's name expresses who God is. Let all I am praise all that God is. "Soul" in an expansive sense is not a bad translation—the profoundest

---

1. I'm grateful to my colleague Harry Maier for help with this section and often elsewhere.

self, not an interior self separated from body and others and God, but the person God made, took flesh to save, and intends to resurrect.

This psalm represents a "liturgical not-forgetting" (Mays 1994: 326). The benefits of the Lord recalled here radiate out from the speaker to God's vindication of Israel, to all humanity, to the cosmos, to the angels at God's throne, and by the final verse, back to the speaker's soul. The psalmist mixes the praise of a redeemed speaker with the praise of Israel (Kraus 1993: 291). In other words, the psalmist will not let us later speakers forget to praise. And the psalm will not let the speakers praise without intertwining personal thanksgiving with the story of God's faithfulness to his people.

The next section recalls God's benefits to one delivered. Psalm 103:3–5 does this with poetic power by repeatedly using the second-person singular, "you, your." Commentators both ancient and modern have noted the intertwining of "guilt" and "diseases" as the twin ailments from which God rescues "you." Sickness is explained theologically, with guilt as the cause (Frank-Lothar Hossfeld, in Hossfeld and Zenger 2011: 35). The two are linked elsewhere in scripture (e.g., Jer. 16:4). This link could lead to troubling pastoral conclusions. Should someone sick be told their illness is their fault? That true repentance would lead to restored health? Of course not. Cause and effect are not so mechanically linked, and medicine can clearly heal people without repentance as a prerequisite. The link could be defended theologically by saying that the "we" who are ill and need both healing and saving is all of humanity, linked as we are in Adam. "Our" sin causes harm, and we cannot repair it entirely on our own. Already in scripture, the book of Job protests against any one-to-one link of ill fortune and sin (Mays 1994: 163–64). Yet something remains of their association. Karl Barth calls sickness "a forerunner and messenger of death" (quoted in Mays 1994: 163–64). It can make us sigh over "our" sin, even if it is ours only by virtue of sharing humanity with Adam and all others; it can allow us to give thanks for healing even if the benefits come to us derivatively through our membership with others in Adam and in Christ.

I am less sure the psalm begins with thanks for an individual healing than many modern commentators. The benefits in 103:3–5 range from healing to being crowned by God in 103:4. The psalmist exults that God treats "you" like royalty (Limburg 2000: 348). Identity here flows like liquid; it expands like gas. The thanksgiving rendered goes far beyond one person's experience and ranges across many kinds of benefits so the entire assembly can give voice to thanks. The collective "we" here first sins, then is restored, then is crowned like royalty, then gives praise and calls the whole universe to join. An Augustinian glimpse at this would conclude it is the body of Christ, head and members, whose very "soul" is to offer unending praise. Exactly how many individuals on their own are eligible for this sort of healing, this range of praise, the crown of a king, joining with all Israel and all the cosmos in exultation?

Augustine exults in the depiction of healing in 103:3–5. "An omnipotent doctor is never confronted with an incurable disease," he promises (Augustine 2003: 83). He loves to describe Christ as a physician. His use of it here shows how deeply God delights in bodies. While some ancient interpreters may have interpreted "soul" in some narrow sense, exclusive of bodies, Augustine here does no such thing: "He knows how to re-create what he created; he knows how to form anew what he once formed." God is so deeply good that he exults in every particle of what he has made, down to the last hair on "your" head. God himself has descended to the pit to make complete restoration possible. What is crowned in 103:4 is God's own gift. The only danger in this hospital is that the patient would thrust the physician's hands away rather than submit to them. Augustine is quick to make a standard disclaimer: that we don't understand what we're talking about. What patient fully understands how healing works? We can shout with gladness but cannot fully explain God's grace. Yet in Christ "we" receive the benefits of being parts of his body since he took the illness of being part of ours.

This section concludes with a promise of youth renewed like the eagle's. This is not the only place these majestic birds become an analogy for God's flourishing people (Isa. 40:31, most famously). One modern interpreter expounds on the image of the particular bird this way: eagles eat their fill and then seem frail and weak, hobbling and perhaps even falling, until they take flight and soar, "using thermal currents" (Hossfeld and Zenger 2011: 34). This is precisely the sort of observation Augustine welcomes in his *On Christian Doctrine*, where he advises that interpreters of scripture know all they can about zoology, botany, and all else that science can teach so as to teach the scriptures well. To say that the simile is "poetic" is to fail to interpret altogether. Why was this particular image used? Analogies can, of course, be pressed too far. Perhaps Augustine does so when he expounds on the eagle. He draws on the best biology of the time, which suggested that elderly eagles' beaks grow too large. Elder eagles must bash their beaks on rocks to allow themselves to eat. Occasionally, Augustine apologizes for or expresses doubt over an observation about an animal, though here he does not. He simply says the reference to the eagle "was not made by the Holy Spirit without good reason" (Augustine 2003: 89). This repair of the facility to eat is like "a kind of resurrection," and the rock against which the bird causes this life-sustaining injury is itself Christ, drawing on 1 Cor. 10:4 ("and the rock was Christ"). What interests me here is that both Hossfeld and St. Augustine want to ask why the psalmist draws on this particular bird. Hossfeld uses details from science not available to Augustine that he would have gladly drawn on (thermal currents). Augustine uses christological insight available to modern interpreters but not normally consulted. Augustine would change the analogy himself if told the observations were incorrect. He would have no trouble drawing on thermal currents to speak of God's surprising, beautiful work ("Were not our hearts burning within us?" Luke 24:32). The desire to know more about God through nature and scripture is a good one and should be pursued further.

Psalm 103:6–14 is the merciful heart of this psalm, showing the merciful heart of God. For Ps. 103, the blessing doubly invoked in the opening verses and returned to in the closing verses takes the form of not-forgetting. To be blessed is to re-member, to re-form in our bodies God's gracious way with Israel. Even the most historical-critical interpreters sometimes go gospel heavy at this point. Mays calls it a "profoundly evangelical" psalm (1994: 326). Limburg praises the graciousness formula at 103:8 by saying it is "like a creed" (2000: 349). Hossfeld names it the "Magna Carta" of the forgiveness of sins (Hossfeld and Zenger 2011: 36). For Christians, the form of God's mercy is Jesus.

There is a certain danger, however, in reading this section in a noncovenantal way. The word "all" appears so often in this psalm,[2] and descriptions like "as far as the east is from the west" emphasize mercy to everyone so deeply, that God's specific and costly covenant with Israel can be forgotten or underemphasized. St. Augustine, with his rhetorical and homiletical gifts, expounds this way: "Walk tall, human soul, for you are worth so high a price"—the blood of the Son of God (2003: 85). That will preach and is biblically true. Yet the risk is reducing salvation to an individual exchange and excising Israel from God's merciful dealings. The psalm has a contrapuntal note that must be heard as well: "those who fear him" (103:11, 13, 17). These merciful ways are made known *to Moses*—a point we Christians have often downplayed or forgotten. This is not grace showered on the unsuspecting and ungrateful. It is covenantally shaped grace remembered by a people who love the God of the exodus, who "works vindication and justice for all who are oppressed" (103:6).

This section of Ps. 103 represents a careful reading of Exod. 33–34. The graciousness formula of 103:8 appears often in scripture as a thumbnail sketch of

2. Mays points out the frequent use of "all" and the expansive scope it lends this psalm (1994: 327).

God's deliverance of Israel. Psalm 103:6–7 introduces the graciousness formula, and then 103:9–14 comments on it. The section as a whole forms a corporate identity, a "we," on whom God has compassion unending (Hossfeld and Zenger 2011: 33–35).

This compassion is forged in the story of Israel. God's *hesed*, his steadfast love, is God standing by a people who misbehave as gravely as in Exod. 32. The psalmist does not recount the details, but any reader familiar with the Bible will remember that at the very moment God was unveiling himself most intimately to Israel on the mountaintop with Moses with the Ten Commandments, the people were forging golden idols, bowing down to them, claiming they had delivered them from Egypt, and rising up to "play." Punishment was severe: a plague wiping out many, people being forced to drink the idols ground to dust, the smashing of the tablets, and brother killing brother who had engaged in idolatry. This is the sort of humanity whom God remembers with "steadfast love" and, perhaps more impressively, "compassion."

Hesed is often paired with righteousness in scripture, but here "compassion" sticks out. Who can forget the perfidy of Aaron saying, "I threw [the gold] into the fire, and out came this calf" (Exod. 32:24)? Who can have compassion on a people like Israel as described in Exod. 32? The word "compassion" shares a root with the word "womb" (Limburg 2000: 349). God nurtures her people as tenderly as a mother does her child. The psalmist avoids any mention of the infamy. The dismal events of Exod. 32 are passed over in silence. God can recall mercy to Israel while forgetting its sin, removing it as far as east is from west (Ps. 103:12). God is not interested in going to court as accuser (103:9); the New Testament's description of the Spirit as "Counselor" will strengthen this turn of the courtroom from place of judgment to place of restoration. Exodus's description of God's memory is vastly disproportionate on the side of mercy: God keeps *hesed* for a thousand generations and visits iniquity of parents on children only to three to four generations. God is some three hundred times more gracious than vindictive. Psalm 103 explodes the math altogether. Mercy is "from everlasting to everlasting," righteousness "to children's children" (103:17).

"As far as the east is from the west," the psalmist proclaims, "so far he removes our transgressions from us" (103:12). Elsewhere scripture promises that God will remember his people's sins no more (Jer. 31:34). It is worth lingering on this notion of divine memory and forgetfulness. According to this psalm, God *does* remember something: we are dust (103:14). The dirt from our making is still under God's fingernails. What do you expect of mere dust? God remembers our creation just yesterday, a moment ago, and considers our sins understandable. I have told stories as a preacher about God forgetting our sins. They work because Christians believe God is eternal, all-knowing, and wise. The idea of God *forgetting* has traction, teeth. Some Christians have wanted to revise such attributes of God as relics of Greek philosophical thought, arguing that the Bible, in passages like these, suggests a more malleable notion of God. I do not. The notion of God forgetting is, like all our speech about God, anthropomorphic. It is an analogy, and it fails in certain respects, like all analogies. God does not forget our sins because God is flighty or confused, nor is God surprised when we misbehave anew. God forgets our sins because God is merciful, and God puts strictures in place to curb us toward holiness. We call those strictures "the church." The all-knowing God chooses to forget. It is good biblical theology to keep the tension in the language in place.

For this psalm, God's unimaginable difference from creatures is a profound mercy. God is like a parent in his compassion. God is greater, older, stronger, and wiser than us, and that makes for grace. Other places in Israel's scripture describe God's elect as beloved children (Exod. 4:22; Hos. 11:1–7; Jer. 31:9). Limburg sees Luke 15's story of the prodigal son as an "expansion" on Ps. 103:13 (2000: 349). The New Testament takes this tradition further to describe the Son's very relationship to the one who sent him, into which the Spirit ushers all us forgiven sinners. Every time we say, "Our Father," we name God the way Jesus named him, which Jesus himself learned from passages like Ps. 103:13.

Psalm 103, then, gives the lie to clumsy Christian atonement theories that speak as though God the Father had to kill his little boy to forgive us.[3] Grace, expressed here in the psalm, gave rise to Israel's later self-understandings, including Jesus's. God is plenty capable of expressing mercy without sacrifice, as the psalms regularly attest. For God remembers we are dust. God remembers lifting a handful of dirt and blowing life into it, us. What could we expect of such frail creatures but to disintegrate back into dirt? To say that God somehow *must* punish sin to be faithful to himself is to fail to be fully biblical.

We should say instead that God has worked in the most beautiful way possible.[4] God is constrained by nothing other than God's own character. And that character

3. Arguably, the church never taught that, though a misunderstanding preacher can stray from the tradition and do great harm, of course. See Fleming Rutledge's magisterial *The Crucifixion: Understanding the Death of Jesus Christ* (Grand Rapids: Eerdmans, 2015).

4. David Bentley Hart's essay on this is justly famous: "A Gift Exceeding Every Debt: An Eastern Orthodox Appreciation of Anselm's *Cur Deus Homo,*" *Pro Ecclesia* 7, no. 3 (1998): 333–48.

has God's hand always in the dirt, making life from lifelessness. God bends low in his constant care for Israel, his children. God bends lowest in Jesus. In his Word, God has made himself "a brother to that grass," St. Augustine says. We should not find it unbelievable that we mere dirt-creatures could become daughters and sons of the divine. God became human to show us it is so. Augustine is constantly thickening the mystery of scripture. Do you find it incredible that God could forgive? Even more incredible that God would become grass, dirt, human, frail, for us, "that grass might not despair of itself" (Augustine 2003: 103)? Isaiah 40:6 is a clear parallel to Ps. 103. Grass withers and flowers fade, but the word of the Lord stands forever. Psalm 103 suggests the "love" of the Lord stands forever (103:17). With God, the Word and the Love are one and the same. The Son and the Spirit are, with the Father, one God, one of whom is made into grass like us to join us to this triune life. Those in Christ will not be surprised to see such trinitarian fullness throughout the scripture. But without the scripture we would have no idea what we were seeing, no language for God's work, and so no hope.

Psalm 103 illuminates its resounding hope with a glance at the angels. All God's messengers, all God's hosts, his ministers, should do his work (103:20–21). There is a vision of heavenly plentitude here, of fullness, nearly overflowing from heaven, erupting in frail grass, consummating with a cosmos in which all do God's bidding. There is one alone who blesses the psalmist's soul in 103:1–2, 22: God, in whose Son all creatures become one, and all the worlds become praise.

PSALM 104

Two things especially stand out about Ps. 104. One is its portrait of creation. It not only offers thunderous praise. It does so relatively uninterrupted by danger or threat (except for 104:35). Even the young lion and the leviathan in the great sea—fairly dangerous creatures to human beings—praise God by their roaring and playing. Unlike other psalms in praise of creation, such as Ps. 8, human beings make barely an appearance here, clocking in for work as the lions close their shift (104:22–23). God presides gracefully over a created order that hastens to follow commands, looks to God for food and water in due season, and demonstrates God's glory simply by being what it is. "There lives the dearest freshness deep down things," the poet Gerard Manley Hopkins said.[1] And all things shout the grandeur of God with which they are charged.

Second, God's Spirit is mighty and active in God's world. If Ps. 103 describes God's merciful and redeeming work, which Christians understand as appropriate to the Son, Ps. 104 describes God's creating and sanctifying work, appropriate to the Father and the Holy Spirit. Psalms 103 and 104 together describe both the intimate nature of God and the cosmic testimony of God's works (Limburg 2000: 352). Psalm 104 is assigned for the day of Pentecost in the lectionary and has given rise to such prayers to the Holy Spirit as this: "Come Holy Spirit, fill the hearts of your faithful and kindle in them the fire of your love. Send forth your Spirit and they shall be created. And You shall renew the face of the earth."[2]

1. Gerard Manley Hopkins, "God's Grandeur," in *Poems and Prose* (New York: Penguin Classics, 1953), 27.
2. "Prayer to the Holy Spirit," in *A Book of Prayers* (n.p.: International Committee on English in the Liturgy, 1982), available at https://www.loyolapress.com/our-catholic-faith/prayer/traditional-catholic -prayers/prayers-every-catholic-should-know/prayer-to-the-holy-spirit.

The Spirit who broods over the waters at creation longs to make all things new. The scope of his work stretches from the farthest planets and stars to the intricacies of each heart. No grave is safe from his life-giving power. One modern commentator notes that we have here a "building block for a biblical pneumatology" (Hossfeld and Zenger 2011: 61). But few of us ever actually build the thing. Fulsome Christian readings of the Old Testament are discouraged, and the mainline Western church leaves the doctrine of the Spirit neglected. The two phenomena are not unrelated.

Commentators *are* often quick to point out the deep similarities between this psalm and the religious and devotional literature of Israel's ancient neighbors. There are similarities with the Egyptian Hymn to Aten (Hossfeld and Zenger 2011: 50). The portrait of God riding on the waters is similar to praises of a Canaanite storm god. Mesopotamian visions of divine conquest of the sea as the origin of creation may inform the psalm. The Babylonian Enuma Elish describes gods wearing "mantles of radiance."[3] The god Nergal is described as surrounded by a "fearful shine" (Hossfeld and Zenger 2011: 49). Images similar to those in Ps. 104 appear among Assyrians and Akkadians, and from Susa and Phoenicia, and in doubtless other places. This suggests several things. One, God is not so ungenerous as to provide no knowledge of himself to people who bother to look (104:27–28). Two, more boldly, animals and waters and light *do* reflect God's grandeur. That is why and how God made them, as this psalm makes clear. As commentators wax enthusiastic about Israel's neighbors and their similar scriptures, I am tempted to lament that we can find whatever other religions are "present" in this psalm but are forbidden from finding Jesus or the Holy Spirit there. But that is unfair. More circumspect commentators admit it is difficult to posit any causal relationship between other people's stories and Israel's. There may be some, or causation may run the other direction. Biblical people ought never to be surprised to find God's truth liberally sprinkled throughout creation, especially among those who pray and try to imagine a who behind the what of things. Nevertheless, Israel's particular emphases shine through in our canonized text. The God of Israel is not limited in his power to the daytime. He is not another creature among his creatures. God's creating and sanctifying work shine through all that is, and are renewing the face of the ground right now.

Psalm 104 presents us with a theology of dust. All living things are drawn from it and will return to it, as funeral liturgies attest. Christian theology takes a step

---

3. William Brown, *Seeing the Psalms: A Theology of Metaphor* (Louisville: Westminster John Knox, 2003), 272.

farther: God is dust. God's taking of flesh means God, like the rest of us, is walking dust, as red as the earth from which Adam is first formed. The only difference is that the incarnate God is already raised in his flesh; the rest of the dead wait.

This sort of dust-affirming faith should make for a world-affirming one. But it often has not. Poet Wendell Berry may be as responsible as anyone for pointing out the biblical mandate to be a responsible part of the interdependence of creatures in a way that brings glory to God, that causes God to delight (104:31). He also asks environmentalists who blame Christianity for our planet's ills to follow the first rule of criticism and "read the book first."[4] The Bible is an outdoor book. God's glory is everywhere in creation. It is as common as raindrops and blades of grass. "Everything that is, is holy," William Blake said, expressing the psalmist's sentiments. If Christians hope to see God's love in Christ (John 3:16), they must also love the world the way God does. Berry's point—his interaction with Blake and with John 3:16—would be strengthened by more fulsome trinitarian and christological emphases. Our environmental problems spring from an insufficient valuation of dust. All things are made of dust and God's "spirit." And creation, as this psalm suggests, is inextricably mutually intricate. No part is separable from any other, in life or death.

For Christians, "spirit" is not vaguely divine; the Spirit is God. Dust is not just the building block of all creation. Dust is also the garment God wraps himself in. Christian faith is dust-affirming even though, of course, the church's actions have often fallen short of our faith. Scripture has frightful things to say about God's people having, and *not* heeding, God's word. Perhaps a first step is reacquaintance with a word more in our hands than in our hearts.

Psalm 104 presents what one commentator calls "a grand tour of God's creation."[5] The psalmist exults in the living creatures, all of which look to God for their provision and thrive in the place graciously given to them. Yet this is not a nature poem alone. It is a celebration specifically of God's dominion over all things, since God made and delights in them (Alter 2007: 362). There is not a single godless particle in all of creation. All things, looked at aright, bear witness to God's creating and resurrecting goodness.[6] The accent in this story of creation is on frivolity and delight. Creation did not have to be this diffuse, this extravagant,

---

4. Wendell Berry, "Christianity and the Survival of Creation," in *Sex, Economy, Freedom, and Community: Eight Essays* (New York: Pantheon, 1993), 94.

5. Brown, *Seeing the Psalms*, 271.

6. There is also, of course, nearly unfathomable evil that mars creation, against which the Spirit groans (Rom. 8). To see that shadow is part of seeing the fuller picture of creation.

this various, this full of life. Yet it is, and we hardly notice. The psalmist offers us the Bible's first "hallelujah" (104:35; Mays 1994: 336). Jesus warned that if the people acclaiming him as king stayed silent, the stones would cry out (Luke 19:40). He needn't have. The stones already do, as does the entire choir of creation.[7]

"Bless the LORD, O my soul"—Ps. 104 opens as it closes, just as had the previous psalm. Only Pss. 103 and 104 open and close this way (Limburg 2000: 352). Psalm 103 also extolled the Lord for his works. It also closes as Ps. 104 opens, with an invocation of God's angels, messengers, or ministers (103:21; 104:4).

This psalm differs from its predecessor in its visual portrayal of God, "clothed with honor," "wrapped in light," setting the beams of his "chambers on the waters," each mini-portrait equally dazzling (104:1–3). The great linguist and interpreter Robert Alter points out that the verbs here form a chain of present participles, which suggest a flurry of activity on God's part: wrapping and stretching and setting and making and walking.

Augustine suggests that the psalm is rich enough literally. Those content to be dazzled with divine beauty in the natural world or on the letter of scripture are not wrong. But there are further delights here for those who would go deeper: "To those who contemplate them these works are pointers to God. . . . He has never ceased to display his works before our eyes" (Augustine 2003: 107). To uncover these hidden delights is not the job of the virtuoso interpreter alone. "Your desires will help us in Christ's name as we seek" out the spiritual sense, Augustine tells his assembled congregation. Their shouts will guide the preacher's exposition; presumably (though he does not say this!) their silence or disapproval would guide it as well.

Who is the "I" in the psalm? This question bedevils many biblical interpreters. For example, tell me who the "I" is in Rom. 7. Is it Paul? Israel? All creation? Every person? Similarly, we should ask who the "I" is in the psalms. Is the "I" David? Another writer? Israel? All of "us" who enter into the psalm? Augustine has an answer that will dissatisfy some but surprise no one: the "I" is the body of Christ, the church to which our psalm speaks (2003: 110). Even a modicum of historical consciousness will give us pause here. But the claim makes sense on Christian grounds. Gentiles have access to this scripture only insofar as we are grafted into Israel by grace (Rom. 11:17, 24). Unless we are the circumcised and law-obedient people of God, this is not "our" book. The "my" in Ps. 104:1 refers to God and the people God is graciously making part of himself—that is true for

---

7. I'm sure the stones observation has been made before, but I first heard it from Frederick Buechner.

Jews and for Christians. The only people for whom it is not true are those going out of their way to display false humility and maintain a safe and critical distance.

"Bless the LORD, O my soul." What does it mean for the speaker to bless with her soul? God is already great. Human blessing adds nothing to God's already-overflowing grandeur (Augustine 2003: 110). To praise this way makes *us*, the ones praising, great. It aligns us with the grain of the universe.[8]

"O LORD my God, you are very great. You are clothed with honor and majesty, wrapped in light as with a garment" (104:1–2). This visual portrait of God inspires thoughts of the incarnation. Patristic thought generally assumes that "visual" or "projected" portraits of God refer to the Son and the Spirit.[9] Cyril of Alexandria, for instance, sees the splendor of 104:1 as referring to the second coming of Christ. Augustine, more daringly still, sees the church in the reference to inestimable beauty—this from the patristic figure who insisted more than any other on the church's morally compromised nature. The church is a group of sinners, full stop, since saints are inextricable from the sinners till the end (Matt. 13:24–30).

God is beauty itself, as other scriptures testify (Song 1:2 and Ps. 45:2 sound this theme in a nuptial context). But God is not content being beautiful alone. Beauty by nature beckons to others. "Now I am going to make a bold statement," Augustine the preacher promises. "To render her beautiful he loved her even when she was ugly," referring to the church (Augustine 2003: 111). Already on thin ice, he inches out farther: "More daring still, since I find it in scripture: to make her beautiful he became ugly himself." He immediately apologizes, "That would not have been a fitting statement to make in the presence of people who love him, but for the fact that scripture bore witness to it before I did." In our era, William Willimon muses that even a coward can stand behind the text and explain, "I would never say this to you, but God seems to, so here you go."[10] Augustine, one with his fellow preacher in the communion of the saints more than a millennium and a half before, makes such a claim.

God in God's self is inherently and unimaginably beautiful (Song 5:8–16). Yet scripture suggests that God takes on human deformity and ugliness. He does not

---

8. I take the language from Stanley Hauerwas, *With the Grain of the Universe: The Church's Witness and Natural Theology* (Grand Rapids: Brazos, 2001).

9. Origen, *Homilies on Leviticus* 12.3.3, and Cyril of Jerusalem, *Catechetical Lectures* 15.1, in Wesselschmidt 2007: 227–29. Augustine has arguments against this in his *Trinity*, fueled by worries about subordinationism, or diminution of the Son and Spirit. Augustine, *The Trinity*, 2nd ed., ed. John E. Rotelle, trans. Edmund Hill, OP, Works of Saint Augustine I/5 (Hyde Park, NY: New City, 2012), books 2–3.

10. Channeling Walter Brueggemann, Willimon says this sort of thing often. I heard it during my time as a TA for Willimon in a course on Karl Barth and preaching at Duke Divinity School in 2001. The course material eventually became his book *Conversations with Barth on Preaching* (Nashville: Abingdon, 2006).

resent or judge or lament them. He puts them on, as texts like Isa. 53:2 suggest ("he had no form or majesty that we should look at him"). God, who is beauty itself, takes on our ugliness with Christ's descent into our flesh. This descent reaches its lowest point with the cross, where mockers despise his lowliness. But not for long: "The heads of the mockers necessarily go on wobbling until he whom they mocked becomes their head" (Augustine 2003: 112). They—we—do not realize that God puts on human ugliness to clothe us in his beauty.

The church has its own beauty, described in passages like Eph. 5:8 ("Once you were darkness, but now in the Lord you are light"). Ours is a derivative beauty, borrowed splendor, reflected glory. It is the church with which God wraps himself in Ps. 104. And if it is hard to believe that a sordid, ordinary body of bickering believers shines like the sun, Augustine thickens the mystery. Is it harder to believe that God would take on ugliness or that we can be glorious? God already did the former; can and will God not do the latter?

This sort of interpretation grates on modern ears. But what is its alternative? Increasingly complex theories about the religious prehistory of the text? Observations that go as deep as "Wow, that's a gorgeous metaphor"? Augustine has drawn his reasoning from the deep logic of the incarnation. He has not merely bent words in the direction of Christian teaching, as if to make the psalm pass theological muster. He has tried to ascertain the incarnation with these particular words. The *res*, the thing itself, is already known: God in flesh to save. The *signa*, these particular words on the page, have to be figured out in that light.[11] Augustine is often maligned with the rest of the ancient church as a world-and-body-denying Platonist. Here he has God in flesh lowlier than any creature on behalf of those who mock him. It would be hard to be more world-affirming. How much more beautiful than staying safe and unsullied in the distance is a God who comes so unbearably close as to wear our sin and bear torture at our hands to save us?

"You stretch out the heavens like a tent, you set the beams of your chambers on the waters" (104:2–3). One explicit reference is to the second day of creation, in which God erects a dome in the midst of the waters, to separate waters from waters (Gen. 1:6).[12] Above that vault are the upper waters, where God builds "upper chambers" (Alter 2007: 363). This verse may hint not only of God's bringing order

11. Augustine describes *res* and *signa* in *On Christian Doctrine* 1, trans. D. W. Robertson (Upper Saddle River, NJ: Prentice Hall, 1958), 8–10.

12. Martin Luther, *Lectures on the Psalms II*, trans. Herbert J. A. Bauman, ed. Hilton C. Oswald, vol. 11 of *Luther's Works* (St. Louis: Concordia, 1976), 318.

out of chaos but also of God's bringing redemption through water, drawing on the exodus or on the stories of the Israelites' neighbors (a Canaanite storm god is a particularly popular suggestion). Amos sounds a similar note, asking

> who builds his upper chambers in the heavens,
> and founds his vault upon the earth;
> who calls for the waters of the sea,
> and pours them out upon the surface of the earth—
> the LORD is his name. (Amos 9:6)

Psalm 104 is a test of literalism. We know cosmologically that there really is no ocean above a physical vault above our heads—these are just metaphors. But then the "really" and the "just" in those sentences should be interrogated. These are words from God, meant to flesh out our salvation. They ought not to be damned with faint praise. They "really" refer to God, not "just" to their ostensible literal referents, and they refer to the people of God and the hope of all the earth. How so?

The psalm suggests that for God, creating the universe was no more difficult than it is for a person to stretch an animal skin (104:2). Plain enough. Augustine takes this further: it is "unmistakable" (patristic rhetoric of certainty tends to ramp up precisely where modern incredulity does) that the verse refers to Christian preaching. Paul has shown the way in this, interpreting the heavenly signs of Ps. 19:4 ("their voice goes out through all the earth, and their words to the end of the world") with reference to Christian preaching in Rom. 10:18. Augustine continues by drawing on Gen. 3 and God's preparation of skins for the disgraced creatures to wear (Gen. 3:21). Animal skins are a sign of human mortality, brought on by the fall. And scripture is written down by mere mortals (Augustine 2003: 115). God used those destined to die to stretch out immortality-making words. And how, technologically, was that done from biblical times to Augustine's and long after? On animal skins. In the incarnation God came to where he had always been but mostly unseen previously. God stretched a skin for us, a sky full of signs, a scripture crammed with marvels. God stretched the skin of mere mortal lives, extending their influence unimaginably. And God took on human skin himself. Scripture is an almost physical extension of the incarnation, both frail, tenuous media to bear something so decisive as salvation. Augustine is working on, and reorienting, what we see when we see the sky. Physical beauty is good. Pressing deeper, one can see scripture's beauty amidst the frail lives of its authors and those now trying to live it out. God's own frail flesh makes sense in this sequence and also crowns it. Augustine interprets the psalms and Genesis the way St. Paul has taught him.

Augustine also borrows the language of Jesus in John 7:38, "Out of the believer's heart shall flow rivers of living water." He follows in the trajectory of St. Paul here: "God's love has been poured into our hearts through the Holy Spirit that has been given to us" (Rom. 5:5). In a Christian lexicon, descriptions of waters shut up above, as in Ps. 104:3, bring to mind the Spirit whose descent is a cascade of God's love. The building blocks of a biblical pneumatology are here. We simply have to pick them up and assemble them.[13]

"You make the clouds your chariot, you ride on the wings of the wind, you make the winds your messengers, fire and flame your ministers" (104:3–4). Biblically attentive readers will think immediately of Elijah caught up in the whirlwind to heaven by a chariot and horses of fire (2 Kgs. 2:11–12). St. Cyril's observation is simple and profound: "Most things about our Lord are two-fold." Christ's first coming is quiet, like the dew. His final coming not so much (*Catechetical Lectures* 15.1, in Wesselschmidt 2007: 227–28). The twofold fire and flame in Heb. 1:7 are read as a divine description of angels. As great and mighty as they are, they are less than the Son, for they are creatures and not to be worshiped. In Ps. 104:4 they are portrayed as God's messengers, missive-bearers, ministers in the world. Angels are not spoken of terribly often in mainline church circles—Orthodox and Catholics have greater resources for such commentary. But perhaps this reticence is biblical. They do not come up in scripture often. When they do, angels bear messages from above, about not their own greatness, but God's. Fire and flame suggest a dangerous, godly presence (Exod. 3:2). Their flame cauterizes, heals, makes holy, and brings glory not destruction.

The description of God riding on the wind refers "literally" for Augustine to the ascension of Jesus ("A cloud took him out of their sight" in Acts 1:9). For Augustine, "literal" does not mean what the author had in mind when putting pen to paper. It refers to what these letters mean in a biblical universe, a canonical context. Figurally, the clouds refer to our coming ascent. Wherever Jesus goes, his people will follow. Augustine cites 1 Thess. 4:16–17, a passage beloved by devotees of the rapture in our day, as a context to read more spiritually ("Then we who are alive, who are left, will be caught up in the clouds together with them to meet the Lord in the air"). This refers to the Lord who commands physical clouds (Isa. 5:6),

13. Robert Jenson's two-volume systematic theology attempts to redress the West's historic avoidance of the Spirit. Jenson, *Systematic Theology*, 2 vols. (New York: Oxford, 2001). James Howell, *The Kiss of God: 27 Lessons on the Holy Spirit* (Nashville: Abingdon, 2004), does so also for a broader readership.

whose preachers water the vineyard that is God's people. The cloud raining at that time apologized: "This particular cloud who is talking to you has no more energy left today" (Augustine 2003: 128). Whimsy mixes with warning: "The Judge will come on the heels of the preacher" (Augustine 2003: 128).

"You set the earth on its foundations, so that it shall never be shaken" (104:5). Anyone who has been through an earthquake knows otherwise. In early modern times, verses like this were taken as a reason not to acknowledge the Copernican revolution. But Galileo had no reason to fear Ps. 104:5 in Augustine's hands (in fact, his dearest wish should have been that the inquisitorial Catholic Church leaders had been better readers of the Augustine they hallowed). According to Augustine, the "earth" refers to the church, which is the Lord's coveted possession in Ps. 24:1, will stand forever according to Jesus's promise (Matt. 16:18). With the *res* established, Augustine returns to the *signa*—this earth is thirsty, it cries out for moisture, as the psalm suggests (he adds references to Pss. 42 and 142 for good measure). If God provides rain for all kinds of terrain, will God not water his thirsty church? Astronomers have nothing to fear here. Except the same thing all creatures must fear—lack of life-giving water.

Psalm 104:6–14 describes the cascading of that water ever downward to its place. It also echoes the story of the flood from Gen. 6–9, when the water rose above the mountains (104:6), after which God promised no future deluge (104:9). As destructive as that story was, this piece of praise has God noticing the wild asses and their thirst, the birds of the air who sing after the rain (104:11–12). Everything, however unlikely, looked at aright, bears witness to God's provision. Scripture is trying to train the artist's eye, one that notices detail, that exults in the seemingly ordinary, that pauses long enough to notice, say, ordinary waterways and thirsty animals.

Reading Augustine and Luther on these verses, I was alternately impressed and annoyed by one recurring theme: material provision for pastors. What an obscure, intramural church fight to wage, I thought. Then, as a pastor, I found myself embroiled in debate over compensation for folks working hard and fruitfully on my pastoral staff. And in those committee meetings I found myself quoting Ps. 104. God sees that water descends to the proper terrain so that all types of animals can drink. How much more must God want to provide for those who work to give cups of cold water to his children (Matt. 10:42)? The form of life of pastoral ministry matches the form of life of scripture's commentators and writers. The further we are from the church the more foreign these ways of reading scripture will feel.

"You . . . bring forth food from the earth, and wine to gladden the human heart, oil to make the face shine, and bread to strengthen the human heart" (104:14–15). In the middle of the psalm is a joyful, life-affirming, incarnationally shaped bit of delight. The verses were some of John Calvin's favorites.[14] No dour-faced Puritan, the French Reformer noted that the different tastes of food and wine show God's exuberant goodness. The variety is not necessary. It's just delightful. Commentators often make mention of the oil in this verse. Luther describes the oil that makes a face shine as the offer of mercy to those who don't deserve it.[15] The oil reminds Cyril of Jerusalem of 2 Cor. 3–4 and Paul's promise of the glory of the Lord shining in believers' faces from one degree of glory to another. Oil is a sign of chrismation in Christian liturgy—a mark of the seal of the Holy Spirit for confirmation, ordination, healing, or last rites. Bread is a sign that we need more than bread to live (Limburg 2000: 353). These three gifts signify the Eucharist. God uses ordinary, delightful, naturally grown and human-manufactured gifts to give life. And also new life.

The animals in Ps. 104:17–30 present a "sprawling zoological panorama," as Alter puts it, like the voice out of the whirlwind in Job 38:1. Yet there is none of that voice's accusation or cross-examination. The panorama is simply lovingly catalogued. Origen marveled that God has created a home not only for us but for all animals (*Against Celsus* 4.75, in Wesselschmidt 2007: 230).

"You have made the moon to mark the seasons; the sun knows its time for setting" (104:19). Of course, at a basic level, the orderliness of creation bears witness to a choreographing creator. More deeply, the moon waxes and wanes as the church does, growing and shrinking like any time-bound institution (Augustine 2003: 160). The church has often glimpsed Christ in the "sun of righteousness" in Mal. 4:2 and in descriptions of the sun's course across the sky like Ps. 19. If the sun "knows" its waning, then Christ knew his passion and loved it (104:19).

"The young lions roar for their prey . . . and Leviathan that you formed to sport in it" (104:21, 26). God provides for each creature. Augustine sees the lions as a sign of evil. They slink around in the dark, roaring. He notes the surprise for those expecting to see a hint of the Lion of Judah (Rev. 5:5). Just because Christ is a rock does not mean we should see Christ in every rock, he insists (Augustine 2003: 165). A lion can signify Christ's reign or the evil that God allows to survive, that God even feeds (see 1 Pet. 5:8, where *the devil* is a roaring lion). So too the leviathan, a great beast of the deep, in this psalm reduced (or enhanced?) into

14. Brown, *Seeing the Psalms*, 272.
15. Luther, *Lectures on the Psalms II*, 335.

a house pet with whom God plays. Elsewhere in the psalms (say, Ps. 91) and in Job (chap. 41), the leviathan is a sign of evil. The Hebrews were not particularly seafaring people. The great sea beasts stir terror enough for those confident on the water, let alone those not accustomed to sailing. But here Leviathan is a sign of mirth. Perhaps this can be allegorized by saying evil should be squashed when young (so Augustine). Perhaps it is a sign that evil should be mocked, as God makes sport of Leviathan. Perhaps it is a sign that even evil, allowed to work to its purposes, cannot but eventually come around and bless the designs of God. It has no independent existence; it serves finally to confirm God's glory, as all creatures will one day do.[16] Evil is a parasite without independent existence. No one can go and pick up a handful of evil. As a teacher of mine put it once, if you grab the devil by the scruff of the neck and examine the label in the uniform, it will say "property of the triune God." Whatever (mysterious) allowance evil has for now, these will ultimately—inadvertently for the devil, providentially for us—work out for good.

God speaks only one word: Christ. All other words can be brought into obedience to his story, by telling of his incarnation, death, resurrection, and eventual reign. It is as if Augustine takes John 1 literally. With the anchor that is that one word, all else can be a figure.

The last portion of Ps. 104 deals with God's breath especially. Verses 28–30 are the reason the psalm is assigned for Pentecost. They are the building blocks for that biblical pneumatology. It is, perhaps, not surprising that the church's liturgy delivers that pneumatology. St. Francis's canticle of creation sounds similar notes to the psalm from which he learned, praising God for brother wind, sister water, mother earth, and all God's servants. The prayer mentioned above ("Come Holy Spirit, fill the hearts of your faithful and kindle in them the fire of your love. Send forth your Spirit and they shall be created. And You shall renew the face of the earth"[17]), works as a prayer for the dawn, for new birth, for renewal in the church, for the bringing of the kingdom. The Spirit has sometimes been spoken of as the "shy" person of the Trinity.[18] The Spirit never seeks attention but rather

---

16. I do not mean here to endorse universalism, but only to have the scope of eschatological praise of God be as expansive as the psalm does. Augustine is perfectly happy to say that all God has made will one day give praise—the wicked do so by attesting to God's judgment.

17. "Prayer to the Holy Spirit," in *A Book of Prayers* (n.p.: International Committee on English in the Liturgy, 1982), available at https://www.loyolapress.com/our-catholic-faith/prayer/traditional-catholic -prayers/prayers-every-catholic-should-know/prayer-to-the-holy-spirit.

18. Vladimir Lossky, *The Mystical Theology of the Eastern Church* (Crestwood, NY: St. Vladimir's Seminary Press, 1997), 168; and Howell, *Kiss of God*, 19, where he cites Frederick Dale Bruner to this effect.

defers that attention to Jesus. If Jesus is ever or anywhere worshiped and adored, the Holy Spirit is surreptitiously at work.

Psalm 104 brings that hidden work into the light. Here the Spirit is praised as the one who gives breath to all creatures and who then withdraws breath from them, bringing their dismay and return to the dust (104:28–29). The Spirit creates and renews all things (104:30). In traditional trinitarian theology, the works of the Trinity *ad extra* are indivisible. Every work of God is an act of the Father's done through the Son in the Spirit. To show the persons' equal grandeur, we can use the preposition "and" occasionally, as Matt. 28:19 does. Every work of God is done by "the Father, the Son, and the Spirit."[19] These works, then, are not the Spirit's alone, just as creation and reconciliation are not the Father's or the Son's works alone. Yet the scriptures *appropriate* those works to one or the other person of the Godhead. So it is fitting to speak of creation as the Father's work and atonement as the Son's, as long as we remember the Trinity can never act separately.

If that is so, creation's existence, sustenance, and eventual renewal are all the works of the Spirit, according to Ps. 104. God's creation will one day be filled with the glory of God so that the very ground is renewed—that is the Spirit's holiness-making work. Not a single particle of the creation that God made, treasures, and presently laments over will be lost eventually. All will be recovered and shine with his glory. The scope of redemption is cosmic, from the tiniest creeping thing (there may be ten quintillion creeping things on earth, this preacher learned from Google) to the farthest star to the tiniest change of color in a crystal buried so far under the earth no creature will ever find it. The only thing incapable of bearing God's glory is sin; therefore, for much of Christian tradition sin is not a *thing* at all, just a lack (104:35). All that truly is bears witness and will one day shine.

19. These arguments draw from St. Basil the Great, *On the Holy Spirit*, trans. David Anderson (Crestwood, NY: St. Vladimir's Seminary Press, 1980).

PSALM 105

In graduate school we read Gregory of Nyssa's great work *The Life of Moses*. "Great" doesn't always mean interesting, and most of us students were bored with the classic. Gregory recounts the events of the exodus once, and then recounts them again, offering more spiritual readings, but still boring to the mostly mainline, Western, middle-class students. One class member, though, a Romanian Orthodox priest, was surprised by our lack of interest, and explained his perspective: "To me, hearing the story over again was like being read your favorite story by a beloved grandfather."

The priest's way of reading is what is required for a psalm like 105. The story of God's people, Israel, is so familiar we glide over details. Yet for the attentive, there are treasures. Like children listening to a deeply familiar story, we should notice when our grandparent changes something in the telling, even ever so slightly.

There is no mention of sin here, nary a note of Israel's—and so humanity's— regular contribution to the potluck of its life with God: stiff necks, grumbling, rebellion. The psalmist is so focused on God's faithfulness that human recalcitrance does not register in Ps. 105. Psalm 106 more than makes up for this omission. Psalm 105's attention to God's providence is a little like Karl Barth's vision of divine redemption. God's majesty and grace are so predominant that human participation barely appears. Humanity is elect in Christ, such that it is difficult to imagine any outside the sweep of God's embrace. The point is not "universalism." The point is that God's victory is so all-encompassing that it is hard to conceive space outside redemption's reach.

As the psalmist turns to the events of the exodus itself, the crossing of the Red Sea and the drowning of the Egyptians do not come up. Neither do Sinai or the giving of the law (cf. 105:45). The focus is on God's faithfulness during foreign oppression, from Abraham's first calling to Egypt to Canaan to now. Modern scholars suggest Ps. 105 has its home in Israel's later traumatic uprooting from God's land. Exodus is retold here "in the colors of the exile" (Mays 1994: 339). The psalm's uninterrupted note of gratitude is directed at people in the midst of recent devastation. The one who accompanies them on the road to and from Babylon also accompanied Abraham, Joseph, Moses, and Aaron. This God has a track record and can be trusted. He has never allowed his people to be oppressed unendingly.

Some textbook accounts of theology distinguish Western and Eastern Christianity by saying that Western Christians focus on Christ's death and atonement while Eastern Christians focus on Christ's resurrection and the coming renewal of creation. It is the sort of overly tidy typology that can mislead. Yet if it works, this is an Orthodox psalm more than a Catholic or Protestant one. The emphasis is so pronounced on God's life-restoring power that sin and death are obliterated in its light, and we, the psalm's readers, are made one with God's pulsing, over-flowing life right now.

Psalm 105 opens questions for Christians about the nature of our election. Israel cannot remember God's faithfulness at all without specific mention of its ancestors by name (e.g., Isaac is mentioned only here in the entire Psalter) (Hossfeld and Zenger 2011: 70). The emphasis is less on God's numerous descendants (an easier covenant promise for Christians to read ourselves into, as in Gen. 12, 15, and 17) and more on God's gift of the land. What does it mean for those grafted into this covenant by grace, against our nature, to read about "our" ancestors and God's thousand-generation covenant with "us" (Ps. 105:8)? If the Israelites' identity as people of the Lord (105:24, 25, 43) is rooted in genealogical relation to these ancestors, what about us Gentiles, who lack biological descent from Abraham? Christians must remember the gift character of this psalm, and so of all scripture. This is not our book by some sort of inherent right. The promises are to someone else—namely, the Jews (as Ps. 105 makes clear throughout). But God, in vast creativity, working through Israel, has invited even us to his table. We should never presume. Only give thanks and marvel.

Psalm 105 opens with a bossy tone. One scholar calls Ps. 105 "an imperative hymn" (Kraus 1993: 308). The first six verses include ten imperative verbs: give thanks, call on, make known, sing, glory, rejoice, seek, remember, and more (Limburg 2000: 358). This is a liturgical workout. The admonition to praise asks us "inwardly to appropriate, and urgently to explore the great wonders of Yahweh in the history of his people" (Kraus 1993: 310). The psalm's roots stretch deep into Israelite worship; 1 Chr. 16 repeats much of the first part of this psalm in a story about the tent of meeting, where the Levites are appointed to give praise with these words. The events narrated here come from the patriarchs and the exodus, but the Chronicler places them in the time of the monarchy. The actual psalmist probably sat in exile in Babylon. The New Testament picks up this psalm's themes in several places to recount God's faithfulness (the Magnificat in Luke 1:46–55; 1 Cor. 10:1–4). God can be trusted, whatever present evidence to the contrary.

St. Augustine draws our attention to Ps. 105:4: "Seek his presence continually." A more faithful translation from the Hebrew has a stronger admonition for the reader: "Seek his face always." Infinity was not a beloved concept in ancient thought. It is like a number that won't settle down, can't be measured, runs amok. Ancient Christians came to think differently about infinity.[1] God's nature is so vast and unimaginable as to be infinite: not only in the sense of being a lot bigger than us, but in the sense of being without measure, qualitatively different and not just quantitatively. Human beings can grow in grace unendingly without ever tiring of their growth in love or exhausting divine fullness. Augustine asked, on these lines, if God is "always" to be sought, is he ever found? Yes, he answered, we *do* possess a glimpse of the vision of God in this life. If God were never to be found at all, the prophet would not command us to seek him (Isa. 55:7). And yet we seek God in hope, since we can never grasp God fully (so Rom. 8:25). The psalmist urges us to search for God unendingly since we will never tire of the divine presence. For every aspect of God we come to grasp, every gift of God's grace that inhabits our souls, there is vastly more we do not understand, more of God with which to fill us up (Augustine 2003: 186).

The psalm shifts gears at 105:5, from more timeless admonitions to descriptions of God's acts in time. Good thing for us: we can only understand things that take place in our time (and even then just barely!). God condescends to work and be among us. Augustine uses strongly feminine descriptions here: God nurtures and nourishes and accommodates us. God's actions characterize who God is (Hossfeld and Zenger 2011: 69). God is the one who works in history. The theologian Robert Jenson makes this point unmistakably: God is whoever raised Israel from Egypt and Christ from the dead.[2] My local university recently had a panel on the-

---

1. See Robert Wilken, "Seek His Face Always," in *The Spirit of Early Christian Thought: Seeking the Face of God* (New Haven: Yale University Press, 2003), 80–109.

2. Robert Jenson, *Systematic Theology*, vol. 1, *The Triune God* (Oxford: Oxford University Press, 1999), 63.

ism, agnosticism, and atheism, in which participants argued whether objectively observed evidence points to the existence of a god. The Bible does not address directly such an abstract question. Scripture gives us one who works in history, leaving a paper trail, vulnerably sticking a neck out, for and with us.

God's way of doing this is by choosing a people. An unlikely people. The great Baptist preacher Charles Spurgeon gets nervous with this claim (he is thinking of election to salvation more than God's election of the people Israel, but his points still stand). Reformed thinkers like him love the doctrine of election. So they guard vigilantly against its misuse. Election is not a couch for ease but a demand for diligence (Spurgeon 1976: 439). Spurgeon quotes a certain Folengius, who worries about no "care or sorrow" more than that of ingratitude. In election God chooses the unlikely or even the impossible—in the psalmist's words, the "few in number," wandering aimlessly (105:12–13). Spurgeon points out that God chooses the owners of not land but only of a cave for a burial (Gen. 23:19–20). As the cliché goes, God does not call the equipped; God equips the called. And that calling, received by such unlikely beneficiaries as us, is a source of wonder, gratitude, and awe. We bring nothing to this exchange—human contribution to the election depicted here is "irrelevant" (Hossfeld and Zenger 2011: 70). It is God alone who renders "judgments," putting opponents in their place (105:5).[3]

We see here the first of several anachronisms. Abraham is described as God's "servant," a title the psalms often give to David (Pss. 78:70; 89:3), here awarded posthumously to the patriarch (Kraus 1993: 69). It is not the last time in Ps. 105 alone that later language will be applied to Israel's earliest beginnings. Such an anachronism is surprisingly appropriate. For here, a postexilic Israel is being invited to identify with a preexilic Israel. Current identity is being forged in ancient terms and vice versa. The same thing is happening when anyone reads the psalm rightly.

"He is mindful of his covenant forever, of the word that he commanded, for a thousand generations" (105:8). *A thousand generations.* That's a long time. It's a long enough time that ancient Christians would see a verse like this as a wrinkle in the letter—a signal to read more deeply. A thousand generations would be some twenty thousand years, or a large, round number meant to signify the "forever" that the psalm also promises. Viewed overly literally, the psalm is rendered untrue. Israel often lost the land of Canaan—including in the psalmist's recent

---

3. Kraus (1993: 310) suggests the language here is punitive in nature, as in Jer. 1:16 ("I will utter my judgments against them, for all their wickedness in forsaking me") and 4:12 ("Now it is I who speak in judgment against them").

memory. Christians might immediately fall back on old supersessionist habits here, as Augustine does: the old covenant is called "old" precisely because it has been replaced. Christians trying *not* to be supersessionist will realize that if God can break such promises as Ps. 105:8, then we have no reason to trust God. Christian scripture supports this promise being read as eternal (see Mary's Magnificat at Luke 1:55, "to Abraham and to his descendants forever"). Psalm 105 suggests, with its complete omission of Israel's human failings, that the covenant remains intact by God's virtue despite our vice. God has some eschatological work to do to validate this song and Mary's.

"To you I will give the land of Canaan as your portion for an inheritance" (105:11). This is the most solemn vocabulary available, the sort of language that a sovereign would use in making a grant of territory to another king (Mays 1994: 339). Deuteronomy makes similarly authoritative promises of possession of the land (1:8; 4:31; 8:1). The psalmist's rearticulation of Genesis's promises leans heavily on the promise of the land, leaving aside the promises of countless descendants and other nations being blessed through Israel (see Gen. 12:1–4; Limburg 2000: 359). The latter two are, of course, the portions of the promise to Abraham most often drawn on by Christians like St. Paul (e.g., in Rom. 4:16). These are omitted in Ps. 105. The portions of the promise that are most awkward for Christians—the pledge of the land of Canaan—are here lifted up most. How are Christian readers to respond? One, we should grant our Jewish elder siblings in faith a hearing when they speak of God's eternal promise of the land. Zionism is enormously complicated, but it is not easily dismissed as unbiblical.[4] Two, Christians must give an account of our own practice and thinking with regard to land. Ours is a *placed* faith: biblically in Canaan, Egypt, Sinai, Jerusalem; in church history inching westward to Europe, the Americas, and now to the Global South. These places are not promised to us the way Canaan is to Israel in Ps. 105. The church can relocate geographically in a way that differs from genealogical Israel.[5] Wherever we are, God calls us to tend the land and work for its good (Jer. 29). And to tread lightly on it. Specific geography is not our ultimate promise. But Ps. 105 suggests a placed faith is at least of penultimate importance. Those trying to construct a

---

4. Good resources for this weighty question include Walter Brueggemann, *Chosen: Reading the Bible Amidst the Israeli-Palestinian Conflict* (Louisville: Westminster John Knox, 2015), and Gerald R. McDermott, *Israel Matters: Why Christians Must Think Differently about the People and the Land* (Grand Rapids: Baker Academic, 2017).

5. I take the description "genealogical Israel" from Mark Kinzer's gloss of St. Paul's "Israel according to the flesh." Kinzer, *Searching Her Own Mystery: Nostra Aetate, the Jewish People, and the Identity of the Church* (Eugene, OR: Cascade, 2015), 24.

biblical ecology will find much to like here.[6] That we have made our lives on the lands of First Nations people, who lived here long before us and did not invite our presence, offers much on which to meditate. Finally, Christians might hear in God's promises of land a prefiguration of God's enfleshment. God is not disdainful of the created world. In fact, God becomes part of that world, a vulnerable part that Christians must cling to as Israel before us clung and clings to its land.

The next verses of Ps. 105 connect loosely with the story of Genesis. When was it, precisely, that Israel was few in number, wandering from nation to nation, yet unoppressed by any foreign king (105:12–14)? Augustine wonders whether this is a secret history, not present in the scriptures, delivered perhaps by an angel. More reticent commentators shy away from such a potentially gnostic suggestion and note parallel language elsewhere. Alter sees a parallel with Gen. 34:30, when Jacob rebuked his sons Simeon and Levi for treacherously carrying out revenge for the rape of their sister Dinah: "My numbers are few, and if they gather themselves against me and attack me, I shall be destroyed." As the psalm promises, only God's protection keeps Israel from being crushed (Alter 2007: 369). There's no mention of the brothers' treachery in this psalm, however. Hossfeld hears an echo of the mini-credo of Deut. 26:5: "A wandering Aramean was my ancestor; he went down into Egypt and lived there as an alien, few in number." All readers of the Bible can see God's people on the move, without state protection, in the form of refugees. If there is a consistent command throughout the Bible, it is to take care of those who are defenseless—for God's people remember in their scriptures, in their bones, what it is like to have no protection but God.

When precisely were kings rebuked on Israel's account? Most commentators suggest the sister/wife stories, in which a patriarch passed off his spouse as a sister or cousin to save his skin (Gen. 12; 20; 26). Again, the more unflattering details of the story are omitted here in Ps. 105's glowing portrait of human faithfulness.

When precisely were God's "prophets" done no harm (105:15)? Abraham receives the title of prophet in Gen. 20:7, but it is not a common description for him. More troublingly, when did God forbid anyone to touch his "anointed ones"? In what way were the patriarchs anointed? One commentator wonders if the description is here democratized, with Israel as an anointed people, as in Exod. 19:6, or the suffering servant in Isa. 61:1 (Kraus 1993: 311). Alter (2007: 371) suggests a mere historical conflation: later monarchical language is anachronistically

---

6. E.g., Ellen F. Davis, *Scripture, Culture, and Agriculture: An Agrarian Reading of the Bible* (Cambridge: Cambridge University Press, 2008); Norman Wirzba, *Food and Faith: A Theology of Eating* (Cambridge: Cambridge University Press, 2011).

stuffed back into Israel's older memory. For Augustine this must be a glimpse of the incarnation before the fact, evidence of believers in Christ among God's chosen. These "anointed ones" are literally "Christs," already there among the patriarchs. In Augustine's mind, this is not surprising. For the church is just an extension of Israel's story, in which God makes good use of the bad actions of human beings. Most poignantly for us, Ps. 105 is so dedicated to tidying up the stories of Israel's ancient indiscretions that it can only obscurely refer to the stories of Genesis. Say anything more about being "few in number" or "kings" being rebuked, and unpleasant details about Simeon and Levi and polygamy would have to be addressed. Psalm 105 is presenting a merciful portrait of our ancestors, showing their best side (Hossfeld and Zenger 2011: 70). It is grading on the curve. Christians call it grace. We hope God will remember our story in a similar way, making note only of his faithfulness, not of our unendingly creative ways to avoid God and hurt one another (see Ps. 103:12).

The retelling of Israel's story in Ps. 105 assumes its hearers have heard the story before (Limburg 2000: 359). This is not how one tells a brand-new story. It is how one retells a beloved story, punctuated with praise. If so, some details are odd. Those who love the story most will notice the smallest changes. When precisely was Joseph's neck in a collar of iron and his feet in fetters (105:18)? This can be inferred from his imprisonment, but those specific details are new here. When exactly did he instruct the elders of Egypt (105:22)? Again the psalm may be inferring. Augustine points out the new details. It makes sense that if Joseph instructs Egypt in how to run Pharaoh's kingdom, he would also instruct about the one true God: we shouldn't imagine Joseph "to be solely intent on nourishing bodies in Egypt" (Augustine 2003: 194). We see here a glimpse of Christians' responsibility in our world today. Joseph lives as a child of the covenant and blesses his community with no need to choose one over the other. Christians have often been caught in a feedback loop of asking whether to be faithful to the gospel or to serve the present age.[7] Of course if the ultimatum is put in such binary terms, those who remember the martyrs will cling to the gospel at the cost of their lives. But it is rarely the case that we must choose one or the other. Joseph, like Shadrach, Meshach, and Abednego later, serves his pagan ruler well. Of course, as that later story hints, and Joseph here learns, such service can be fraught and dangerous. The point for now is simply that Christians must serve their communities and civil leaders, and we must do so as Christians.

7. This is especially true of my teacher Stanley Hauerwas, his students, and our critics.

In this retelling of events, the Lord's *sovereignty* is emphasized more perhaps than elsewhere. As Spurgeon puts it, God summons famine like a master would a servant (105:16; Spurgeon 1976: 441). Spurgeon goes on to see the rest of the story of Joseph's kenosis as a template for the life of the church. Throughout being tossed into a well by his brothers, bought by slavers, sold at market, and thrown into prison, Joseph was ever led by God: "God's way was the surest, the wisest, the shortest." For Joseph and those who follow this covenant-keeping God, "Our road to glory runs by the rivers of grief" (Spurgeon 1976: 441). Yet those fetters were a preparation for Joseph to wear chains of gold. All the Lord's people go from prison to a throne. Spurgeon sees this as the form of the individual spiritual life: few can bear the sudden miracles foisted on Joseph "without pride," so Joseph had to be humbled to stay modest. That is a fine reading, though perhaps too limited. The language here hints at Christ's harrowing of hell. Joseph was led down to Egypt, down a well, down to prison, down to the total loss of reputation, and back to exultation, status, position, power. Of course, Joseph's people would descend as well before God raised them up in the exodus. The whole pattern of the story from one man, Joseph, to a nation led by God through Moses, suggests Christ's kenosis, descent to hell, and miraculous rescuing of a people through water.

Those who first heard this psalm did not know that culmination of the story explicitly. They just knew they sat in exile, longing for the land promised by a God who said he would never leave them. And as they looked back in their stories and praised in a strange place, they saw a God *with* them no matter their circumstances or level of despair. They saw a God who did not leave this people in sorrow unendingly. The one who accompanied them on the road to and from Babylon previously led Jacob to Egypt and Moses to freedom (Hossfeld and Zenger 2011: 68).

The NRSV's language for Ps. 105:19 is perhaps not strong enough: "until what he had said came to pass, the word of the LORD kept testing him." Alter suggests "until the time of his word" for the first phrase, and the verb "purged" for the second. The word of the Lord *purged* Joseph. Augustine is aware of the odd formulation as well. He suggests that Joseph was "kindled," set on fire by the Lord's utterance. Augustine finds a parallel in Paul's charge in Rom. 12:11 that we should all be so kindled, ardent, ablaze. Sounds . . . painful. And sure enough—the Lord is responsible for all these actions. Ancient Christian notions of good and evil struggle under the weight of such texts. It is crucial to say God never causes evil; God can only be the source of unending good. This psalm as a whole supports that contention (despite verses like 105:16 and 105:25). For God's covenant mindfulness is so overwhelming that Israel's misdeeds hardly register in Ps. 105 (Ps. 106 will more than make up for this lack!). Augustine is quick to insist that God does not turn the Egyptians to hate. But God does make good use of bad agents. We human beings often reverse the favor, making *bad* use of *good* agents. God does send favor and blessing on some, like Joseph at the beginning and the end. And God's blessing can incur others' envy and wrath, like the rest of Joseph's story. The spiritual question is this: Who wants to follow a God who treats people this way?

The order of the plagues is another unusual deviation from the story. Anyone who has read Exodus knows immediately something is amiss. They preach as they ever do: God controls events; the natural order rises up to do his will against the arrogant oppressor; no one is safe from any plague, not ruler or priest, not the wealthy or the poor. But why is the ninth plague (darkness) from Exodus listed first? The first and second plagues from Exodus follow, then a conflation of the fourth and third, then the seventh, the eighth, and finally the tenth, with no appearance either by the boils on the skin or the pestilence against the livestock (Exod. 9:1–12; Kraus 1993: 311). The psalmist seems to have reordered the plagues to "display the structure" of the creation in Genesis (Hossfeld and Zenger 2011: 72). The darkness recalls God's separation of light from dark. Water to blood reminds of creation of the land and the holding back of the water. The plagues that harm animals recall their creation and naming. And the death of the firstborn is positioned to match the creation of Adam and Eve. Creation itself is here undone among the Egyptians. Israel's current oppressor had best take note. God has power over creation, and God takes sides.

Israel had best take note too. Its charge is to be a people who remember and keep the Lord's laws. Zion is hardly mentioned here, yet when it is, it is made the point of the entire endeavor: "That they might keep his statutes and observe his laws" (Ps. 105:45). This psalm has been at pains *not* to mention Israel's misdeeds or sins. Stories of the rock providing water (105:41), quails dropping from the skies, and manna appearing from heaven (105:40) are told without the disobedience, grumbling, or God's impatience. They are told solely with joy and singing, like Miriam and the women do in Exod. 15. The psalm actually lurches backward in time at 105:43. It had moved past the exodus and gone on into the wilderness and God's provision before returning to the pinnacle of God's liberating power. Other portions of scripture speak of a second exodus. Isaiah envisions another liberation with rejoicing in places like 35:10, 48:20–21, 51:11, and 55:12. Israel shall "come to Zion with singing" and "go from Babylon, flee from Chaldea, . . . say, 'The Lord has redeemed his servant Jacob!'" and "the mountains and the hills before you shall burst into song." The exodus does not stand alone. God's character is always to be bringing about liberation.

Christians, of course, see this second exodus in Christ's death and resurrection, in our baptism, and in God's gathering of all nations, including us, to worship Zion's God. The psalmist's and Isaiah's exalted, world-encompassing praise leads to wonder: Is not our hope too small? We call on God for "spiritual" things, perhaps healings, interior peace, grace for others. Scripture speaks of a God who undoes creation under the feet of enemies, who causes rocks to burst and mountains to skip, who demands that people keep his gracious laws. A steady dose of scripture is necessary to keep our vision of salvation from constricting. The New Testament, which draws on the same hope of the psalmist in such places as Mary's Magnificat, Paul's retelling of Israel's wanderings (1 Cor. 10), Steven's pre-martyrdom speech (Acts 7), and perhaps the saints' resurrection and their enemies' dread in Rev. 11:10–11, has a hope not less cosmic in scope.

On a final note, Augustine, for one, is uncomfortable with the plundering-of-the-Egyptians tradition, present in Ps. 105:37. We should obey God not for material reward but for God's own sake (Augustine 2003: 202). The church has long drawn on this passage to speak of God's provision of wisdom to all the earth. Just as the departing Israelites accepted the Egyptians' treasures, so too when we see genuine wisdom in pagans' writings, we should eagerly receive it. All truth is God's, wherever it is to be found. Other Christians had imagined this Egyptian treasure as a future means to beautify God's tabernacle and temple. Augustine does not utilize those particular readings here. He is more attracted to an argument for justice: this is back pay, reparations, for service rendered in slavery. He suggests that God makes use of the Egyptians' iniquity and the Israelites' weakness in the same way, "to symbolize and prefigure what needed to be revealed through these events" (202).

This is the character of God: to make use even of our failures. And this is the destiny of humanity: to cast down our crowns at his feet.

PSALM 106

What is worse than misery? Misery without meaning.

One would think misery sent by God would be the worst fate imaginable (Ps. 105:15, 17–18, 26–27, 40–42), but it is not so. The worst would be random, inexplicable misery. For despite all of Israel's misery, there *is* a God to whom to lament, one good enough to bring relief, with a history of offering grace precisely where it is least deserved. There is a haunting beauty in Ps. 106's dismal review of Israel's history. If God can forgive all of this, how could anyone ever outrun God's mercy?

Psalm 106 is the mirror opposite to Ps. 105, which remembers the stormy love affair between God and Israel with the sort of affection that causes amnesia about the lover's vices. Psalm 106 relates *only* Israel's vices. Israel holds up a mirror to itself and points out its own flaws, one by one. "We have sinned in the sins of our fathers," 106:6 says (more literally than most English translations) (Mays 1994: 341). And yet, however much Israel grieved God, God came to the rescue every time. Israel pleads with God to do so again (106:47). The poetry of the psalm, recounting history from the exodus to the exile, almost numbs the listener, making forgiveness seem unlikely or even impossible. If God can still save Israel after such a litany of misdeeds, God may do so again. For God is nothing but mercy, and Israel could use some of that. Now, please.

Psalm 106 is a guide for any people seeking mercy from God. The pastor stands up and makes this bold declaration: "We have sinned against the Lord. Come, let us confess our sins." Heads bow, lips move, sins are confessed. The unfamiliar church attendee may be puzzled or even offended: "How does that pastor know I have sinned? I'm not so bad." But the uninitiated then notices something strange.

Those belaboring their sins seem . . . happy (106:3). Recitation of any litany of misery brings relief. This is true on anthropological grounds—confession is good for the soul and brings healing, as addicts in recovery can attest. The psalm testifies further that confession is good for the soul for theological reasons—because of the specific character of the biblical God. Confess away: there is a good God listening. And before the prayer is even out of our mouths, God has pronounced forgiveness. There is a joy on the far side of confession, and a misery that stops short of confession. Those who confess receive mercy. Those who do not confess do not receive mercy. Modernity has often tried to insist that the good news is that there is no bad news. The gospel suggests the good news is that there *is* bad news that, when confessed, yields unimaginably good news.

We Christians have often critiqued our own doctrine of original sin—and there is much to bemoan. God's original word over us is blessing, stamped as we are with the divine image (Gen. 1:27). *Almost*-original sin might be better language. Augustine—a hero in this volume and in the memory of the church—speaks of original sin as though it is almost a biological pathogen passed down from parent to child in the sex act itself. His stance is not the best moment in the history of doctrine. But Ps. 106 suggests there is something to original sin, biblically speaking. Our sins are not ours alone. They include all the sins of those who have come before us. It is uncommon among historical psalms to weave together individual pleas (106:4–5, "remember *me*," "that *I* may") with the first-person plural "we," encompassing the entire history of Israel (Karl Jacobson, in Van Harn and Strawn 2009: 280). Psalm 106:1–4 and 47 speak to God in the second person; the rest of the psalm speaks of God in the third. The people are braided together, I and we, now and historically, in their (sorry—our) great need for grace.

Paul includes Ps. 106:20 ("They exchanged the glory of God") in his own equally dreary litany of human misdeeds in Romans: "They exchanged the glory of the immortal God for images" (Rom. 1:23). Paul follows the deep logic of Ps. 106 as he turns on his hearers in Rom. 2:1: "You have no excuse, whoever you are." Everyone who condemns another person has done just as bad or worse. And God's response is to give us up, so to speak (Ps. 106:15). Those who choose something other than God receive the misery of what they have chosen. But they also receive the mercy of the God who cannot be other than mercy. Paul learns his gospel from the sorrow and comfort of the psalms. God does not save because the people are so good. God saves the people for the sake of his name (106:8)—that is, because God is so good.

This is counterintuitive good news at best for North Americans. Political debates get heated quickly when you bring up the question of whether white people today bear guilt for their ancestors' historic sins against African Americans and First Nations peoples. But Ps. 106 cheerfully signs up for corporate guilt. Only with corporate guilt can anyone receive corporate grace.

It is striking that such a litany of gloom begins and ends with the language of praise. This presents a difficulty. We must praise—that is our vocation as human beings. Praise of God is part of the "righteousness" that those who are "happy" *do* at all times (106:3). But "who can utter the mighty doings of the Lord"? Who can "declare all his praise"? We certainly cannot, sinners that we are (see 106:6–46). Scripture itself names our dilemma and offers us a remedy: only those being redeemed can know themselves *as* sinners. Only in the light of redemption can we discern the long shadows cast by our obstinance. Sin is not mere misbehavior. "Mistakes were made," public-relations firms instruct disgraced celebrities to say. No—sin is our fault, even though we cannot stop ourselves. One theologian titled a seminal book *The Joy of Being Wrong*.[1] Only those already being put in the right can notice how wrong they *have* been.

Psalm 106 opens and closes with praise. Commentators note that it closes the fourth book of the Psalter—hence the note of jubilation (see also Pss. 41; 72; 89; and 150) (Augustine 2003: 203; Kraus 1993: 316). There are other litanies of Israel's failures (e.g., Ps. 78), but they tend not to open and close with exultation. This is the puzzle of Ps. 106: How can such misery be bookended by such raucous doxology? Perhaps a short tour in the history of doctrine can help.

In the history of the church, we have had two general strategies for telling outsiders, and reminding ourselves, why the gospel is compelling. One is to say that Christians make the best people. Our gospel must be true because our saints are so beautiful. Origen employs this strategy regularly in his *Contra Celsum*. He refutes pagan mockery of Christianity by pointing to the virtues of Christians: we don't visit only our own people in prison; we visit pagans in prison. We don't take in abandoned babies from among only our own number; we'll take in absolutely everybody. Stanley Hauerwas's work in our generation is a sort of revitalization of this strand in Origen's thought. If the gospel produces people no better than any other, then why bother? You can hear this strategy unwittingly reflected in the common criticism that Christians are hypocrites. Our critics actually want us to be better than we are. For our gospel is better—and they know it.

---

1. James Alison, *The Joy of Being Wrong: Original Sin through Easter Eyes* (New York: Crossroad, 1998).

St. Augustine's approach to human sin and redemption is rather different. He offers his book *Confessions* as a sort of anti-apology. His opponents and naysayers have been busy since he was kidnapped and forced to be bishop of Hippo against his will. They have heard what a sinner he is. He used to be a Manichaean, a group the church claims as heretical. Some say he still is. He had a longtime mistress who bore his child. There is talk of other women. And have you met his mother? (The ecclesial gossip machine is no recent innovation.) Augustine's response to his detractors is treasured in the church as a model for confession. He hears his opponents and says, in effect, "You're right to say I'm a sinner. In fact, I'm going to show you how much worse I am than you already think. Because only then will you know how great God is, to save and use such a one as I." If Origen thinks outsiders should believe the gospel because we make the best people, Augustine thinks outsiders should believe the gospel *because we have the most forgiving God.* Augustine can glory in his depravity because it shows the lengths to which God descends in Christ to redeem him.

Both Origen's and Augustine's perspectives contain truth. But you can guess which church father's heart thrills more to Ps. 106. "Confess to the Lord, for he is good," Augustine paraphrases 106:1, in a translation more faithful to the Greek Septuagint than the Hebrew (*Sermon* 16A.5, in Wesselschmidt 2007: 248). It is a fool's errand to try to run away from God's mercy. The farther and faster we try to escape, the more quickly we will find ourselves dashing into his arms (see too Ps. 139). It may seem paradoxical to our ears, but it was not to Augustine's: confession of sin has to be accompanied by praise. If we confess what we are, God will transform us into what we are not (Augustine 2003: 209–10).

Most peoples, historically and today, tidy up their histories, shading them to be, as much as possible, a series of ever more glorious successes, discretely leaving out or justifying failure. Not the psalmists of Israel. Psalms like Ps. 106 detail Israel's misdeeds. Why? Because the more Israel sins, the more grace it receives from God. St. Paul's explanation to the Romans why they ought not to go out of their way to sin so as to receive more grace (Rom. 6:1–4) is one every pastor who preaches grace biblically should employ. Psalm 106 gives comfort and direction to a frequently unfaithful church. We should not cover over our faults, historical or contemporary. We should recount them in confession. It is the only way to meet God's mercy.

The bulk of the psalm attends to the specifics of Israel's attempts to outrun God's mercy. The psalmist must first show just how not-good the people are and always have been. Even before they are out of Egypt, they are sinning against the Lord—at the sea itself (106:7). Fresh in freedom, with the Passover meal still in their bellies, God's people already turn forgetful. As the prophet Ezekiel would also say, in typical prophetic hyperbole: the Israelites never did let go of the idols of Egypt (Ezek. 20:8). Having seen God split the sea, they soon forget and exchange his image for that of grass-eating beasts (Ps. 106:13, 20). They make sacrifices to the dead and mingle with their foreign neighbors, serving false gods (106:28, 36). They sacrifice their own children (106:37–39). The very heirs of the covenant, promised to Abraham to be more than the sands on the sea or the stars in the sky, become mere fodder for offerings to lifeless godlets. The prose here is not quite as purple as Ezekiel, but it is on the way—Israel is like a whore who pays her clients; the nations are actually embarrassed for her (Ezek. 16:27, 33–34).[2] One could do worse than simply to read Ps. 106 and prophets like Ezekiel in church. It would be healthy starch amidst a liturgical diet that tends more to the saccharine.

When Israel, standing in for all humanity, is at its worst, God shows mercy and relents from punishing. Moses stands in the breach for the people, to keep them from being destroyed (106:23). Moses, like Abraham before him, talks God out of destroying the people for their infidelity (Exod. 32:11–14, as in Gen. 18:22–33). Michael Walzer writes that Moses had rather more success with God than with leading the people![3] God often accedes to Moses's entreaties and keeps the people from suffering the full deserts for their sins; his people are harder of hearing. Similarly, Phinehas acts on behalf of God's people to intercede and stop a plague (Ps. 106:30). The psalmist doesn't delve into the gruesome details of the Phinehas story. In Ps. 106, Phinehas merely prays. In Num. 25 he responds to the Israelites' intermarrying with their Midianite neighbors by spearing two together in their act of passion. The act has prophetic depth to it in addition to its Freudian echoes: You want to be together? Then die together. It also has horror in it. Not a few self-appointed zealots for the Lord have styled themselves as having the zeal of Phinehas. God grants Phinehas his "covenant of peace" and names him to the "perpetual priesthood" because of this "atonement" he made (Num. 25:12–13). The psalmist elaborates that Phinehas's intercession "has been reckoned to him as righteousness" (Ps. 106:31). That language appears only here and in Gen. 15:6 in Israel's scripture. There, Abram's faith in God's promise was reckoned to him as righteousness. Here, Phinehas's covenant-restoring zeal was so reckoned.

2. Mays (1994: 341) makes the comparison to Ezekiel.
3. Michael Walzer, *Exodus and Revolution* (New York: Basic, 1985), 67. I'm grateful to James Howell for this wonderful observation.

The language of "reckoning righteousness" is, of course, extremely important in the thought of St. Paul and to churches for which justification by faith is a cornerstone doctrine. N. T. Wright has pointed to this language as a description of the zeal for which Paul of Tarsus was proud—he was willing, like Phinehas, to do violence to defend Israel's exclusive covenant (Phil. 3:6).[4] Yet Paul now considers that and all privileges loss for the sake of Christ (3:7). For Wright, God reckons as righteous those who will be found to be among the true Israel on the day of judgment. In Christ, even Gentiles can be reckoned righteous by our trust in God's promises (Rom. 10:9)—namely, that the end of the ages has come in Christ, so Jews and even Gentiles are streaming to worship Israel's God on Mount Zion. Israel's exclusive access to the covenant was good and right for a time. With the Messiah's coming, our zeal had better be directed elsewhere—to assault on our own sins, a plague on any idolatry, and a view of Gentiles that would see us blessedly scattered among them for mission (Ps. 106:27). By the end of the psalm, Gentile captors are pitying Israel and occasionally enlisted in its service (106:46). Elsewhere in scripture, marriage to Moabite wives is a blessing to such biblical heroes as Moses and Boaz. The Old Testament has a mixed witness with regard to the status of the nations before God. In the New, the gates of the kingdom are broken open, to the Jew first and then the Gentile (Rom. 1:16–17). Passages like Ps. 106 that praise Phinehas have to be read contrary to the letter, super-literally if you like, with the zeal of martyrs rather than that of blood-stained crusaders (e.g., Paul in Phil. 3:10–11). Psalm 106 shows us how to do this by emphasizing Phinehas's intervention and remembering it as vicarious prayer to make undeserved atonement on his people's behalf, with the violence excised.

God does not leave the people without advocates, those who stand in the breach on Israel's behalf—Moses and Phinehas prominently among them. But at times, in the litany of misery, no Israelite is mentioned as standing up for the people and bringing about their deliverance. God himself can do that on his own and be faithful even if every one of us is faithless (e.g., 106:7–8, 44–45). Yet the presence of Moses and Phinehas, acting on behalf of the people, says something important about the mediation of the saints. Kraus describes them as offering a sort of penal substitution on behalf of the people (1993: 316). Augustine speaks of their example as a demonstration of the great power of the prayers of the saints (2003: 213). St. Pachomius, one of the desert fathers, said on the death of his friend St. Theodore that he "always interceded with God on our behalf to save

---

4. N. T. Wright, *Paul and the Faithfulness of God* (Minneapolis: Fortress, 2013), 81–89.

us from the hands of the devil." Now that Theodore is gone, he'll continue to be "an ambassador for us in the presence of God" (*Life of Pachomius* 208, in Wesselschmidt 2007: 248–49). Protestants have been nervous to attribute agency to mere human beings in the salvation of sinners. Yet the psalm strikes a careful balance. God does not need people to remember to be merciful because God has no way other than mercy. And yet God creatively enfolds the acts of Moses and Phinehas in his dispensation of mercy to his people. We who pray and praise with the psalm are encouraged to pray for God's people not because God will forget his mercy if we do not but because dangerous, sacrificial intervention on behalf of the people is what scripture commends, glorifies, beautifies, and invites us to emulate.

The rest of the psalm's historical account, 106:34–46, proceeds at a gallop, leaving behind place names and specificity, giving a sense that these are perpetual patterns of sin by which Israel defies God's mercy.[5] They do not destroy but mingle with the people and their gods. They sacrifice their children to demons. They pollute themselves by their acts. Many of these charges are common in the prophets and the historical books such as Judges and Kings. And there is no intercessor to stand up on the people's behalf. Moses is gone, by the Israelites' handiwork. Phinehas's work, while remembered forever, is not imitated by a new priest. God himself intervened for the sake of his name in Ps. 106:8. But here, remarkably, with no divine or human mediator at all, God "regarded their distress when he heard their cry" (106:44) and he did this "for their sake" (106:45). For *their* sake? For these people who sleep with foreigners, commune with demons, and commit child sacrifice? This is the pattern with God and humanity: we cry, God hears, and God delivers (Exod. 2:23–25).[6]

The psalmist may originally have sat in exile in Babylon (106:27, 41, 47). Israel often views its history from its seat of sorrow in Babylon as one of failure to be faithful, causing God to "give them up" to their own subhuman choices (106:26–27). They lost the land because of their infidelity, and they trust God to be gracious to return them to it in due course. God does not leave the people Godless forever. God must come and save, for that is God's character, revealed to us by the psalm. Psalm 106 forms a perfect counterpart to Ps. 105. Psalm 105 cannot but forget Israel's sins in light of God's disinfecting light. Psalm 106 cannot forget Israel's sins in light of God's severe mercy. A people who praise this way will remember,

5. Hossfeld's exhaustive commentary on these verses is crucial for what I say here throughout (Hossfeld and Zenger 2011: 81–95).

6. I am grateful to my Vancouver School of Theology colleague Pat Dutcher-Walls for this observation: the God who makes exodus also restores from exile.

with God, the history of faithfulness into which we are grafted (Ps. 105) and the history of rebellion in which we take part (Ps. 106). A psalmist and community dislocated anew remember when they were dislocated before. God was faithful despite everything. Take heart, their praise implies, God will be faithful again.

"These things happened to them to serve as an example, and they were written down to instruct us, on whom the ends of the ages have come" (1 Cor. 10:11). This "us" to which Paul refers is a bunch of Gentile Christians living geographically far from the times and places recited in Ps. 106, but spiritually we are no different. We too are to flee idols, to shun sexual immorality, to not put God to the test, and we are to trust God (1 Cor. 10:13). Human sin is boringly cyclical. The same ones come back up again and again. Divine mercy, by contrast, is creative. God has mercy sometimes for his name's sake, sometimes through an enemy king, and sometimes via Moses's costly intervention or Phinehas's singularly zealous intercession. The psalmist portrays Israel's sin so unrelentingly to show the depths of divine grace. Try though we may, nothing we can do can fail to show God's magnificent mercy, which always triumphs over judgment (Jas. 2:13).

Eventually. Mercy does have a way of taking its time completing this strange triumph.

PSALM 107

A soldier was serving her second tour of duty in Iraq. She drove a truck in a convoy, which meant that she was no stranger to being under fire. Only this time she was in an uncountably long line of trucks, each having to switchback between the barricades designed to stop suicide bombers. The danger this day was not suicide bombers but mortar fire raining down on the convoy helplessly below. She was sure she was going to die. "And then," she said, "I prayed for the first time in my life."

Not that she hadn't prayed before, for a grade on a test or the attention of a boy or to get out of trouble. But this was her first "guttural" prayer, where she really needed God to respond in a matter of life and death. She was in trouble, and she cried out. The result was a Ps. 107 sort of prayer.

Psalm 107 opens the last of the five books of the Psalter. Both Pss. 106 and 107 begin with the basic biblical admonitions to offer praise and thanks to the Lord, but Ps. 106 proceeds to detail the people's failings. Psalm 107 gives four paradigmatic stories of human distress, a plea, divine rescue, and praise. The heart of the psalm is thanksgiving. Yet for all their differences, there are deep links between these two psalms. Psalm 106:47 offers its own guttural prayer. Psalm 107:3 suggests that God has made a swift answer to that prayer in gathering his people from exile to offer praise. The concluding axiom of 107:43, "Let those who are wise give heed to these things, and consider the steadfast love of the LORD," sounds like a response to the call in Ps. 106:7, "Our ancestors . . . did not consider your wonderful works; they did not remember the abundance of your steadfast love." Israel there forgot and suffered. Israel here remembers and gives thanks.

And those two Israels are, of course, one and the same.[1] The Israel in misery in Ps. 106 is being miraculously gathered from the places to which it is scattered in Ps. 107 and throughout the final fifth of the Psalter.

"O give thanks to the LORD, for he is good; for his steadfast love endures forever" is a recurring prayer throughout the scriptures. Psalm 118 makes it the chorus in a liturgy of praise. The motif appears in the story of the exodus and in God's self-revelation at Sinai (Exod. 34:6–7). It appears also in the writings of the prophet Jeremiah in response to God's restoration of the land (Jer. 33:11), and in Ezra as God's people shout for joy at the laying of the foundation of the new temple (Ezra 3:11). Here the events of Israel's first paradigmatic deliverance, the exodus, and its second, the return from exile, are overlaid, and praise is offered for each in similar terms (Mays 1994: 346). The echoes of the exodus are unavoidable here in the people's redemption (twice at Ps. 107:2) and in God's triumph over the chaos of the sea (107:23–30). The echoes of redemption from exile are just as clear in the psalm's regular use of language from Isa. 40–66 and Job[2] and in its universalizing thrust—it is not obvious here that one has to be a member of the covenant community to cry out to God for rescue. Yet, of course, the whole story is steeped in the language and prayer of Israel. This is perhaps a hint of a way forward for inter-religious conversation. All those crying out can surely learn from and befriend one another. God is close to those who call on him, who cry out to him for help. Yet this God who is ready to rescue whomever asks is none other than the God of Israel.

Hesed, the NRSV's "steadfast love" in Ps. 107:1, is complicated to translate. Some interpreters relay the word as "kindness," others as simply "love," others as "mercy." All get some purchase on the term. Yet I wonder if these descriptions are too passive for the God described in Ps. 107. Here *hesed* is a rescuing love, a redeeming one (107:2). "Steadfast" suggests an unmovable posture, that the love holds the line no matter what force is arrayed against it. Limburg suggests translating it here "amazing grace," which, hackneyed liturgical use aside, conveys the sense of *hesed*'s proactive nature and humanity's doxological response. "Covenant faithfulness" has become a sort of standard translation since it wraps God's fidelity around the promises made to Israel and reminds of divine love despite human frailty (so Ps. 106:43–45).[3]

1. Eric Zenger points out the myriad links between Pss. 106 and 107 over against a historiography that has overemphasized their differences (Hossfeld and Zenger 2011: 110).
2. See, e.g., Isa. 51:10 (God dried up the deep), 62:12 (they shall be called the Redeemed), 63:4 ("the year for my redeeming work"), and 35:9 ("the redeemed shall walk there"), and the deep resonance between Job 5:11–16 and Ps. 107:33–41 (Mays 1994: 346).
3. I'm grateful here again to Pat Dutcher-Walls.

Some historians have argued that Ps. 107 was born in the people's praise rather than in a solitary scholar's study. This psalm is a liturgy of thanks, designed to allow as many points of entry to as many kinds of rescued people as possible (Nancy L. deClaissé-Walford, in Van Harn and Strawn 2009: 281). Kraus compares it to a mass wedding or a mass baptism, designed for a throng to say together (1993: 326). Zenger is cool toward this imagined historical reconstruction. The four kinds of rescue presented in this psalm are vivid but also indistinct; they aim to be comprehensive but not precise. The rescues from hunger and thirst, from the pit, from a deadly illness, and from trouble at sea signal "the narrow and dangerous boundary between life and death" (Hossfeld and Zenger 2011: 100). The psalm is less like a dated church bulletin and more a declaration of the way God always works in history. Psalm 107 presents the end of the exile in a miraculous rescue by God and the renewal of Israel on stage before the nations (Hossfeld and Zenger 2011: 102). "Let the redeemed of the LORD say so, those he redeemed from trouble" (107:2) is political language more than religious (Alter 2007: 383). Zenger calls it language from family law—a member of the family who is endangered or enslaved has been restored, thus returning the family to wholeness (Hossfeld and Zenger 2011: 103). It is also exodus language—a return to the touchstone of all of scripture—reminding those praying of the God who sets free from oppression (Exod. 6:6, "I will redeem you with an outstretched arm"). It is also restoration from exile language, such that "redeemer" becomes a title for God (Isa. 41:14, "Your Redeemer is the Holy One of Israel"). To belabor the obvious for a moment, there are patterns in the Bible. The God who rescues in the exodus, who gathers the exiles, who redeems from bondage, who raises Jesus—this God is one and the same. So one astounding act of rescue by God can be spoken of in terms of the others.

God's people also follow a pattern. This is why interpreters both ancient (Augustine: "It is the baptized who are invited by the Psalm to speak" [2003: 225]) and modern (Mays: "The psalm teaches the congregation and its members to see themselves as the redeemed" [1994: 347]) inscribe themselves and their worshiping communities into the text. The rescuing God has included *us* among his people being rescued.

There is a translation problem in 107:3: "and gathered in from the lands, from the east and from the west, from the north and from the south." A more literal rendering would have "from the rising of the sun to its setting, from the north and from the sea." One can see why translators and interpreters make these points on the compass. There is a symmetry that way, leaving the speaker and the restored community at the center of the gathering movement of God, in the heart of the reconstituted Israel (Hossfeld and Zenger 2011: 99). One interpreter sees the east as the place where one wanders lost in the desert (107:4–9), the west as the place where the sun goes down, leaving us in darkness (107:10–16), the south as the direction of the sea (107:23–30), and the north as the direction from which trouble is always coming to Israel (Nancy L. deClaissé-Walford, in Van Harn and Strawn 2009: 281–83). Zenger is probably right to see these as mythical rather than geographical points, with a restored Zion as the navel of the universe (Hossfeld and Zenger 2011: 104). Augustine (2003: 225) sees here the gathering of the Christian church (Matt. 8:11, "many will come from east and west and will eat with Abraham and Isaac and Jacob in the kingdom"), gathered from all nations (Matt. 28:19; Rev. 5:9).

Psalm 107 is simple and elegant. Each of four sufferers describes their straits. They cry out to the Lord. The Lord redeems them, and they give thanks. The concluding portion of the psalm refers to the character of the God who has intervened for these four. Other psalms describe hunger and thirst (Pss. 42–43). Some others describe deliverance from the pit, the grave, or *sheol* (Pss. 130; 142). Others also give praise for a restoration after an illness approaching death (Pss. 6; 38; 88). But no other psalm describes redemption from peril on the sea (Mays 1994: 345). Older commentaries used to point out that Israel was not a particularly sea-faring people. Images of the sea, the deep, its monsters, and its chaos and disorder always signal fright and terror. Newer commentaries tend not to make blanket statements—*someone* in Israel was sailing, fishing, trading. It is no surprise that hymnody and literature about the sea rooted in scripture has drawn on Ps. 107—from *Moby-Dick* to the twelfth-century poet Judah Halevi ("The waves of the sea and the wind of the west; Let them propel me to the place of the yoke of Your love") (Alter [2007: 386] makes these connections). William Whiting's 1860 hymn "Eternal Father, Strong to Save," although not commonly sung now, has been popular in navies and among seafarers ("Oh, hear us when we cry to Thee, for those in peril on the sea!").

The rescue on the sea and the rescue of the hungry and thirsty wanderer form a chiasm in the psalm. Both are blown about aimlessly, chaotically, perilously. Those near a desert know to avoid desert wastes on their own and rather to travel in caravans along rivers via inhabited towns. For whatever reason, these travelers have not done so, and their heart has "fainted within them" (107:5). They cry out, God delivers, and they give thanks (107:6, 8). God does more than provide them with bread and water, crucial as those are. He leads them to an inhabited place, to safety, to other people (107:7). As ever, these descriptions function literally and also more deeply than the letter. Scripture insists that God's is the right path. To leave that path is to court disaster (e.g., Ps. 1). St. Augustine, himself no stranger to wandering aimlessly and perilously, assigns John 14:6 as a sort of antidote to the ailment of 107:4–9—God has to interrupt our wandering and move us to the "way" of Jesus.

Another figural reading more rooted in the psalm's historical origins is its reference to a homebound journey for Israel returning from Babylon. Isaiah promises that God can make a way in the desert, a highway that is straight and navigable in a place where on Israel's own there would only be death. The ransomed will return that way, and they shall hunger no longer (Isa. 49:8–12; 51:9–11, which compares that desert way back to the exodus) (Kraus 1993: 328). As Ps. 107:8–9 makes clear, divine rescue brings about public praise.

This is the seed for a full-grown theology of evangelism. How can we not tell others, when the Lord has rescued us from absolute despair? Spurgeon quotes a contemporary who notes that the only payment Christ ever asked from one he healed was that that one go and tell others. "Words seem a poor thing," except that Christ is God's own Word. To tell others near and far about God's saving work is to step into the relationship between God and the Word that is God's very self.[4]

The second cry for rescue also forms a chiasm with the third. Both of these, unlike the first and fourth, include mention of the sin of the one crying out as a reason for his distress (107:11, 17). This is not held against him. God does not reserve saving help for the deserving. God lavishes it also on those who got themselves into the mess they're in and can blame no one else. Psalm 107:10–16 describes a prisoner in a pit. This may be a cistern, wide at the bottom and narrow at the top, so that an individual cannot climb out (Kraus 1993: 328). As with the psalmist elsewhere (Ps. 40), as with Joseph tossed in the well by his brothers (Gen. 37:24), there is an element of debasement here, of humiliation, and shame. Unlike those others, this plaintiff is actually in irons (107:10). The last thing this one can do is save himself. All he can do is cry out. Augustine reads this sufferer metaphorically as one who knows the truth intellectually but cannot muster the wherewithal to engage in right action (Augustine 2003: 228). All efforts wasted, the prisoner slides back into the unscalable mud and cries out. The cry is answered. The psalmist is delivered (107:13–14). The rescued one thanks the Lord publicly.

4. Spurgeon 1976: 461, quoting John Trapp, who is drawing on Gregory Nazianzen.

Ancient Christians need what I've called elsewhere "a wrinkle in the letter" to read figurally.[5] Something in the letter has to signal a need to read more deeply. The wrinkle here is 107:16, "He shatters the doors of bronze, and cuts in two the bars of iron." What doors of bronze? What bars of iron? This complainer is in a cistern, at the bottom of a mud-walled well. Surely God could have thrown in a rope, like Joseph's brothers did (Gen. 37:28). This violent jailbreak sounds more like Jesus's harrowing of hell on Holy Saturday, more like an angel initiating a jailbreak for Paul and Silas (Acts 16:26), more like the rolling away of the stone and stripping the gears of death (Matt. 28:2).[6] A people saved by such bold intervention would be hard-pressed not to see it here. For a parallel reading from the Old Testament, the language in Ps. 107:16 closely echoes God's calling of Cyrus in Isa. 45:2, where God promises, "I will go before you and level the mountains, I will break in pieces the doors of bronze and cut through the bars of iron" (Hossfeld and Zenger 2011: 108). God's surprising anointed one (Isa. 45:1) conquering Israel's enemies seems a more fitting use of such a loud, boisterous promise. Later, another surprising Anointed One will bring about redemption for Israel and the world at an even greater scale.

The third complainer is also in straits because of sin (Ps. 107:17). His illness is so advanced that food itself makes him retch. He is close to death (107:18). This one also cries out, is delivered, and offers public praise in the form of "thanksgiving sacrifices" (107:22). The description of the celebration is not unlike a Christian liturgy—he tells of God's saving deeds, they celebrate a sacrificial thanksgiving together, and they sing songs of joy.

Some historic interpreters have seen more Christian specificity in these verses. "He sent out his word and healed them" (107:20) sounds like "Word" could be capitalized and spoken of as the preincarnate Logos. What does Jesus do during his incarnation more avidly than heal? Spurgeon cites a contemporary, William Romaine, who applies the biblical portrait of God "with healing in his wings" to Jesus's healing ministry in Galilee (quoted in Spurgeon 1976: 463). Origen points to this verse multiple times in his *Contra Celsum* as evidence for the Logos's divinity (Wesselschmidt 2007: 254). Eusebius—not usually noted for having a high Christology—makes the same move (*Ecclesiastical History* 1.2, in Wesselschmidt 2007: 254).

In a different register, Augustine sees here the spiritual malady of one who tastes no sweetness in prayer or scripture. The very idea is detestable (107:18). Such a

---

5. Byassee, *Praise Seeking Understanding* (Grand Rapids: Eerdmans, 2007), 205–19.
6. E.g., Theodoret of Cyrus (an Antiochene theologian, and so supposedly more averse to allegory) reads 107:16 as a reference to the resurrection in his *Letter 151*, in Wesselschmidt 2007: 253.

person does well to remember that when the spiritual disciplines do taste sweet, this is no personal achievement (Augustine 2003: 232–33). Conversely, we might say when they repel, it is not necessarily due to personal failure. The spiritual life comes in waves like that. The question is whether we will follow despite adversity or ease. Spurgeon quotes another contemporary on the question of who responds to the preached word of grace. Try though we may, our words can renew no one's soul. Only when God himself sends God's own word does a soul revive (George Swinnock, quoted in Spurgeon 1976: 462). And lest such spiritual readings seem only premodern things, both Zenger and Kraus note that the feast of sacrifice that effects union between host and guest is not a little like a Christian Eucharist (Kraus 1993: 328; Hossfeld and Zenger 2011: 111).

The fourth plaintiff has the longest litany (107:23–31). Sailors see the Lord's might in the deep before they're terrified by it (107:24). The specifics of the remedy are detailed (107:29–30). This fourth and final complaint forms a bookend with the first, in that those lost in the desert and those lost on the sea are each in places of life-threatening chaos. Unlike in the middle complaints, there is no suggestion of wrongdoing on the part of the complainant. Of course, God is still merciful simply to hear our complaint. God more often hears from us when we are in distress, and the psalm shows that God is willing to hear prayers offered from fear (Spurgeon 1976: 464).

There are fewer stories of rescue at sea in Israel's scripture than other sorts. The story of Jonah comes to mind. Paul's multiple shipwrecks do as well. The storm in Ps. 107 is so profound that the sailors' wisdom, or "craft," is useless, and they stagger like drunks (107:27; Alter 2007: 386). More profoundly, the story has primal echoes of a God who defeats the chaos of the sea in bringing life-teeming land into existence, a God who conquers the sea in redemption, a God whose rescue of Israel from exile is described as a sort of mythical sea battle in places like Isa. 43:2 ("when you pass through the waters, I will be with you") and 51:10 ("was it not you who dried up the sea . . . ?") (Hossfeld and Zenger 2011: 108). No wonder Christians, as those brought to life through the sea in baptism, see our own redemption here as well.

Translations vary for 107:30. The NRSV likes "haven"; Kraus likes "harbor." Alter prefers the older English "bourn" since it suggests the ship can launch anew from there. Whatever we call the place of refuge, it brings to mind the church, as the "inhabited town" did in the first complaint (107:4, 7). Augustine sees in the ship at sea an image for the church. Previous spiritual maladies in the psalm were error, concupiscence, and ennui, and now the threat of shipwreck is for those who lead in particular. We thought the helm's chair looked appealing until we took it over. By our own plans, we're tossed around like drunkards. God alone can deliver us from primal chaos, from heretics, from our own pride. Images of the church as a ship on a dangerous sea go back so far we cannot date them—they are already present in catacomb drawings, drawn typologically from Noah's ark. Augustine compares the storms to the church battling with heresies. God must have some reason for heretics—1 Cor. 11:19 ("there have to be factions among you") on Augustine's reading suggests God uses them to clarify true doctrine and to turn our pride into trust. Storms must continue. And God will be faithful through them.

The last part of the psalm pivots from the four complaints to a hymnic description of the character of God (107:32–43). God doesn't just make a way through hunger and thirst, prison, sickness and sea. God also turns rivers to desert, fruitful land into waste (107:33–34). God is always reversing things. The "normal" and the "expected" are subverted and rearranged. Psalm 107 is far from alone in this portrait of God's upside-down way of working (1 Sam. 2:4–8, and Mary's Magnificat that depends on it; Job 5:11–16). God's awesome power works both to destroy and to create (Alter 2007: 387). For all the penchant for the dramatic rescue that this psalm shows, it also has space for quiet life together and quotidian blessing (107:36–38; Limburg 2000: 370). Similar themes echo through Isaiah. Amos warns of a "futility curse," in which the people build and plant but others live in those houses and enjoy the land's yield (5:11). Isaiah promises God will undo that and every curse (65:21–22).[7]

There is a quick history of Israel in the concluding verses of Ps. 107 (Hossfeld and Zenger 2011: 109). God subdues the proud and exalts the weak in the exodus and the entry into the land (107:33–35). Israel lives happily in its God-given land for some time (107:36–38) until the corruption of Israel's princes causes it to fall and go into exile (107:39–40). We already know by this point of the psalm that God will gather from the farthest parts of the earth what was scattered (107:3, 41–43).

The patristic and medieval eras like to see in the biblical motif of God's reversal the supersession of Israel and the replacing election of the church (107:33–35) (Eusebius, *Proof of the Gospel* 6.7, and Origen *Commentary on the Gospel of John* 28.212–15, in Wesselschmidt 2007, 255; Augustine 2003: 233–34). The danger there is the pride of the church's superiority and the violence it has wrought. If God's character is indeed such that he reduces the proud and exalts the humble,

---

7. So Pat Dutcher-Walls in private correspondence.

what will become of the proud church and humbled Israel? Further, what can God do with a church that fails to learn to love Israel from its own scripture (John 4:22; Rom. 11:26)? Better to say that when God afflicts, it is out of justice; when God deals mercifully, it is for no reason other than his good pleasure (David Dickson, in Spurgeon 1976: 464). If God deals with us on an economy of merit, we are truly lost. Any reading that sets us up in a place of judgment and puts down another deals death, not life.

A better reading puts us, and our lives, in light of Israel's life, as works of God's love. The Lord of Israel saves those who cry out and those who are in pain, not those who are special or worthy. This first psalm of the fifth book of Psalms sends the message that God is gathering his people Israel back to his bosom. The great heart of Ps. 107 is simply this: life is a thing for which to thank God. Ideally, we wouldn't need a death-defying rescue to see it. But when we have such a rescue, we have words of praise here with which to give appropriate thanks. The psalmist dismounts with a return to biblical wisdom, with which the entire Psalter originally opened (Ps. 1). Wise readers will notice the patterns by which God works—and the steadfast love, *hesed*, by which the God of Israel orders the whole.[8]

This rich psalm presents a textured theology of God's nature as one who saves. It also reads like a sort of *ordo salutis* in evangelicalism, or a robust tropology (having to do with the moral life) in medieval readings of scripture. Augustine identifies the four complaints as four stages of a soul, from one in total error, to one who knows the good but cannot do it, to one who takes no delight in things that should delight, to a ruler of a church battered by the waves. Historical-critical readings probe behind the text for clues about its origins or transmission. Augustine probes *in front of the text*, at the place where it interfaces with our souls. Augustine's individual readings may not be right on a variety of grounds. But his *way* of reading has to be right: scripture has to be a map for souls, a guide for the church, a life-structuring order of praise, or we should stop reading it. Is it any wonder that a modern church under the tutelage of historical criticism has done precisely that?

Augustine's way of reading is indefensible if God is not one and if Jesus does not save. If not, these words apply only to Israel, not to the rest of us. But who is the one who satisfies hunger and thirst (Matt. 5:6)? Who is the one lifted up out of the pit who breaks the bonds of death (Ps. 40)? Who is the great physician who shares our ailment to share with us his cure? Who is the one with power to

8. This paragraph relies heavily on Hossfeld and Zenger (2011: 110–11).

calm the wind and the waves? The disciples ask this very question in Mark 4:41. Those who read their psalms, who are in this boat being redeemed by this strange Lord, will be stunned to find themselves mouthing an answer.

The soldier under mortar fire in Iraq experienced her first answer to prayer immediately after her first request. A swarm of dragonflies descended over the valley she was in, covering trucks and mortars, friends and foes, every inch of ground. Her attackers could not see to fire; she could not see to flee. She was delivered in what seemed to her a biblical miracle. As soon as her tour was up, she set out to find out more about this God who had appeared to her so powerfully. She gave thanks, and plans to spend the rest of her life telling the story. It was a Ps. 107 sort of answer.[9]

9. Natasha Sudderth Schoonover, interview by Therese Strohmer, February 4, 2013, Women Veterans Historical Project (University of North Carolina at Greensboro), 35, http://libcdm1.uncg.edu/cdm/ref /collection/WVHP/id/9687.

PSALM 108

Psalm 108 is something of a stepchild in a cobbled-together family, patched and spliced from bits of Pss. 57 and 60. It tends to get dismissed by modern interpreters. The footnotes in my edition of the NRSV pass this judgment: "Neither the form nor the contents of the two psalm parts fit well together. The psalm must be the result of an error made by a copyist." These commentators treat the psalm like a stereotypical Victorian would an illegitimate child: they ignore it (Harrelson 2003: 854–55). Kraus points the reader to his comments on previous psalms and glowers, "The interpretation of individual verses need not be repeated here" (Kraus 1993: 334). In a somewhat more hopeful note in an ecological age, Limburg titles Ps. 108 "Psalms Recycled" but says little more about their repetition. Modern lectionaries ignore the psalm.

Yet this psalm is a new thing, cobbled together perhaps, but different from either of its sources. The same words in a different setting do not signal the same thing. Premodern interpreters are more inclined to see God's handiwork rather than editorial clumsiness. "The Holy Spirit is not so short of expressions that he needs to repeat himself," Spurgeon observes (Spurgeon 1976: 465). Augustine, however, seems more annoyed at the recycling. He comments briefly on the slight differences between Ps. 108 and its sources before glimpsing the incarnation in the two psalm superscriptions that are *not* part of this one. Psalm 57 mentions a time when David was hard-pressed, and Ps. 60 a time when David had the upper hand. "We could have no clearer indication that both the earlier psalms are oriented to a single end not in their superficial historical sense but in the depth of the prophecy they express" (Augustine 2003: 240). Israel's greatest king, both in weakness and in power, summons our praise of God. We are not surprised that Augustine finds

Jesus here (in fact, the adamant insistence, "We could have no clearer indication," appears when the christological connection is more tenuous). But then Augustine stops commenting and moves on, like his modern counterparts.

Interpreters agree that the first part of Ps. 108 (1–6) is an individual hymn. Its attention to the dawn and the sun's course over the day recalls Pss. 8 and 19. It is called a psalm of David, like many earlier in the Psalter (Pss. 3; 51–72). The reference to music also connects Ps. 108 with the other Davidic psalms. The second portion of Ps. 108 (7–13) is a national lament and request for God to act militarily on Israel's behalf. It imagines the Lord parceling out territory that does not now belong to Israel, a conqueror dividing the spoils (108:7–9). This is an imagined future of an Israel restored to its glory under David, admired by the nations (108:3–5). The placement of this material, then, in the fifth book of the Psalter shows its importance for imagining a reconstituted and renewed Israel under a new king (Hossfeld and Zenger 2011: 122). If the spliced psalms did not fall together by some sort of scribal inattention, what might we say about their merger?

I recently learned the term "upcycling." In old-fashioned recycling, materials are returned to their elements and made into something altogether different as if from scratch. Upcycling turns unwanted materials into something more precious than they were before. A coffee company here in British Columbia took unneeded coffee sacks and paid a seamstress to sew them into tote bags for sale. Those bags did not fall together. An expert made something new from them.

Psalm 108 begins as an individual psalm of praise, as if to flatter God into hearing the request coming in part two. Psalm 108:7–13 lays out Israel's national predicament in light of its far-flung regional hopes to reign, unmolested and admired, by its conquered neighbors. Psalm 108:10 wonders who might bring this state of affairs about—could it be, perhaps, the God praised in the opening verses? Yet God is not presently helping, despite repeated promises to do so (108:11). The psalm concludes with a confidence that the faithfulness God has shown in the past will be shown again—for a God praised like this always delivers like this (108:13).

"My heart is steadfast," 108:1 exults. The life-giving, constantly pumping organ is unmovable here, like an axle around which a wheel spins (Spurgeon 1976: 465). One interpreter whom Spurgeon quotes describes the heart as needing to be steadfast so as to soak in scripture the way Mary "pondered" God's surprising faithfulness in her heart (Luke 2:19) (John Wells, cited in Spurgeon 1976: 465). Those who fix their attention on the text's particulars, as Mary did, will notice the few changes. Psalm 57:10's exultation of God "as high as the heavens" becomes 108:4's "higher than the heavens." It would seem difficult to improve on the exaltation of God "to the heavens," but Ps. 108 has done so (Hossfeld and Zenger 2011: 115).

"I will awake the dawn," 108:2 promises, in a reversal of normal events. Spurgeon quotes the Talmud on the reversal, that a midnight breeze would play the strings on David's instruments so that he would awake and busy himself with Torah until the dawn. He also quotes Rashi: "The dawn awakes the other kings; but I, said David, will awake the dawn" (Spurgeon 1976: 466). The psalm's attention stretches from first light to the highest heavens and compares that vast expanse to the extent of God's endless love. Alter's translation of 108:6 is pleasingly fresh: "Loom over the heavens, O God. Over all the earth Your Glory" (2007: 390). Even the Gentiles spend the day awash in God's mercy in the form of sun and rain. Even they will see God's glory stretched and resplendent. "This is truly a missionary prayer," Spurgeon exults (1976: 466). And sure enough, the biblical hope that all nations will stream to Zion and worship its God is one in which the church of all nations has always seen itself. Israel is God's beloved, sure enough (108:6). The Hebrew describes the Gentiles here as "non-nations," more a mob than a people (Hossfeld and Zenger 2011: 119–20). A future church drawn from Israel and all nations, gathered around Israel's Messiah, can look back and see itself mysteriously forecast in the psalm. What is a step beyond admiring? Joining. The New Testament takes a step beyond pagan nations' admiration of Israel to being grafted into Israel's relationship with the one true God (e.g., Rom. 11:13–24).

Scholarly opinion sets this in a variety of historical settings. Many see this as a postexilic prayer for the reconstitution of Israel under a new king as glorious as David of old. Others see a more specific referent in the period of the Maccabees (Hossfeld and Zenger 2011: 117–18). Both historical backdrops could have had influence, of course. More important than the imagined historical backdrop is what the psalm says. It reaches back to David as the charismatic musician and man of prayer and liberator from Israel's enemies. Its grouping in Pss. 108–110 shows hope for a new sort of David to reign and for the Lord to grant victory and divvy up the spoils. The oracle of 108:7–9 promises a newly minted Israel, with Ephraim and Judah both as points of pride (108:8) and Israel's neighbors back under its control (108:7–8). The heart of the psalm is a restoration of Israel from the scattering of exile to the power over its neighbors remembered under a once and future monarchy. Other portions of scripture express hope for this glorious renewal as well: "I will set up over them one shepherd, my servant David" (Ezek. 34:23; see also Isa. 11:1–16). This can only happen, of course, if YHWH acts. The Lord's hand is what brought Israel to ruin in the first place; the Lord's hand can deliver his beloved as surely and mightily as it did of old (e.g., Exod. 15:3, "The LORD is a warrior").

Moab and Edom come in for special degradation in the oracle. Moab is reduced to a mere washbasin, a place for purification of hands and cleaning of feet. Edom is reduced to a servant, its location as a place to which the master of the house hurls shoes (108:9; Spurgeon 1976: 466). Historically, to hurl the shoe is a metaphor of conquest. God's renewed faithfulness will begin as Israel succeeds in an assault on Edom (108:11). Israel's historic enemy, imagined in Genesis as an estranged sibling, comes in for prophetic denunciation often in scripture (Num. 24:18; Ps. 60; Ezek. 25:13; 35:6; Obadiah). Psalm 137:7 remembers Edomite sycophants cheering on the Babylonians in Judah's greatest hour of need. It is natural then that Judah's restoration will begin with an assault on Edom (Amos 9:11–12).

It is not obvious how Israel will go about this reconquest. Who will lead it against Edom? Psalm 60's contribution to Ps. 108 is a lament that God no longer goes out with our armies (108:11). Israel is certainly not strong enough to deliver herself, let alone to conquer anybody else, on normal military calculus. Yet the psalmist holds out hope that God will be faithful. Despite recent evidence to the contrary, God's right hand will deliver again. Cast into a spiritual key, Spurgeon says, "David . . . relied upon Him when Israel seemed under a cloud and the Lord had hidden his face" (1976: 467). Against all reasonable expectation, God can be counted on to bring about the oracle's promise of Israel's renewal, reconstitution, and reign over itself and its neighbors (108:12–13).

Some commentators seek an "interruption" of this theology of holy war. Zenger notes that the heavy emphasis on divine initiative, and the near absence of any human action, lessens the trust in the might of arms in Ps. 108. The glance back at David, the shepherd boy and musician, suggests an alternative kind of power besides geopolitical conquest. Psalm 108 ends with a sort of political impotence, with no actual conquest, just a wish for it.

I remember here an elderly Welshman for whom a friend cared on his deathbed, whose last words were, "I had always hoped I would see a free Wales. I suppose I won't now." Psalm 108 ends in a similarly far-fetched hope (Hossfeld and Zenger 2011: 123). Israel's hope is more weighty still, even if the hope of Welsh nationalism can grant us a glimpse. The restoration of Israel is linked with the end of the world, the fulfillment of all God's ancient promises, and God's people's greatest hopes.

A theology of holy war deserves its own lengthy treatment elsewhere. For now, we can speak as a church constituted on the far wings of Israel's hopes (108:3–5). Our grafting into this covenant comes only with a king who reigns from a tree, a conqueror subdued by his enemies and ruling only by the force of his resurrection. For those who see Israel's hopes in this sort of king, a washbasin is no insult, the handling of shoes no ignominy (see Mark 1:7; John 13:1–17). Nations farther afield than Edom and Moab stream to Zion to worship him, making music like David, "our" ancestor, in a renewed Israel that none but God could have imagined, let alone brought about.

PSALM 109

I used to think Ps. 137 was the most morally difficult in the Psalter, with its blessing on those who dash infants against the rock. But then I stewed in Ps. 109 for a while. The church has called it the *Psalmus Iscariotus* and has seen here a portrait of God's eternal condemnation of the Jews. The word "horror" seems too slight. "May his children be orphans, and his wife a widow" (109:9). "May his posterity be cut off" (109:13). May his father's sins be in the Lord's face (109:14). And may the God of all mercy ever see the sins of his mother. May his very prayers be counted as sin (109:7). This is not just a prayer for the desolation of someone's family in this life. It is a prayer for damnation for him and his parents and the total eradication of him from the community's memory (109:15). May he be made ghastly. May he be a thing of total religious reprobation. His kids too. And his parents. Forever.

Who prays this way?

Perhaps we can begin to approach the prayer if we think of the memory of the Nazis, to use an obvious example. They stand out in current cultural memory as the ultimate horror, and we wish any sign of them cut off. A 2011 documentary called *Hitler's Children* interviewed descendants of famous Nazi leaders about how they deal with their surnames and the blood in their veins.[1] One descendant voluntarily sought out sterilization. "I cut the line," he said simply. The psalmist's wish for no future generation made costly sense to the descendant of Nazis. Who could stand the thought of a pious Nazi at prayer after his atrocities? A counter-prayer that such an offering would add to his sin could begin to make sense (109:7).

1. *Hitler's Children*, directed by Chanoch Zeevi (Maya Productions, 2011).

There is something macabre about Western culture's memory of the Nazis. America's enemy in the last "good war" parades across our TV screens as a sort of desperate self-reassurance for how good we are to have opposed them. This cable channel fetish may be a sick interest in being voyeurs of evil at its uttermost. But radical evil is not cut off from the earth. Christians in South Sudan have seen their homes bombed, their children made orphans and forced to walk thousands of miles in a desperate bid for safety. In the Rwandan genocide, the horror over one hundred days was on such a scale that everyone alive in 1994 either has blood on their hands or benefited from a miraculous delivery. The scale and perversity of slaughter in Syria is the newest entry, as of this writing, to this wretched fraternity. Who doubts there will be more?

The Christian doctrine of original sin suggests that we shouldn't fetishize the Nazis' evil as a unique category. As sinners, we are all capable of committing horrors, if subject to the right pressures. The basic point is that our moralistic hand-wringing at Ps. 109 could swiftly turn to sympathy if we ourselves were among the countless victims of genocide. Emmanuel Katongole describes the Rwandan case in particular as a "mirror to the church."[2] We look, not to see how bad someone else is, but to see who we all are as human beings.

But what about the Jews?

The book of Acts describes the need to elect a replacement for Judas with a reference to Ps. 109:8, "may another seize his position." St. Augustine, my hero on matters hermeneutical, interprets the entire psalm as a blanket condemnation of Judas and the people for whom Judas typologically stands, the Jews. Augustine does stop short at a few points. He emphasizes the Jews' temporal condemnation with the destruction of Jerusalem in AD 70 rather than the more eternal imprecations of 109:6–19. He is fully aware that in the mystery of election God can call individuals to conversion. I have argued elsewhere that Augustine's habit of turning prayers of imprecation into prayers for transformation into friendship (an approach he studiously avoids on Ps. 109) could inform how Christians ought to read anti-Jewish portions of scripture.[3] But reading his work on this psalm is horrifying. It is not a far stretch to see the anti-Judaism here as an ingredient in the stew that became twentieth-century European anti-Judaism.

2. See Emmanuel Katongole and Jonathan Wilson-Hartgrove, *Mirror to the Church: Resurrecting Faith after Genocide in Rwanda* (Grand Rapids: Zondervan, 2009).
3. See my *Praise Seeking Understanding: Reading the Psalms with Augustine* (Grand Rapids: Eerdmans, 2007), chap. 4.

Perhaps a better approach to the *Psalmus Iscariotus* is to look at its heart of darkness, shake our head, and ponder the handing over of Jesus. It is a mystery how one who shared everything with the Lord would share him with his enemies for money. Who can explain it? Scripture speaks of Judas's betrayal both as intended by God (John 13:18) and as an atrocity worthy of the worst condemnation (Matt. 26:24). At that point—where the worst we humans can do and the saving work of God coincide—the mystery is thick indeed. Somehow the darkest deeds of which humanity is capable came together to make a total horror—religious horror included—of the sinless Son of God. And somehow that dark human and life-creating divine cooperation yielded the world's salvation. Psalm 109 suggests that the worst in scripture and the worst in us can, surprisingly, signal our salvation.

And precisely there, words fail again. Who can explain how our intimacy with Jesus turns into betrayal each time we sin, and how the resurrecting God breathes new life despite our acts of death?

A key question with Ps. 109 is whether it is indeed a psalm of imprecation at all. The translators of the NRSV think not, and so have inserted a "They say" at 109:6 to indicate that the diatribe of 109:6–19 is a complaint made against the psalmist by unknown false accusers. Kraus and Alter agree. Zenger is unequivocal: "The description that has been repeatedly assigned to [Ps. 109], 'a psalm of cursing and vengeance,' is completely wrong" (Hossfeld and Zenger 2011: 128). It is, instead, a justice psalm. In contrast, Mays and Limburg think the most natural reading is to take the curses as the words of the psalmist himself. As Mays points out, even if the psalmist is quoting his accuser, at 109:20 he asks God to turn those accusations back against his enemy, so the interpretive problem stands (1994: 349).[4] The precritical tradition was unaware of the possibility of 109:6–19 being the words of an accuser.

Augustine sees here a perpetual curse of the Jews. He prays, "May God punish them for eternity."[5] As a frequent apologist for Augustine, reading him on this one psalm makes me want to repent for his work and mine. Spurgeon is at least more circumspect. He calls this "one of the hard places of scripture" and prefers to leave it mysterious than to figure it out (Spurgeon 1976: 468–74). I hope the

4. Zenger translates 109:20 without the "return to sender" curse (Hossfeld and Zenger 2011: 125).
5. Augustine 2003: 252. In fairness to Augustine, he is innocent of modern scientific racism that describes curses in terms of bloodlines. If a Jew converts, Augustine would be glad to welcome her or him. For a more positive assessment of Augustine's theology of Israel, see Paula Frederiksen, *Augustine and the Jews* (New Haven: Yale University Press, 2010).

NRSV is correct, even if some of today's interpreters may be reacting partly to the sins of the history of interpretation. Even so, the tradition read the psalm the way it did, we cannot pretend otherwise, and we have to do business with such readings as part of ours.

How do we make sense of God's written word cursing in this way, especially when the Lord of the scriptures, God's Word fleshed, commands (not just "advises"[6]) us not to curse? Several points here. First, Limburg (2000: 377) helpfully points out that cursing in the ancient world and in the scriptures is a sort of convention. The vocabulary is "typical" of the time: "break the teeth in their mouths; . . . let them be like the snail that dissolves into slime" (Ps. 58:6–9), "let them be blotted out of the book of the living" (Ps. 69:23–28), "happy shall they be who take your little ones and dash them against the rock" (Ps. 137:9).[7] Those suffering are undergoing something like a return to the chaos before which God created—they ask for something similar for their oppressors. Second, such maledictions are not wishes. The Bible's hope is that such horrors *not* come to pass. Augustine often points out that Jonah's prophecy against Nineveh did not fail, precisely because Nineveh repented in response to his preaching and so was not overturned or destroyed (Jonah 3:4). Prophecy was fulfilled in the deepest sense: God desires the conversion of sinners, not their destruction. The curses catalogued in a place like Deut. 28:15–46 are so horrific precisely so that signees to a treaty won't break it. Third, tempted as we may be, the church cannot afford to avoid the cursing psalms in our worship. Martin Tel gives a twentieth-century example: when the church in Nazi-occupied Holland could not risk outright rebellion, congregations could pray the psalms of imprecation aloud. Those praying knew who the enemies were. Those occupying could be told they were just chanting biblical songs.[8] Fourth, these maledictions in Ps. 109 suggest something deeply wise about sin: it is its own reward. Evildoers always fall in the pit they have dug for someone else. This is present in 109:16–19—it is not that God notices and then punishes wickedness; rather, wickedness is its own desert. Those who reject Christ's way of enemy love are not then handed some other punishment. Their punishment is not to be in that way which leads to life. Finally, the fact that this psalm depicts malediction with such vividness does not leave us without

---

6. The infelicitous phrasing of Limburg 2000: 378.

7. It is a rhetorical convention of our time as well—and we don't always "mean" it except to entertain our listeners. The ancients were at least more serious about the effects of their words.

8. Martin Tel, "Necessary Songs: The Case for Singing the Entire Psalter," *Christian Century* 131, no. 1 (December 26, 2013), https://www.christiancentury.org/article/2013-12/necessary-songs.

interpretive creativity. God, in Christ, *becomes* a curse for us (Gal. 3:13, quoting Deut. 21:23). Everything of human horror has been absorbed by the God-man at Golgotha. That theological commitment, coupled with modern translators' work, helps us read the psalm well.

The psalm's superscription as a psalm of David sets it in a certain context, a "Davidized" one, one "saturated with royal theology and messianism" (Hossfeld and Zenger 2011: 131, 136). Modern interpreters often ignore the superscriptions; ancient ones can overemphasize them. Here the superscription helps: placing the psalm in the mouth of Israel's prototypical king makes it a prayer of a powerful person advocating on behalf of the poor (109:31). This psalm's language—of love, help, thanks, the saving right hand—accords deeply with Pss. 108 and 110. The christologically crucial Ps. 110 asks for deliverance from Israel's external enemies. Psalm 109 asks for deliverance on an internal matter not less existentially dangerous (Hossfeld and Zenger 2011: 136).

"Do not be silent, O God of my praise" (109:1). Commentators regularly point out that in this psalm full of devastating accusations, there is one plaintive complaint against God, "How long, O Lord?" God is simply noted as silent. But the psalmist's accusers are anything but silent: "For wicked and deceitful mouths are opened against me, speaking against me with lying tongues" (109:2). The formulaic nature of the complaint could mask an important observation: this is the language of one falsely accused. Mouths are open like wild beasts. "They beset me with words of hate, and attack me without cause" (109:3). The psalmist is surrounded by a mob, like Israel often is, with enemies on all sides (Kraus 1993: 339).

"In return for my love they accuse me, even while I make prayer for them. So they reward me evil for good, and hatred for my love" (109:4–5). Christians have thrilled to these verses—they sound like Christ's command to pray for those who persecute, enacted on his cross (Matt. 5:39, 45; Luke 23:34). Even Augustine, whom I criticized above, sees enemy-love here. "The Lord himself renders good for evil," he exults, citing Rom. 4:5 (Augustine 2003: 242). "All this happens *while* the psalmist has been praying for" his enemies (Limburg 2000: 375, emphasis added). Or maybe not. A more literal reading would render 109:4, "And I am all prayer" (Alter 2007: 391).[9] Christian mystics of all ages have asked that God make us altogether prayer: our whole life, including love of enemies, immersed in Jesus as fully as our bodies were under the water in our baptism, entirely offered to the Father by the power of the Spirit. Zenger translates, "For my love they accused me,

9. Alter gives this translation before preferring a Syriac variant that "*may have* worked from a Hebrew text" that indeed reads, "my prayer is for them" (2007: 391, emphasis added).

but I am a prayer" (Hossfeld and Zenger 2011: 124). He sees here a reference to a false accusation (as in 2 Sam. 19:22; Job 1:6–9, 12; 2:1–4, 6–7; Zech. 3:1–2). This one in particular has hindered the efforts of the one praying on behalf of the poor and has made him hated among those he means to help—*not* that he prays for them *while* they abuse him (Hossfeld and Zenger 2011: 132). Zenger may be overreacting to an interpretation that sounds too Christian. His own translation is open to a christological reading, as is his interpretation—Christ is a powerful one, "great David's greater son,"[10] who acts on behalf of the poor and so is set upon by a mob.

Even Augustine (2003: 246) notices a change at 109:6, though he doesn't know what to do with it: "They say, 'Appoint a wicked man against him; let an accuser stand on his right.'" Suddenly, it is only one man being accused, whereas 109:1–5 and the close of the bookend, 109:21–31, both speak of multiple accusers. Psalm 109:6–19 does not address God in the second-person singular either, though the outer portions do (Hossfeld and Zenger 2011: 130). Kraus (1993: 338) compares the passage to King Hezekiah laying another's imprecations before the Lord (2 Kgs. 19:14–19). This is a quotation of the psalmist's enemies. The speaker is accused of neglecting the poor—the very marginalized people on whose behalf the king is expected to advocate (Ps. 72; Prov. 31:9). The plaintiffs can destroy the defendant, powerful as he is. So the king lays out his case before the only higher court of appeal: YHWH. These are not the speaker's curses. These are the curses of an accuser, a "satan" (109:6), one appointed only for destruction.

Christians have invoked similar arguments to just war theory for what they take to be Ps. 109:6–19's intent (call it "just cursing" perhaps?). Augustine notes that we are forbidden to curse by Jesus himself. Yet the psalmist, he claims, is calling for justice—something that should delight our hearts. To ask for justice is to wish for good where an adversary wished only for ill (Augustine 2003: 245). One of Spurgeon's sources argues that magistrates have to consider the good of an entire community. To spare a moral monster would be like "sparing" a mad dog; to bless such a one would be to become complicit in his wickedness (Spurgeon 1976: 473). Both judgments are correct. Christians have argued that we should not do violence in our own defense but only on behalf of a weaker, defenseless neighbor. Still, the psalmist curses far more widely than on behalf of a weaker neighbor here, calling down specifically religious malediction against multiple generations of a family. Psalm 109:8–13 hopes the one cursed will be

---

10. James Montgomery, "Hail to the Lord's Anointed" (1822 hymn), in *United Methodist Hymnal* (Nashville: United Methodist Publishing House, 1989), 203.

like Cain, marked, homeless, wandering, dependent (Gen. 4:12). The next verse, Ps. 109:14, assumes his parents had committed a great number of sins to produce an offspring so wicked (Alter 2007: 393). The extinguishing of this accursed one and of his house and three generations of his family is as severe as anything that happened to the northern kingdom of Israel (1 Kgs. 15:29; 16:12).[11] Commenting on Ps. 109:28, Augustine wonders at how futile the curses of human beings are (2003:258). In the economy of God's mercy, our human curses often fall harmlessly to the ground.

Psalm 109:16–20 gets specific about the nature of the accusation: "For he did not remember to show kindness, but pursued the poor and needy and the brokenhearted to their death. He loved to curse." The accuser asks that these curses seep into the curser's very marrow (109:17–19). Augustine sees the beginnings of something hopeful in the mention of water and oil in 109:18—an obscure (especially for him) prefiguration of the water of baptism and the chrismation of the Holy Spirit. Here is a hint leaking through of a theology that says the one cursed is Jesus, that those joined to Jesus suffer with him and so are glorified with him (Rom. 8:30; Augustine 2003: 257). Jesus is a rescuer in need of rescue.[12] The Father, in resurrecting him, answered this prayer. Those still in need of rescue, against whom unjustified curses like 109:6–19 come, can still pray this psalm.

Psalm 109:21–25 marks another switch in voice. The accused speaks in his own voice, seeking justice against his accusers, especially in light of the brevity of human life. This could be the all-too-familiar cycle of revenge in which the formerly oppressed become as cruel in revenge as anything their opponents did when they were in power. But the psalmist's plea for justice is made *for the sake of the Lord's name* (109:21; Spurgeon 1976: 474; Alter 2007: 394; Limburg 2000: 377). The Lord alone can act to make wrong into right and judge between competing human claims to righteousness. Enemies may curse, but the Lord can turn a curse against Israel into a blessing (Num. 23:11; Kraus 1993: 341). The name of the Lord is good, as the psalmist never tires of repeating (see Ps. 118). More than that, the name of the Lord evokes memories of the exodus and the God who is known in his rescue of oppressed Israel from its wicked enemies (Exod. 3:7–15; Hossfeld and Zenger 2011: 134).

11. During Barack Obama's presidency, Ps. 109 was often taken up against him and his family, from the early days in 2009 on billboards and bumper stickers to Senator David Perdue in 2016. See David Graham, "David Perdue's Prayer for Barack Obama," *Atlantic*, June 10, 2016, https://www.theatlantic.com/politics/archive/2016/06/david-perdue-obama/486587.

12. The language, which hints of Karl Barth, comes from Hossfeld and Zenger 2011: 138.

It is odd for a royal figure, for one in a powerful office (109:8), to claim to be "poor and needy" (109:22). Yet even the powerful can be unjustly accused and become impoverished, in a variety of senses. Leaders do tend to accrue more enemies, and human *schadenfreude* at the sullying of a good reputation seems to be relatively universal. Speaking more biblically now, God has promised to act on behalf of the poor and needy (Ps. 107; Hossfeld and Zenger 2011: 131). It is the Lord's—not just the king's—very job description to protect the poor (Pss. 10:16–18; 12:6; 35:10; 40:18; 72:4, 12–14; 86:1; 145:11–19; 146:7–9; 149:2–4). But because the Lord loves the poor, so too should the king and all the rest of us. Later, when a claimant to rule Israel acts on behalf of the poor, biblically attentive observers will know with whom he is identifying. For now, the shadows lengthen, and the psalmist is like an insect flicked away (109:23). His knees are weak (109:25), and his enemies scorn (109:6–19). Only the rescuing Lord can turn such curses as these into blessings (109:28). It is *God* who stands at the right hand of the needy (109:31), *not* the satan, the accuser (109:6). Therefore, the psalmist will give praise, not curses, and tell the throng of the Lord's deliverance anew (109:30).

The most important question of this psalm is the most important question of the Bible: What is the character of the God here described? He is the one turned into a religious horror (109:6–25), left generationless by the frenzy of a whipped-up mob (109:9–15) because he is a monarch who is poor (109:22), who petitions the God of the Bible for justice (109:26–29), who is miraculously delivered, so that the whole world hears good news (109:30–31). This must indeed be a God whose character it is to bless in the face of every human curse (109:28).

PSALM 110

Ask average Christians to list their favorite psalms, and it would likely take a while for them to get around to mentioning Ps. 110. Yet Ps. 110 is the most-quoted psalm in the New Testament. It appears in three Gospels, Acts, Romans, 1 Corinthians, Ephesians, Colossians, and the Petrine Letters. It comes in for extensive and creative treatment in the book of Hebrews. The language of this psalm is quoted in the Apostles' Creed. American Christians have loved Psalm 23 at least since the Civil War for its comforting imagery in the face of death.[1] But the popularity of Ps. 110 shows that the New Testament church sought something other than comfort. When they sought to ponder the mystery of the relationship between God the eternal Father and his incarnate Son, the beloved words of the royal Ps. 110 leapt to mind.

We do well to listen when the Bible talks to itself.

First, we hear some static and garbled conversation. Verses 1 and 4 of Ps. 110 are clear enough in what they say, though of course some Christian interpreters question the New Testament's use of them.[2] This psalm may have once celebrated the crowning of a new king in Israel. For the New Testament, Ps. 110's king is David all over again and a new kind of eternal priest, ruling over a renewed Israel and subduing its enemies by the power of God alone. Psalm 110:2–3 and 5–7 are

---

1. William Holladay, *The Psalms through Three Thousand Years: Prayerbook of a Cloud of Witnesses* (Minneapolis: Augsburg, 1996), argues that Ps. 23 took on its outsized importance only with the American Civil War.

2. Kraus writes that it is wrong to apply Ps. 110's "messiah image" in a way that "transcends history and is Christologically shaped" (1993: 109). Of course, Christology done with appropriate attention to the humanity of God never transcends history. It is rooted in history and rooted in God's eternal life in equal measure.

more troubled in their manuscript transmission, translation, and interpretation. Portions of scripture like these garbled ones remind us that God's word is one fully accessible only to him. God graciously shares that word with us in scripture in some ways that we can understand. But we cannot understand fully. We are frail creatures to whom the word has been entrusted—we make mistakes, we err. Yet scripture is powerful and does not fail to produce fruit, even when we fail to understand fully. Thankfully, life with God is not solely a matter of understanding. It is a matter of God having plunged into life in our flesh to subdue the enemies of creation and establish a way between God and humanity that cannot be undone.

"The LORD says to my lord, 'Sit at my right hand until I make your enemies your footstool'" (Ps. 110:1). As important as this verse is, it does not stand above critical inquiry. By itself it cannot "prove" Jesus's divinity. Alter translates the second "lord" reference as "my master" (Alter 2007: 396). The psalmist is referring both to the Lord who speaks and to the king who is offered a place at God's right hand. There are additional interpretive dangers. If this is a christological psalm, it can look like an adoptionist Christology: Jesus is promoted into the ranks of divinity while God alone does the work (110:2, 5). The Synoptic Gospels' references to Ps. 110:1 could give rise to another misreading: Jesus is *not* a son of David, since he is, instead, Lord (Matt. 22:44; Mark 12:36; Luke 20:42–43).[3] The clearest verse in our most important christological psalm brings grave interpretive peril.

Psalm 110:1 and 4 are the words by which God, through a prophet, bestows royal office (Mays 1994: 351). Psalm 110 concludes a short series of psalms attributed to David in their superscriptions (Pss. 108–110). Perhaps this one is God's answer to the prayers for deliverance in Pss. 108 and 109 (Ross Wagner, in Van Harn and Strawn 2009: 285). David's life is not presented with any specificity or attention to history. Rather, the David invoked is a new or renewed one of some sort, and the Israel over which he presides is restored, or nudged forward, into the purposes for which God has always intended it (Ezek. 34:23–24; Isa. 11:1–9; Hossfeld and Zenger 2011: 147, 152).

The right hand is a place of special honor (1 Kgs. 2:19; Pss. 45:9; 80:17). In English we still refer to someone in power as trusting a "right-hand" man or woman (Limburg 2000: 380). Yet over against the way we use the phrase in English, here

3. The gnostically inclined and proudly anti-Jewish Epistle of Barnabas reads Ps. 110 precisely this way: Jesus is *not* a son of man but instead the Son of God. Whatever else the virgin birth may mean, it *cannot* mean Jesus is not as fully human as the rest of us (indeed, he is the most human one). The church had to slowly learn that the two natures of Christ mean we must speak of his divine and human agency as cooperative, not conflictual (Epistle of Barnabas, in Wesselschmidt 2007: 261).

it is God who does all the work of conquering. The king—the right-hand man—does nothing. The impression is like that of Exod. 14:14, "The LORD will fight for you, and you have only to keep still." It is common in the ancient Near East for royal enthronements to include descriptions of the defeat of the king's enemies. Surviving artwork often depicts the enemies of the king as a literal footstool carved into the foot of the monarch's throne (Wagner, in Van Harn and Strawn 2009: 286). One can see why Ps. 110 would work as a coronation psalm. Kraus suggests that the king may have mounted a royal chair and been carried into the holy of holies with the reading of this psalm (as in Jer. 30:21, "I will bring him near, . . . for who would otherwise dare to approach me?") (Kraus 1993: 348). Perhaps the king sits to the right of the ark of the covenant, the symbol of God's very presence and "palladium" of holy war. The king, God's viceroy, represents the Lord's holy power, and God acts through the king (Kraus 1993: 349). Zenger is more doubtful that we have a concrete historical situation here, though he agrees the psalm is very ancient (Hossfeld and Zenger 2011: 144, 149). He describes 110:1 as a sort of co-enthronement. The king participates in the royal rule of YHWH. Even so, it is the Lord who is the genuine king of the world, and the one on the throne is a companion to him. The Lord's enemies are the forces of chaos (as in 1 Cor. 15:20–28). And to rule is the royal duty of human beings. Our original vocation in the garden is restored by God's gracious power (Gen. 1:26, 28; Hossfeld and Zenger 2011: 147–49).

In a way, the many New Testament references to Ps. 110:1 function as mini-commentaries. They are also themselves biblical and so highly authoritative commentaries, at the very least! They show us how Christians are to read Ps. 110. The Gospels feature it in a controversy dialogue toward the end of Jesus's ministry as the friction grows between him and his fellow Jewish leaders. No one dares ask him any more questions after, and the crowd listens with delight (Matt. 22:46; Mark 12:37). Like the parables, this statement from Jesus in Matt. 22:41–45 seeks to befuddle as much as to clarify. St. Augustine catches the drift that this is a deliberately puzzling passage—he asks how it is that anyone could be both master and son. But he points out that even an earthly king who is son of a nonroyal father would be that one's son *and* his master (Augustine 2003: 267). Augustine never seeks to make the mystery of God fully transparent. He often points out that even our normal human relationships defy interpretation. He works to thicken the mystery. You think God is incomprehensible? We can't even fathom ourselves; how much less God? Later Christian tradition would come to understand that the only way for Jesus to be both son of David and Lord of David is for him to be human, descended from his stepfather Joseph's royal line (as Matthew himself already makes clear in Matt. 1:1–17), and divine, begotten of but not lesser than God. The church fathers would elaborate on the relationship between the Son and the Father. Some teachers of the church thought that Jesus's descent made him less than his Father in rank. The Father does all the work in Ps. 110; the Son does nothing. Pro-Nicene writers from Ambrose forward argue that this verse refers to Christ's work in his incarnation. Prior to the incarnation, the Son was not less divine than the Father; then during his incarnate life he was indeed less—in his human nature he was less even than his divine self. Then after his suffering, he "returns" to the right hand from which he came, and the Father honors him. It is no reduction for God to become human to save. It is, on the contrary, God's most elegant act of divinity. Maximus of Turin describes the Son as the great victor returning from his deed of conquest, after which he deserves to be seated at the right hand of the Father, having just "unlocked the underworld" by his resurrection (*Sermon* 40.2, in Wesselschmidt 2007: 263).

The relationship between the grandeur and the lowliness of Christ is not just the way out of an exegetical conundrum. It is the way God has made in Christ's flesh for our salvation. In Christ, God both reveals himself and hides himself. Reveals so that we may find, and hides so that we may seek all the more. For now, Augustine says, we can see Christ's enemies subject to him, as all nations become part of the church.[4] We cannot yet see his divinity. But we have seen something, so we continue to trek toward the hope that we may see God's face in full (Augustine 2003: 265–70).

The use of Ps. 110:1 in Acts and 1 Peter may be the source of the creed's "seated at the right hand" language. God has vindicated Christ in his resurrection and ascension and in the outpouring of the Spirit in the birth of the church. And folks who talk this way may get themselves stoned (Acts 2:33; 5:31; 7:55–56). Paul transforms the image of enemy kings subdued into the forces of chaos and disorder conquered by Christ's cross (Rom. 8:34; 1 Cor. 15:25). Ephesians 1:20 suggests that God's power is available to us, and Col. 3:1 uses Ps. 110:1 to direct our thoughts toward Christ above. Hebrews 1:13 quotes it to suggest the Son's

---

4. This is slightly more triumphalistic than Augustine tends to be later in his life, especially when the barbarian hordes are at the gates of Hippo as he lies dying. Clearly the adoption of Christianity by the Roman Empire has not meant the easy progressive submission of one nation after another to Christ's reign. I prefer to say, in language influenced by John Howard Yoder, that this portion of the psalm is not yet fulfilled, as many nations take advantage of the time of God's patience *not* to obey. For the underexplored relationship between Augustine and Yoder, see Charles Collier, *A Nonviolent Augustinianism? History and Politics in the Theologies of St. Augustine and John Howard Yoder* (PhD diss., Duke University, 2008).

vast superiority over the angels. The creed, reading these verses well, suggests that God has vindicated his Lord and Messiah, who was divine from all eternity, became human for our sake, and will return triumphantly.

As a pastor I was struck by how often I was asked where Jesus is. Why doesn't he just come down and show himself and make faith clear and easy? The answer is, of course, that he is at the right hand of the Father. Where is that? We don't know. But it suggests Jesus's victory. He is not, of course, absent here: he is present in the body of Christ, in the church's sacraments, in the poor, in the word preached and lived out. In response to the question, we can say that Jesus *has* come down and shown himself. The church bears good news of his incarnation through time to us. Faith in such good news is not clear or easy. Not yet anyway. One day it will be. For now, it is arduous but worthwhile, as we catch glimpses of Christ's lordship made possible by his humility.

"The LORD sends out from Zion your mighty scepter. Rule in the midst of your foes" (110:2). The psalmist describes the ruler surrounded by enemies and ruling nonetheless. As in Ps. 2, the nations conspire in vain, and the Lord laughs (2:1, 4). The king may be embattled for now, but his rule over his enemies is certain (Ross Wagner, in Van Harn and Strawn 2009: 287). To rule is also God's original vocation to human beings (Gen. 1:26, 28), so the psalm can be seen as a restoration of that which was ruined (Hossfeld and Zenger 2011: 149). Ancient Christians saw here the birth and expansion of the church as God's royal people, beleaguered yet advancing. For Justin Martyr, the king's scepter is the "powerful teaching of the apostles" (*First Apology* 45, in Wesselschmidt 2007: 264). The power of the Lord's word compels many to abandon demons. A summons to reign through victory in war becomes a victory over human misbegotten allegiance to powers that destroy. Centuries later, Augustine argues that Christ's rule begins with Christians and expands as forgiveness of sins is preached from Jerusalem outward (Luke 24:47; Augustine 2003: 270). Christ *has* dominion in the midst of his foes—Ps. 110:2 is being realized.

On any account, 110:3 is difficult. Ancient versions differ sharply from one another and from the Masoretic Text (Hossfeld and Zenger 2011: 141). Zenger wonders whether the psalmist had to use "veiled language" to hide his meaning from Persian officials in exile (although if so, he hardly veils 110:1–2) (Zenger 2011: 144). Robert Alter describes the Hebrew as two words, "Your-people acts-of-volunteering" (Alter 2007: 397), which the NRSV expands to "Your people will offer themselves willingly on the day you lead your forces." Zenger renders it similarly, "Your people are eager on the day of your power" (Zenger 2011: 149).

The sense here is clear enough: the Lord's troops are eager to stand for him, offering their lives to further his rule. For a very different reading, Kraus translates the same words, "Round about you stand noblemen in the day of your power" (Kraus 1993: 344). Here we have the Lord surrounded by his court, as in Ps. 29:1, "Ascribe to the LORD, O heavenly beings, ascribe to the LORD glory and strength." Whether these are soldiers or courtiers, the Lord is not alone but is surrounded by powerful advocates and loyal surrogates.

The next part of the verse is more garbled still. Most translations talk of wombs: "From the womb of the morning, like dew, your youth will come to you" (NRSV). The English rendering of Augustine's version has "From the womb before the morning star I begot you." Early Christians naturally enthused over talk of begetting. These are not physical descriptions with literal purchase, of course. God doesn't have a literal womb any more than God has a literal beard or is sitting on a literal throne. But the words do give us trustworthy knowledge about God (I am tempted to call it "super-literal" rather than "not"). Mothers don't birth children of different species. They birth the same sort of creatures as themselves. So too, mutatis mutandis of God. Athanasius points out that scripture refers to us creatures as God's handiwork, but talk of a divine heart or womb signifies that the one "born" is of the same nature as God (*Discourses against the Arians* 4.27, in Wesselschmidt 2007: 266). A womb is a hidden, secret place; it is the mother's very self, her intimate substance, and it is from there that the eternal Son is eternally begotten (Augustine 2003: 273). Modern readers are, of course, more circumspect about talk of eternal generation in this confusing verse. Kraus speaks with more caution about images of hope and change—holy mountains, a rosy dawn ("from the womb of the rosy dawn, have I begotten you like the dew"). Alter renders it similarly, following the Septuagint (which ancient Christians also tend to follow), with the reference to the "dew of your youth" signifying the warrior-king's energy. Ross Wagner offers a reading of both possible translations: 110:3b could refer to God's young fighters and their abundance on the mountains, like dew in the morning (2 Sam. 17:12 or Ps. 133:3) or it could say, like Ps. 2:7, "I have begotten you." The translation is difficult, but the point is surprisingly clear: the Lord alone is the source of the king's might, and God generously chooses and protects Israel's monarch (Van Harn and Strawn 2009: 288). For Zenger, the king, like the rain, brings fertility to the land and the people (as in 2 Sam. 23:4 and Ps. 72:6; Hossfeld and Zenger 2011: 149).

A passage that is difficult to translate can still be worked with. It should remind us that the God we talk about is beyond all human words—even easily translatable ones! These are occasions to learn from the best linguists and historians. They are a check on our pretension to speak well of God. Our knowledge of God is always mediated by frail human beings and institutions. Yet God has so abundantly shared himself in the incarnation that we always have more than enough to say. Our tongues are not tied because of any tragic lack of knowledge of God (though if this psalm verse were the only verse of scripture we had, that might be so!). Rather, God has shared so much of himself and come so unbearably close that we can never describe God sufficiently. I love Mays's understatement here: "For the purposes of preaching and teaching, it is best to admit that the perspicuity of scripture is missing here" (Mays 1994: 352). I wonder if we should preach such difficult passages more often. Church people often don't know they're there, and yet they are plentiful. To see us preachers stammer in the presence of a God whom our words cannot capture, but whose Word has captured us, might be a rare gift.

"The LORD has sworn and will not change his mind, 'You are a priest forever according to the order of Melchizedek'" (110:4). For Christian readers, this verse is nearly as significant as 110:1, with the two verses in one psalm presenting an embarrassment of riches. One historical-critical approach is to read the verse against the backdrop of the end of the monarchy in 587 BC (Hossfeld and Zenger 2011: 150). In other words, the verse is written and historically curated at a time when it is already *not* literally true of Israel's monarch.[5] While historical reconstructions have to be held tentatively, this is a fruitful suggestion for Christian use of the verse.

At the other end of the spectrum of a *sensus plenior*, a fulsome sense, Alter translates the final phrase as "my righteous king," a true Hebrew rendering, but one that avoids intentionally any reference to the man called Melchizedek in Gen. 14:17–24. For Alter, Ps. 110:4 is a pun (Alter 2007: 397). Most agree, however, that the reference is to the cryptic story of Abraham's encounter with a Canaanite priest-king who appears out of nowhere to bless Abram after his victory in a battle, presenting bread and wine, receiving a tithe of everything Abram has, and offering these words: "Blessed be Abram by God Most High, maker of heaven and earth; and blessed be God Most High, who has delivered your enemies into your hand!" (Gen. 14:19–20). Melchizedek, king of Salem, is accompanied by another, an unnamed king of Sodom, who proposes that Abram take spoil, which he refuses to do. Kings of Israel seem to have played some priestly roles: Saul makes

---

5. In a very different context, Elesha Coffman's book *The Christian Century and the Rise of the Protestant Mainline* (New York: Oxford University Press, 2013) argues that by the time the description "mainline" was coined, the churches that fit that description were already in decline. In other words, there never was an ascendant mainline, only a declining one.

an offering (1 Sam. 13:9); David dances before the ark, makes offerings, and blesses the people (2 Sam. 6:13–18). The psalm represents a hope for a renewed Davidic priestly kingship, rooted in the trustworthiness of the God who will not forget his promise in 110:4.

Ancient Christians were impressed by many of these details, as were their contemporary Jews and gnostics, with the lines between these groups fluid at times. Who is this great King of Peace, so much greater than Abram that he can bless him, that the great patriarch of Israel can offer him the tithe that goes to God, that he holds eucharistic elements in his hands, that he heads an order into which later kings of Israel are inducted (Ps. 110:4)? Thomas Long says this is a "signpost in the old order," a story and language that shape the imagination so that the events of Jesus's life and rule have an existing vocabulary with which to describe them.[6] Walter Brueggemann (2014: 135–36) does not see in Gen. 14 any ex post facto attempt to legitimate power claims for a future king in Jerusalem. He does see a name for God, *El Elyon*, "Most High God," that only comes to be applied to YHWH the Lord of Israel late in ancient history. This name is a description of functions taken from other gods and assigned to YHWH. Those who worshiped a fertility god in ancient Canaan were actually, insofar as they got anything right, worshiping the God of Abraham, Isaac, and Jacob without knowing it. So too the Hebrews in taking over descriptions of that god into their story were saying that all truth is God's, that any legitimate worship of another deity is actually unaware worship of the one true God of Israel.

We have in Ps. 110 *in nuce* a theology of other religions. Whatever in them can be brought to render homage to Abraham's God, like Melchizedek, should do so. Whatever cannot, as with the king of Sodom's proposal to plunder, should be refused.

Melchizedek is minor in Genesis, though his one appearance rings dramatic and regal. He is minor in Israel's scripture, only appearing in Ps. 110 besides Genesis. But he is major in the book of Hebrews. The author of Hebrews uses Melchizedek to build an entire Christology of Jesus's eternal priesthood (clearly, we should not judge the importance of biblical motifs by the frequency of their appearance!). It is God who appoints Christ as high priest (Heb. 5:6). Jesus does not change from year to year. His is a permanent priesthood by which he can save all who approach God, for whom he makes intercession (Heb. 7:21–25). "See how great he is!" the preacher thunders (Heb. 7:4). Melchizedek is without genealogy, no mother and

6. Thomas G. Long, *Hebrews* (Louisville: Westminster John Knox, 1997), 85.

no father; he just explodes into history (Heb. 7:3). He blesses the patriarch and so must be greater than Abram (Heb. 7:7; cf. 2 Sam. 14:22). Levi is still in Abram's loins when this blessing happens (Heb. 7:10), yet the priesthood of Christ comes through a different tribe, that of Judah. Christ's priesthood does compare favorably with the Old Testament's, but it is not a new story. His is older than the Old Testament, older than Abram, more effectual, and based on an "indestructible life" not inheritance upon death (Heb. 7:16). As another preacher comments, Jesus is God's best wine, but there were foretastes (Brueggemann 2014: 85).

Hebrews is often pilloried for being allegorical, gnostic, floating above history. Arguably, with its detailed talk of loins and tribes and tribute, it is as rooted in history as any other book we have. It is inarguable that I have given a literal reading of Hebrews. It is also a figural reading of Gen. 14 and Ps. 110:4. Is the result literal or figural? Both, really. The lines blur. It is a Christology of Jesus's priesthood offered across the two testaments, remarkably neglected in our day but begging to be rediscovered. Jesus indeed has no human father, only a divine one. He has no divine mother, only a human one. He is descended from Abraham and David through his mother (Matt. 1:1–17). His line of descent via his adopted father Joseph is even important enough to record in the Gospels (Luke 3:23–38). His divinity does not compete with his humanity, contrary to the impression Heb. 7:3 may give. As Long puts it, Levi may be in Abram's loins, but so is Jesus (Heb. 7:10). Psalm 110:4, reflecting back on Gen. 14 and reflected on in Heb. 7, makes this point clearly: God has no other face than the one of trustworthiness and tenderness seen in Jesus, who intercedes powerfully and unendingly for his covenant people (Mays 1994: 354).

The last three verses return to the holy war theme of 110:2 to describe the advance of the rule of the priest-king of 110:4: "The Lord is at your right hand." Here the seating chart has flipped. In 110:1 the king was at the Lord's right hand. Now the Lord is at the king's right hand. It is the kind of switch that suggests the psalmist sees the roles and the persons of the king and the Lord as mutually determining, almost interchangeable. In either case it is the Lord who acts, and the king who is the beneficiary. "He will shatter kings on the day of his wrath. He will execute judgment among the nations, filling them with corpses; he will shatter heads over the wide earth" (110:5–6). None too pacific these images. Scripture turns to such holy warrior images to prophesy about what God will do with Israel's enemies (e.g., Ezek. 32:5–6, "I will strew your flesh on the mountains . . ."). YHWH is a warrior who will shatter heads and pile up corpses on the day of wrath (Ross Wagner, in Van Harn and Strawn 2009: 289). The Hebrew specifies that the Lord will "shatter the head," singular, suggesting there is one universal source of chaos (Hossfeld and Zenger 2011: 151). The "day of wrath" is when the Lord will quell resistance to his rule (Mays 1994: 352).

The last verse is slightly more cryptic. "He will drink from the stream by the path; therefore he will lift up his head" (Ps. 110:7). Could this be a reference to the Gihon Spring, where some sort of anointing of kings may have happened in ancient days (1 Kgs. 1:38–40; Kraus 1993: 352)? Is it an image of a pursuing warrior who stops to refresh himself now that the enemy is routed (Ross Wagner, in Van Harn and Strawn 2009: 289)? Is it an act of hostility to drink another people's water? Is it a sign that this conquering king, like Gideon's chosen men, will not kneel to drink (Judg. 7:4–6)? Perhaps this peaceful image pulls against the violence of 110:2 and 5–6. Perhaps the placement of these verses in the context of the priestly and royal material of 110:1 and 4 balances their call for blood. It is the Lord who lifts up the psalmist's head after all (Pss. 3:3 and 27:6; Van Harn and Strawn 2009: 289). We do well to remember this psalm's birth in a time of exile. Israel has *already* been conquered; its kings' failures are complete; its God's trustworthiness is fully called into question. The confidence of the psalm in God, the king, military rule, and priestly offering has been radically undercut. And yet there the psalm is, offering praise and exuberant confidence. Clearly it hopes for a new David, a renewed Israel, with its vision grander than that filled by any king of Israel prior to or after that time (Kraus 1993: 353; Mays 1994: 353). Except, perhaps, for one.

The explicitly nonviolent New Testament is surprisingly untroubled by the violence in the psalm (Hossfeld and Zenger 2011: 154). The enemy kings of Ps. 110 are transformed in scripture's imaginative world into hostile powers and principalities, including death (Eph. 1:20–23; 1 Cor. 15:20–28). The worldwide conquest of the king becomes the gradual progression of the church from Jerusalem to the ends of the earth (Ross Wagner, in Van Harn and Strawn 2009: 289). St. Augustine continues the New Testament's figural reading trajectory. To shatter a head is to "transform the proud into humble people" (Augustine 2003: 283). The conquering priest-king in YHWH's favor stopping and drinking is a reminder that God in Christ approaches the "course of our mortality," which issues from hidden sources. The "rapid and turbulent stream" of our human life is one from which God draws deeply. In fact, Christ takes to himself "the very depths of the sea," as he is born only to die.

These are all deep mysteries, hidden even as they are revealed.

PSALM 111

Marilynne Robinson writes that hymns she once dismissed as sanctimonious have grown on her as she has aged. "I Come to the Garden Alone" takes an epochal moment—Jesus's resurrection—and includes within it the joy of friend reuniting with friend. "I Love to Tell the Story" sings that "those who know it best, seem hungering and thirsting, to hear it like the rest." Scripture is so fulsome that "every moment and detail merits pondering and can always appear in a richer light." The scriptures seem to change, but we're the ones actually changing while we study. "Of course, those who know it best are those who, over time, put themselves in the way of hearing it."[1]

Hymns can teach. And instruction invites doxology. Psalm 111 is praise of God that teaches the ones doing the praising. The psalm is bookended by two proverbs: "Great are the works of the LORD, studied by all who delight in them" (111:2) and "The fear of the LORD is the beginning of wisdom" (111:10). In between we have a catechesis of adoration. Not just anyone can study the Lord in any old way. God has laid down a means by which human beings can approach in a way that puts all our capacity for wonder and delight to good use.

The "works of the LORD" is the key theme of this psalm. And all the works of the Lord spring from and take their meaning from the central act of God: the exodus.[2] The form of God's very character is exodus-shaped.

As a pastor, I often find folks who are convinced that God's job is to make their lives better. Prayers are lists of outcomes in my life that I would like God

1. Marilynne Robinson, "What Wondrous Love," in *When I Was a Child, I Read Books* (New York: Farrar, Straus & Giroux, 2012), 189–213, here 189–90.
2. Richard Clifford's commentary in Van Harn and Strawn 2009: 291.

to improve. Something good happening is a "blessing"; something unpleasant is not. But every act of God is shaped like the exodus. It is a freedom-granting, tyranny-breaking, provision- and conquest-providing act. God is not there to make our personal preferences come true, like some sort of genie in a bottle, a butler answering a bell. God is there to keep covenant as expressed in the exodus and at Sinai. The question is not how to get what we want out of God. It is to wonder how whatever happens fits into the narrative of God's freedom-granting and law-binding character. Put starkly: God doesn't "care" whether or not we prosper as individuals. What God cares about is our keeping of the law. That eventually makes for our deepest delight also (111:2).

Psalm 111 is like its acrostic poem counterpart, Ps. 112. Each letter of the Hebrew alphabet gets a half phrase in these two psalms rather than a whole verse (Hossfeld and Zenger 2011: 161). Psalm 119 is acrostic writ large. These poems inscribe an argument, showing it rather than telling it: God is to be praised from A to Z, from Alpha to Omega (Rev. 1:8). Everything God has created, tainted though all things are by human sin and frailty, nevertheless bears witness to an unbearable beauty. The exodus is the jewel in creation's crown.

"I will give thanks to the LORD with my whole heart," the psalmist promises (111:1). Any of us who are used to half-hearted commitments from ourselves or others might note, by contrast, the fullness promised here. An American painter friend can go on at length about the virtues of successive fads in Japanese painting, which he does not emulate himself, but after hearing him you might think the whole world should. All-consuming passion is contagious. This hymn is promising similar intensity. Deuteronomy 6:5 commands us to love the Lord God with *all* our heart (cf. Ps. 111:1, 2, 7, 10) (Hossfeld and Zenger 2011: 161). "If you want, you can become all flame," Abba Joseph of the desert fathers promised.[3]

"In the company of the upright, in the congregation." There is no solo praise. No one is dutifully slinking late into the back of a sanctuary. I have served and preached to congregations full of people who, when asked to stand and sing, stand and do no such thing. They listen, grim-faced, while the musicians play. But what if each of us approached God's house to offer fulsome and fervent praise?

St. Augustine hears in "the company of the upright" a sign of the people of God made perfect by Christ at the end of time (Matt. 13:24–30). It is not the preacher's job to root out incorrect believers (though we're tempted—as my judgmental comment in the paragraph above shows). Only Christ can do that.

---

3. Abba Joseph, quoted in Roberta Bondi, *To Pray and to Love* (Minneapolis: Fortress, 1991), 7.

In a very different circumstance of fracturing, think of the nature of the church today, divided as we are into countless denominations, many of which still deny each other's validity. Each shard has something beautiful in it, but no part can easily be reattached to any other. The psalm delights in "Christ's fully perfect body," without fracture or crack, giving thanks to God with one whole heart (Augustine 2003: 285). The Bible offers an eschatological ecumenism.

"Great are the works of the LORD, studied by all who delight in them" (111:2). This adage is a retort to all joyless drudgery in study. Scott Cairns praises the scriptures (and criticizes preachers) this way:

> I love the Word's ability to rise again
> from chronic homiletic burial.[4]

Delight is sacramental. It is a part of God's creation, given to us so that God can meet us there. As Kraus puts it, God "can be experienced by all who take pleasure in his works" (1993: 358). Delight is only there as a conduit through which God can reach us, his people. Whether those taking delight know it or not, it exists only as a glimpse of the overwhelming delight God has for us in Christ and wants us to share with others. God uses scripture to change our desire from self-destructive and ridiculous things into the things of God, exodus-making things, the works of the Lord.

"Wonderful deeds" (Ps. 111:4) evokes Exod. 34:6–7, a piece of praise that anchors Israel's memory in the exodus and Sinai (Hossfeld and Zenger 2011: 164). Commentators point out that the word for "work" in 111:3 is singular (e.g., Alter 2007: 399). God only has one *work*—that of covenant-keeping. God gives the people food so that they might in turn keep the covenant (111:5). Ancient people were more aware than we tend to be of the tenuous nature of food production— there might be a rich harvest, or there might be a very hungry season. The psalm shows that we Christians do well to remember God's graciously provident hand not only at every meal but also at the Eucharist, where God gives us the bread of heaven (Ps. 105:40). The God who gives bread also gives *himself* as bread.[5] Augustine comments that the Eucharist works backward from ordinary digestion. Normally we eat something, digest it, and it becomes part of our body. In the

---

4. Scott Cairns, "The Feast of the Transfiguration," *Huffington Post*, May 25, 2011, http://www .huffingtonpost.com/scott-cairns/the-feast-of-the-transfig_b_669069.html. I'm grateful to Zach Eswine for directing me to this poem.

5. For more here about food, Eucharist, and God, see James Howell, *Worshipful: Living Sunday Morning All Week* (Eugene, OR: Cascade, 2017), 53–64.

Lord's Supper, we eat, *and it digests us* and makes us part of the body of Christ.[6]
Food means much more than sustenance, crucial as that is. It means God. As does
every other created thing, viewed aright.

The church has often seen itself in the Israelites' wandering in the wilderness,
noting both God's magnanimity and our rebellious squabbling. Anyone at all
involved in the church's life knows that dispute, disagreement, and conflict are
just part of it. We bicker no less than our Israelite forebears. Yet God fed them.
God feeds us. And in the scope of eternity, life will not always be so contentious,
nor our wandering so aimless. St. Augustine wonders, if even now God gives to
such sinners as us the Word made flesh, what sort of food will God give to his
fully redeemed people in glory (2003: 288)?

God's demonstration of the "power of his works" is the giving of the promised
land of Canaan (111:6). Modern interpreters are not alone in pointing out the
moral outrage of the conquest of Canaan. Does God really elect people and take
land from other people to bless the elect? Whatever squeamishness we may feel
about it, our God seems to elect a people and to give them the heritage of other
peoples ("houses filled with all sorts of goods that you did not fill, hewn cisterns
that you did not hew, vineyards and olive groves that you did not plant," Deut.
6:11). Scripture is just as clear that God has blessings for all people—Israel's election is for everyone's eventual blessing. Every gift of God is Israel-shaped: each gift
is not for Israel alone; each gift is *through* Israel *for* everybody else. Other portions
of Israel's scripture make clear there is no covenant without outsiders (Ruth is the
most obvious example). And we Christians believe that God has cracked open
this singular election in Christ to invite all of us to share God's provision. "Giving
them the heritage of the nations" (111:6) is literally now about the church's influx
of peoples from all nations. Allegorically we can say more: the conquest is about
God's unearned provision, our ongoing struggle with our spiritual enemies, and
God's not-yet-finished promise to deliver creation fully.

"All his precepts are trustworthy" (111:7). Such ebullient celebration of the
law opens up questions for Christians. If *all* of his precepts are trustworthy, why
do we Christians sideline so much of the Torah? The answer, as ever, is Jesus:
with the coming of Israel's Messiah, God is gathering an eschatological people
from among Jews and Gentiles. The law we keep is also biblical: the law is circumcision of the heart, the Spirit's work of making us holy, the effort to be one
reconciling people around one table, with "one Lord, one faith, one baptism"

---

6. Augustine, *Confessions*, trans. Henry Chadwick (New York: Oxford, 1991), 124.

(Eph. 4:5). This psalm suggests there is a valid ongoing use of the law for Christians. The law is for guiding the praises of the church as we are being redeemed. We are not on our own, morally speaking, making it all up. We are guided by God's own delightful words.

This psalm has no tension or paradox between God's faithfulness and human unfaithfulness (Hossfeld and Zenger 2011: 165). Human infidelity, in Exodus and elsewhere, is overlooked, seemingly forgotten, drowned in the fathomless goodness of God. So despite our frequent and nearly unending creativity in breaking covenant, God remains eternally faithful. This divine faithfulness opens up resources to talk about God's ongoing faithfulness to his people Israel according to the flesh and also to his church. God's invitation to us in Christ is not pinched off or shut down even by our disinterest or adamant refusal.

"The fear of the LORD is the beginning of wisdom," scripture regularly proclaims (Ps. 111:10). The proverb can stand on its own like a bumper sticker. But Ps. 111 is textured with the grain of Israel's specific relationship with God. So the adage here is not unmoored from Israel's story (as perhaps in Prov. 1:7 and 9:10). Job 28:28 develops the theme more deeply. The writer of Job expresses awe at human ingenuity in digging metals out of the ground. Human beings have breathtaking ingenuity. But no one can mine wisdom (Limburg 2000: 384). God has made a way where there is no way—in Ps. 111 that way is the delighted study of scripture. Wisdom comes from living out the covenant God has made that cannot be unmade (Mays 1994: 358).

The psalm tutors us with the praises of Israel. Do we delight as the psalm delights? St. Augustine reads this verse and thinks of Isaiah's sevenfold gifts of the Holy Spirit (the NRSV lists six: wisdom, understanding, counsel, power, knowledge, and fear of the Lord in Isa. 11:2–3).[7] What Psalm 111:10 recommends, the Holy Spirit enables through the gifts poured out on the church. The point of this psalm isn't to dredge up delight to prove our adherence to the God of the Bible. The point is to recognize that only God can empower and enlighten us to read his word not only with understanding and obedience but also with joy. "The fear of the LORD is the beginning of wisdom," and only God can provide that fear. And God has—in the flesh of Christ.

7. Wesselschmidt's translation of Augustine has seven gifts of the Spirit: the spirit of wisdom, understanding, counsel, courage, knowledge, piety, and fear of the Lord. The number of the gifts of the Spirit (seven) has often been taken as a sign of the Spirit in Christian tradition. Modern translations, drawing on the Hebrew, typically list six gifts (Augustine, *Sermon* 248.5, in Wesselschmidt 2007: 269).

The final verse functions as a sort of doxology, Alter says (2007: 400). But so too does the first. It is only with doxology that we study well, and only if study leads back to doxology is it worth the time. One commentator says this verse, 111:10, is inscribed above the library door at his seminary (Limburg 2000: 382). In keeping with this psalm, we would hope to hear constant and raucous shouts of joy erupting from inside.

PSALM 112

Psalm 112 is a small message that tells a great truth.[1] God's righteous people are generous and they lend freely. And then there's this: they are exalted and look down on their foes once God turns existing social conditions upside down.

Is this . . . true? If so, how?

Psalm 112 is a twin with Ps. 111. Psalm 111 is about theology proper—God, without much reference to us. Psalm 112 is about anthropology proper—who we are. The righteousness of God and the righteousness of the one who fears God are linked. Put these two psalms together and you glimpse the two natures of Christ, divine and human, the God who is always giving himself away and a God-man who does likewise.

This interpretation is, of course, reading through thick Christian lenses. No lenses are needed, however, to see that the marks of the righteousness of the person mentioned in Ps. 112 are economic. No interior space of the heart here—just pocketbook practices. The righteous one lends without expecting repayment or charging interest, and the poor are blessed (112:5, 9).

Other psalms are not so sure and lament accordingly (Ps. 73:1–16). It is not always the case that the righteous even have money to lend. Is Ps. 112 an ideal not always reached? An eschatological promise? It is significant that this text is selected for Epiphany season in the Revised Common Lectionary. Perhaps we need special illumination to see such blessedness in this harsh world.

1. Only seventy-nine words in Hebrew (Nancy deClaissé-Walford, in Van Harn and Strawn 2009: 293)! I count 166 words in the NRSV translation.

Psalm 112 opens with a beatitude on one who fears. "Happy are those who fear the LORD, who greatly delight in his commandments" (112:1). Happiness, fear, and delight are an unusual combination. But a biblical sense of fear includes awe, reverence, appropriate regard.[2] Fear means more than reptilian terror in the face of danger. It means recognizing something awe-inspiring, world-as-usual-undoing. This is why scripture commends the fear of the Lord—only a greater fear can drive out a lesser. Either we will not fear God and so we will fear everything else, or we will fear God and so fear nothing else.[3]

To press the point, the psalmist adds delight (112:1). We are not just to fear God but to delight in his commands. For the righteous person, the law is no drudgery. It rather evokes passion, ecstasy, affection. This is not the rote, duty-bound employee; it is rather the enthusiasm of the devotee, the thrill of a lover.

"Their descendants will be mighty in the land" (112:2). How are Christians to read such a promise when historically some of those who delight most in the law are those who foreswear ever having children at all—monks and nuns and priests? Children are undoubtedly a blessing, as those who have struggled with infertility know well. Yet Gentile Christians read this text through Jesus, who himself had no child. Yet he is heir to the promises of God to Abraham to fill the world with Abraham's offspring. There are other sorts of offspring besides biological children, of course. Monks and nuns and priests produce spiritual daughters and sons, offering fatherly and motherly blessing that can affect generations. Kraus suggests the word translated as "descendants" can mean simply "human nature" (Kraus 1993: 364). All humanity is blessed through being born of this one righteous man, Jesus.

Surely "wealth and riches" cannot mean only material wealth. Plenty of righteous people die poor; plenty of wicked people laugh all the way to the bank. Yet the psalmist seems straight-faced. John Wesley worried that faith might indeed make believers wealthy. His eighteenth-century Methodist converts would become disciplined in their newfound faith, they would work and save diligently, and pretty soon they would be wealthy. Wesley feared that a new Methodist, with that new wealth, would then be twice the child of hell as before.[4] Nancy deClaissé-Walford suggests the promises echo those God originally gives to Abraham—to

2. Deuteronomy quotes from Nancy deClaissé-Walford, in Van Harn and Strawn 2009: 294.

3. I interviewed Elvira Arellano about taking sanctuary in a Methodist church in Chicago and asked whether she was afraid of being deported. She said no, because she fears God alone. Byassee, "Sanctuary: Mary, Methodists, and Immigration," *Christian Century*, October 31, 2006, 10–11.

4. Wesley, "Danger of Riches," in John Wesley, *John Wesley's Sermons*, ed. Albert Outler and Richard Heitzenrater (Nashville: Abingdon, 1991), esp. 461–62.

bless him and make his name great (Van Harn and Strawn 2009: 294). God only has blessings that are Abraham-shaped.

Despite the psalm's confidence, it is also heavy with themes of darkness or evil (112:4, 7, 8, 10). But the blessed light up the world, as Jesus preaches in Matt. 5:14–16 (Limburg 2000: 385). Themes of illumination are particularly important at Sinai (Hossfeld and Zenger 2011: 174). God is light itself on that mountain, leading the Israelites with fire, lighting up the worlds, having to shield poor Moses from his unimaginable splendor. Psalm 112 sees the reflection of that world-illuminating light on the righteous keeper of the commands, who reflects God's greater light and so illumines a dark world.

Psalm 112:5–10 describes the demeanor and manners of the just person, the "beneficent" one in the Tanakh's translation.[5] The just person lends "freely," without keeping record or demanding interest (112:9). Our economy depends on that repayment with much interest, and then compound interest on that interest. The psalmist's view of justice is more like our word "generosity." If you try for this sort of justice, be ready for people to call you naïve—to think that one becomes righteous by giving away money! Commentators suggest that usurious lending pauperizes the peasantry of the land (Hossfeld and Zenger 2011: 174). So the just lend without thought of repayment.

What would it mean for the church to rethink our notions of justice along the lines of Psalm 112?

Augustine (2003: 295) notes that the wicked *seem* to prosper now, but the just *are prospered* unendingly. The psalms offer eschatological lenses to see present reality from the vantage of God's coming judgment. Spurgeon (1976: 483) contrasts the just one's unending fame (112:9) with the fate of the mummies unearthed in Egypt, gawked at in his day with "ghoulish curiosity." Once famous, they are now forgotten. How will the achievements for which people walk over one another now look in eternity?

Psalm 112:7–8 promises the just will not fear "evil tidings" or an ill rumor (Kraus 1993: 361). Scripture repeatedly condemns gossip because we human beings consistently love it. Anyone involved in any worshiping community, perhaps any human community, knows the role of gossip. Good gossip involves the transmission of some truth at least, but it is often wrapped up in a greater falsehood. As a pastor, I was often afraid of such gossip because I couldn't get ahead of it; it coursed through the congregation unchecked. I prayed for the lack of fear that

5. I am grateful to Kraus (1993: 364) for the phrase. Tanakh translation in Berlin and Brettler (2014: 1396).

God promises, often fruitlessly it seemed. But now as a parishioner I recognize that I spread gossip as much as anyone else! We are all a batch of contradictions. The psalm promises the undoing of fear of evil tidings, and eventual entirely truthful speech—which by then, eschatologically, hopefully we will be able to bear.

Divine (Ps. 111) and human (Ps. 112) righteousness are combined throughout scripture, so it is natural (if amazing still) to see them combined in the womb of an unmarried Jewish teenager from the sticks. These two psalms are two halves of a mold. The one imaged here is Jesus and all those being shaped after his image by the Spirit.[6] It is not surprising that the apostle Paul, looking for a biblical passage to substantiate his request for an offering of the church at Corinth, turns to Ps. 112:9. It is *God* who "scatters abroad, he gives to the poor; his righteousness endures forever" (2 Cor. 9:9). The righteousness of Psalm 112 has taken flesh among us and is now fleshing out our community—the church—after the image of God.

The wicked only get one verse here (112:10). Gnashing their teeth and looking away is relatively uninteresting, and is also only true eschatologically. One way to view God's judgment is to see in it the promise of Isaiah, reiterated in Paul—that every knee will bow and every tongue confess Jesus's lordship (Isa. 45:23; Rom. 14:11; Phil. 2:11). Such bowing will be a triumph for some, more painful for others. Tim Keller often says that if someone does something for me, I need to know the scope of the favor. Was it minor? OK, cheers, move on. Is it unending salvation? That requires another sort of thanks altogether. What has Jesus saved us from? Life by ourselves, without generosity, teeth ground down to the gums.

---

6. I owe the mold image to Telford Work, *Living and Active: Scripture in the Economy of Salvation* (Grand Rapids: Eerdmans, 2001), 105.

PSALM 113

When I was a teenager, our church loaded up our youth and headed to Guatemala City. One of our first destinations was the city dump, home to tens of thousands of people who pick through it for "valuables" or "edibles." We met with elementary-age children. We played games, sang songs, and then were done. Their teacher linked them all by hand and walked them back across the dump to their homes. Birds of prey circled, and the unimaginable pile smoked. It looked like Gehenna. At the time, I thought it an image of despair. Thinking back now, I wonder whether those linked little arms are an image of victory, reflections of Christ descending into hell.

This psalm suggests that the Lord, seated on high, sees these children (113:6). And raises them up from the garbage pile (113:7). And sits them with princes (113:8). There are occasional stories of street kids becoming rulers. Imagine these children, all of them, seated in the presidential palace in Guatemala City, and you have a glimpse of this psalm's heart.

Psalm 113 is the beginning of the Egyptian Hallel—so called because of the many references to the exodus in Pss. 113–118 (Hossfeld and Zenger 2011: 181). These psalms, which God's people reinhabit at every commemoration of the Passover, offer thanksgiving to God. Mark's Gospel records the disciples singing the hymn as their last act before Jesus's passion—it was likely a portion of these six psalms (Mark 14:26; cf. 1 Cor. 5:7–8). What did their voices sound like? Jesus sang these words as he prepared to be reduced to refuse. In his resurrection, ascension, and coming reign, he will make the lowly great with him.

This hymn of praise begins with exultation (113:1–3) and follows with rationale (Limburg 2000: 388). This first psalm of the group from 113 to 118 functions like the book of Genesis, where God raises life from dirt. The next psalm, 114, is like Exodus, marveling at God's liberating ways. Other ancient Near Eastern deities were praised by their peoples for being high and lifted up (Mays 1994: 361; Kraus 1993: 368). What is unique to the God of Israel is that this lofty one also bends low and lifts up the lowly. Psalm 113 is also highly anthropocentric: God sits, sees, lifts, and gets down with us in the dust to bring about a new order of things. The psalm's metaphor takes flesh in Mary's womb.

"Praise the LORD! Praise, O servants of the LORD; praise the name of the LORD" (113:1). Some have detected the Trinity in the threefold repetition here (Spurgeon 1976: 485). Fanciful, perhaps, but God's triune fingerprints are present throughout creation, if we squint a little. How much more so in the triune God's own scriptures?[1] The next few verses detail the extent of God's blessings through all time (113:2) and all space (113:3). God's praise extends "between all conceivable limits," as Alter puts it (2007: 403). In the words of another commentator, the God who knows no limits must be offered praise without limits (Mays 1994: 361).

This call of praise is pretty conventional. But this is a call for praise beyond Judaism as then constituted, trying to recover from the exile (Kraus 1993: 368). The *Jerusalem Commentary* suggests this helps us with the problem of "other religions." All people praise the Lord *whether they recognize it or not.*[2] Jesus will say later that God's sun rises and his rain falls even on those who give no praise (Matt. 5:45). We might press further and see a charge to go and tell the gospel (Matt. 28:19–20). God is both lofty and low, majestic and redemptively at work in the dust and dunghill.

"He raises the poor from the dust" (113:7). God does more than look at the poor. God acts on behalf of the poor, interrupts social hierarchies, and raises the lowly (Hossfeld and Zenger 2011: 185). The image of God glancing down on us can be threatening, as in other psalms (Pss. 11; 14; 53). Or it can be "full of sympathy," as in Pss. 33, 106, and 138 (Hossfeld and Zenger 2011: 182). I honestly can't tell whether Ps. 113's divine glance downward is a threat or a promise. It is undoubtedly good news for the poor. It's not even clear that the poor man asks for this social elevation. God acts for the poor one because that is God's nature. Perhaps the poorer you are, the better news this is.

---

1. For more of this tradition of the *vestigia trinitatis*, "vestiges of the Trinity," see Peter J. Leithart, *Traces of the Trinity: Signs of God in Creation and Human Experience* (Grand Rapids: Brazos, 2015).

2. Amos Hakham, *Bible Psalms with Jerusalem Commentary (Mikra)*, trans. Israel V. Berman (Brooklyn: Judaica, 2003), 156.

But does God's intervention invert the social hierarchy or level it? This seems not quite a call for reversal of estates between the high and the lowly (Hossfeld and Zenger 2011: 185). That reversal motif is clearer in Mary's Magnificat (Luke 2:41–52) or in Ps. 107:40–41: "He pours contempt on princes, and makes them wander in trackless wastes; but he raises the needy out of distress, and makes their families like flocks." Perhaps the lofty can stay lofty in Ps. 113: "to make them sit *with* princes" (113:8). Those princes just have to move over and make room for others.

This raising up recalls the entire biblical history and future. Human beings only exist because God got down in the mud and molded us into living creatures (Gen. 2). Christians say God himself goes down to the dust in Jesus's burial. The resurrection of Jesus's body promises a future resurrection of all flesh. This is why the church has always honored the bones of the saints. By Jesus's solidarity with our bodies in his flesh we know he will raise all flesh, even that which is now scattered ash.

These themes run through our spiritual practice too. Psalm 113:7 pivots from ash to dung. Our condition is not only dusty. It is crappy. Spurgeon points out "what a dunghill we lay upon by nature" (1976: 487). St. Ambrose points out that Paul counts himself as dung in Phil. 3:10. The wise Christian "manures himself" by being humbled to the earth, for the earth, the dunghill, is the place from which God raises people up (*Prayer of Job and David* 3.2.3, in Wesselschmidt 2007: 277). We can never say that people of the dunghill are far from God. They, we, have a glorious destiny.

So too does the barren woman (113:9). The biblically attuned think of stories of mothers of the faith who believed, prayed gritty prayers, and saw their wombs filled. Isaiah 54:1 imagines Israel itself as a barren woman who bursts into song and shouts, "for the children of the desolate woman will be more than the children of her that is married" (Mays 1994: 362). Songs of barren women miraculously conceiving resonate throughout scripture—in Hannah's song (1 Sam. 2:1–10), in Mary's that echoes it—even in the ears of Jesus, who heard these songs as Mary prayed and sang over her swelling belly. When Christians praise, we join a song already in progress, whose beginnings and endings we cannot fathom. This is especially so when we join with the tears of those who have not yet seen prayers answered, who may never see them answered in precisely the way they want. As scripture is at constant pains to say, God is closer to the degree that one's heart is broken.

Psalm 113:9 begs for spiritual interpretation as well. First Timothy 2:15 unfortunately imagines that women can still be saved "through childbearing" despite

Eve's sin. St. Gregory of Nyssa reads this New Testament verse spiritually via Ps. 113: "Truly a joyful mother is the virgin mother who by the operation of the Spirit conceives the deathless children" (*On Virginity* 13, in Wesselschmidt 2007: 277). Those who bear no biological children can bear countless children in faith. And all people feel barren in the spiritual life at times. Each believer faces "lamentable barrenness," but then occasionally we are visited by the Holy Spirit, and we can bloom like Aaron's rod (Num. 17:8; Spurgeon 1976: 387).

As a pastor, even one not now working in a parish, I am struck by how often I hear about issues of infertility. Especially in a technological era that can work wonders, the ability to have a child begins to feel like a sort of natural right. The sense of entitlement can be enhanced by a verse like 113:9 (it's interesting that the poor don't normally feel themselves biblically entitled to sit with princes!). Scripture is careful to make clear that pregnancy is always a gift, never to be taken for granted. This is why it so important to read verses like Ps. 113:9 flexibly. Whether we have biological children or not, we all have to produce fruit in the life of the Spirit. We can all mentor, tell others about Jesus, model faith for them, live in a way that bears fruit. Such fruit can be far more bountiful than that of biological children. Plenty who have children of "their own" (a telling phrase) are lousy or absent parents; plenty who are Christlike to others become a mother or father to them spiritually. This is what endures in God's economy. St. Augustine preaches, "Your old age must have a childlike quality about it, and your childlikeness the wisdom of age" (2003: 298). God sees fit miraculously to give pregnancy to some closed wombs, and power to some who start in the dust. But we all start in the dust spiritually, with closed wombs, and we all must press through that narrow passage of faith, humbly growing more childlike, wise in matters of the Spirit.

For all our effort, the psalm makes clear it is really God who works—God whose power is beyond every single limit.

PSALM 114

The Appalachians are sometimes called the oldest mountain chain in the world. They have moved, first up with volcanic activity and now slowly down over millions of years. Seas move too, sometimes in destructive ways, as those who live in hurricane country know. The Jordan River is not quite where it was two thousand years ago. The Mississippi is not in the same place it was when the American Civil War was determined on its banks. It even ran backward for three days after an earthquake in 1812. These movements of mountains, rivers, and seas seem believable to us, even though they're amazing.

Psalm 114 doesn't seem believable: mountains dancing, rivers shrieking, a craggy outcrop gushing. God's incursion into our world bends language out of all previous recognition. The only ways to express what God has done is to upset all language, all ecology.[1] The verbs suggest both playfulness and terror. Most interpreters choose one or the other. But the psalmist's point is that in God's presence fear and playfulness are close kin.

Psalm 114 is part of the Egyptian Hallel, the psalms still recited by Jews to be gathered back into God's rescue from Egypt. We Christians stand to learn from our elder siblings in faith that the exodus is not a far-off event. This is the story that makes us *us*. When Methodists baptize, we pray, "When you saw your people as slaves in Egypt, you led them to freedom through the sea. Their children you brought through the Jordan to the land which you promised." It doesn't seem

---

1. I am drawing heavily here on Eugene Peterson, *Where Your Treasure Is: Psalms That Move You from Self to Community* (Grand Rapids: Eerdmans, 1993), 143–62.

odd that Ps. 114 skips from the sea to the river—we do that in our prayer. In the Bible, geography—real places with zip codes—becomes liturgy.

Psalm 114 is unusual. There is no opening acclamation or call to worship. It begins as if in the middle of a thought, without so much as a "hello." Alter (2007: 405) notes the oddity of opening with two subordinate clauses before a verb is then unveiled. A wooden transliteration would be "when-they-went-out, Israel, from Egypt" (Limburg 2000: 391). The psalmist says only enough to skip ahead to the mountains and rivers that skip themselves.

The people the Israelites left is described as having a "barbarous language." Egypt's language *could* be understood by outsiders—Joseph learned it (Gen. 42:23). But Egypt's language is uncivilized, the psalmist says, whatever superficial grandeur its civilization may have seemed to maintain (Alter 2007: 405). For the Egyptians could not understand the language of mercy.[2] Deuteronomy warns against a future nation "whose language you do not understand," as one that is also "grim-faced," "showing no respect to the old or favor to the young" (Deut. 28:49–50). The prophet Zephaniah imagines a day when the Lord will transform speech into pure language, so all will call on the name of the Lord and serve (Zeph. 3:9; Hossfeld and Zenger 2011: 190). The fruit hangs heavy here with Pentecost juice. Augustine says the barbarous language is a sign that the Egyptians don't know how to say "Alleluia" (Augustine 2003: 308).

The exodus story is told with remarkable sparseness. Where are the Israelites? Where are the Egyptians? Where is Moses? Forty years are compressed into a breath. The focus is not on the liberation from slavery. It is on the nature miracles, perhaps influenced by nature worship among Israel's neighbors. Yet the second verse's roots in Judah heighten what is specific to Israel (Hossfeld and Zenger 2011: 192). The God who works these wonders is a specific God, whatever others' claims about theirs.

In Ps. 114:3–4 the sea doesn't stand up on either side, like two walls. It rather darts off in terror, like defeated armies do (Hossfeld and Zenger 2011: 195). Elsewhere in scripture it is nations who take flight (Isa. 17:13; 31:4, 9) or kings who dash for cover (Ps. 48:5). The Jordan doesn't just part to make a way where there was no way. It runs in reverse. It is not surprising that preachers have often seen here a riff on the biblical motif that God's ways are not our ways, that the first will be last. St. Jerome even used this verse to defend infant baptism! God's

2. Amos Hakham, *Bible Psalms with Jerusalem Commentary (Mikra)*, trans. Israel V. Berman (Brooklyn: Judaica, 2003), 161.

ways are often a reversal of what we naturally assume ought to happen (Augustine, *Against Julian* 1.3.10, in Wesselschmidt 2007: 279).

We might contrast nature's pliability to God's commands with human disinterest or active intransigence—the Bible's constant emphasis on human insensitivity to the divine presence. The seas, the mountains, the rivers are entirely in concert with God's will. It is human beings who are stubborn and stiff-necked. Yet God has come nearer to us than God has ever come to a mountain, a sea, a river. Because in Christ *God assumed our nature*. We are one body with him who stills seas and promises easily moved mountains (Matt. 17:20; Spurgeon 1976: 490).

The psalmist taunts the cosmic elements (114:5–6),[3] like slain enemies rotting on the battlefield. There is a hint here too of something even older and more primal—a God who brings order out of chaos, who overcomes the forces of death and turns them into fonts of life-giving grace (Hossfeld and Zenger 2011: 195). But the predominant theme is of playfulness, exuberance, with massive mountains skipping like drunk adults or toddlers in their right minds (Mays 1994: 364). All the movement is enough to make you wonder about churches in which worshipers stand stock still.

The psalm concludes with the water from the rock (Exod. 17:1–7; Num. 20:1–13). Once again, something solid becomes something liquid. Careful readers will remember the surrounding stories: that the Israelites whine in the wilderness and God provides, that Moses strikes the rock instead of speaking softly to it and so is disqualified from entering the promised land (Num. 20:13). The psalm leaves off such details as it focuses on the nature miracles. People whine. People disobey. The psalm doesn't even notice. Meanwhile nature dances, frolics, and gushes.

Psalm 114 has been read in a variety of ways. A letter attributed to Dante used this psalm as an exemplar of the medieval fourfold quadriga (Alter 2007: 405). Literally, the psalm describes the Israelites' redemption in the exodus. Figuratively, it describes Christians' deliverance in Christ. Spiritually, it refers to the liberation to do the right thing rightly. Anagogically, it describes God's promise to make all things new. These readings make sense. The themes in this psalm are the basic building blocks of faith. Israel reads the psalm in another sense at every Passover feast. The psalm invites us also to enter the story, study its magnificent contours, and celebrate at least as much as the hills and the rocks do.

---

3. Richard Clifford's commentary in Van Harn and Strawn 2009: 298.

PSALM 115

The heart of this psalm is in 115:8: "Those who make them are like them; so are all who trust in them." Idols are nothing. Those who make them and worship them become nothing. Israel's God, on the other hand, is life itself and life-giver to others. Those who worship him become alive like him, in the fullest sense. St. Irenaeus made this startling claim: "The glory of God is a human being fully alive."[1] We see that most fully alive person in Jesus, God enfleshed. Those who worship him are on their way to becoming as alive as he is.

Psalm 115 is a response to the taunt from pagan opponents that Israel has no god since its god is not physical. The psalmist taunts right back: pagans make idols with their hands and then worship things they know are lifeless. The pagans' gods have no ability to speak, smell, feel, or walk. These are usually taken to be anthropomorphic metaphors. But can the psalm be taken to mean that the living God indeed has a mouth, eyes, ears, a nose, hands, a larynx? Interpreters ancient and modern are nearly unanimous in seeing these as mere figures of speech. But I wonder whether this anthropomorphic depiction of God prepares the way for an anthropomorphization of God—for the incarnation of the Son. To make fun of pagans' gods for having no functioning fleshy organs is to imply that our God does, or will.

"Why should the nations say . . . ?" (115:2). The psalms often quote the derision of foreign peoples (Kraus 1993: 378). This is typical of psalms in this fifth

---

1. Irenaeus, *Against Heresies* 4.20. I am altering it slightly to be more inclusive—when the ancients said "man" they often meant it inclusively, as we would use "humanity." Irenaeus's actual translation has "The glory of God is the living man, and the life of man is the vision of God." *Irenaeus of Lyons*, ed. Robert M. Grant (London: Routledge, 1997), 153.

book of the Psalter, numbers 107–150, which address the crisis of the exile and its aftermath (Clint McCann, in Brueggemann 2014: 495). But the people of God are always in the position of being derided. The nations are the power players, the brokers who feel they rule the cosmos (Mays 1994: 365). However much or little a surrounding culture claims to be godly, it is always pagan. The Reformers never tire of saying (regarding cultures full of baptized members), "The human heart is a perpetual factory of idols."[2] We go on making these little gods and then bowing down to them. How instead should we worship correctly?

Only by worshiping the true God. That is the lone solution for idolatry. YHWH's steadfast love and faithfulness can drive out fickle love of impish deities. Spurgeon says this of the praise offered in 115:1: "Could we see heaven opened and every angel and every casting crown they'd be quoting this verse" (1976: 492). Only true worship drives out false.

"Our God is in the heavens; he does whatever he pleases" (115:3). Careful with this. God is in the heavens rather than being identified with any manufactured idol. God is not bandied around by worshipers who have to carry him where they want him to go. This verse is often cited for the first line of the Apostles' Creed, "I believe in God, the Father almighty, creator of heaven and earth." Brueggemann (2014: 497) says it breathes the same air as the opening of Genesis, "In the beginning . . ."

But does God do whatever God pleases? The Israelites praying Ps. 115 have experienced the catastrophe of defeat and exile. Prophets and psalms often explain this disaster by pointing to Israel's unfaithfulness. Surely God could have kept the people from being unfaithful, if God does whatever he pleases? The great rabbi and moral sage David Weiss Halivni, struggling with the tradition of God's omnipotence, imagines the archangel Michael insisting that God stop the slaughter of the Shoah. God refuses. Halivni narrates what follows: "Michael went back to his place, ashen and dejected, but could not resist looking back sheepishly at God and saw a huge tear rolling down God's face, destined for the legendary cup which collects tears and which, when full, will bring the redemption of the world."[3]

The story refuses to answer the question of whether God could have intervened. It insists that God is not unaware or uncaring. In fact, the full cup of tears will trigger God's coming to bring full redemption. But for reasons beyond our

2. John Calvin, *Institutes of the Christian Religion* 1.11.8, trans. Henry Beveridge, rev. ed. (Peabody, MA: Hendrickson, 2008), 54–55.
3. David Weiss Halivni, *The Book and the Sword: A Life of Learning in the Shadow of Destruction* (Boulder, CO: Westview, 1997), iii. The story continues to say that Michael is horrified to see that most of the tear misses the chalice.

imagining, the cup is not full yet. Christians should learn from the reticence with which Halivni addresses this biblical theme of divine omnipotence. Our worst instinct is to tell sufferers that God has caused their suffering. Even the hoarsest prophet who has screeched at the people for their sins does not say that. God's way is always to have mercy. The world is a fallen place. Our freedom to sin means we can harm one another and ourselves, endlessly it seems. The bitter fruit of our freedom to fall was tasted most fully by God himself in Christ. One day God will end all suffering and fill the earth fully with his divine presence. Suffering in the meantime is not surprising.

But for God's sake, don't answer the question of why bad things happen to good people with anything more confident or cheerful than the story Halivni tells.

The derision of Ps. 115:4–8 is common in the prophets (e.g., Hab. 2:18–19). Isaiah 40:19–20 imagines a worker carefully choosing mulberry wood so that it won't rot. In Isa. 44:9–20 the carpenter stretches a line and the ironsmith fashions the god, using some of the wood to warm themselves and bake bread. Then they worship what they make. Jeremiah 10:1–16 says their idols are like scarecrows in a cucumber field—everyone who worships them is that stupid. Part of what is happening is a demythologization of the created order. It is not divine. God, who is divine, is quite distinct from creation. Perhaps scripture protests so loudly precisely because idolatry is a live temptation.[4] Other nations have more tangible gods. Israel would like God to turn up, perhaps now in fact (115:2). But Israel cannot just go and physically get its God. He comes in his own time, or not at all if he chooses (115:3). St. Athanasius wisely describes the temptation to worship created matter. God has made everything good, beautiful, and reflective of God's splendor. God, "knowing well its beauty, lest any attending solely to this beauty should worship things as if they were gods," provides us the warning of this psalm (*Against the Heathen* 45.2–3, in Wesselschmidt 2007: 281).

The psalmist implores God to act so the nations will see (115:2). Moses asks why the nations should say that God brought the Israelites out of Egypt to kill them in the wilderness (Exod. 32:12). The opinion of the watching nations matters to the writers of scripture. When God works, the Gentiles should see and worship. Later, after Israel has been defeated, hauled off to exile, denied God's very presence in the form of temple and land, a prophet stood up to speak. We might have expected him to lament the inutility of Israel's God, but instead his mockery falls on his conquerors' gods.

4. Jon Levenson, *Sinai and Zion: An Entry into the Jewish Bible* (San Francisco: HarperSanFrancisco, 1987), 109–11.

It is common to fault the biblical writers for thinking the pagans equate their deities with the gods themselves.[5] But it is hard to imagine the psalmist being impressed if he knew the pagans distinguish between the lifeless idol and the god accessed through it. Augustine (2003: 315) already knows this apologetic: the pagans have the "temerity" to reply that the idol is not the god itself. Augustine continues the mockery of 115:4–8. Mice and snakes are better than inanimate objects—better to worship them. The idolater himself is vastly a better part of creation than the idol he makes.

Augustine suggests that idolatry would be funny if it weren't so serious. Popular misperception in devotion makes space for demons (Ps. 96:5; 1 Cor. 10:19–20). As Ps. 115 itself says, in a far more terrifying claim, to worship nothing is to become nothing (115:8). The psalm is God's offer of a different, better, more alluring song to charm us out of idolatry, "nudging and arousing the minds of men and women by restating to them what they already know" (Augustine 2003: 316). Idol-makers should know their idols are empty. So too should YHWH's people. We have to keep shutting down the factory of idols. It keeps rejuvenating itself.

Alter paraphrases the psalm beautifully: idols are "mere impotent chunks of matter" and "sheer inert stuff" (2007: 408). Yet Israel also has physical aids to worship. Augustine confesses communion chalices and other liturgical objects are important (2003: 316). Yet these are not made to resemble a person or animal, unlike pagan idols (later Catholic statuary may have bothered Augustine). What we make by hand *does* have its place in worship. As Catholics today prepare to offer bread and wine to God in the Mass, they praise it as the fruit of God's creation "and the work of human hands." The Eastern Orthodox Church had to work out a careful argument for the depiction of God in their two-dimensional icons. Certainly, before God took flesh, depictions of God are forbidden by the second commandment. But after God takes flesh we can draw his picture. Not only that, we *must* draw his picture and reverence God's face. If we do not, we will worship a discarnate god.[6]

Idols are a different thing. The rabbis illustrate this with a story about Terah, Abraham's father, who was by profession an idol-maker. One day young Abram, with a precocious sense both of God's grandeur and of God's sense of humor, went around his father's shop smashing the idols. He then put the club in the hand of

5. This is in no way "a sensitive or even perceptive understanding of the role of iconography in those traditions." Levenson, *Sinai and Zion*, 109.

6. See John of Damascus, *On the Divine Images*, trans. David Anderson (Crestwood, NY: St. Vladimir's Seminary Press, 1980).

the one remaining idol. When Terah returned home, he was furious at Abram for smashing up their livelihood. Abram replied, "It wasn't me! It was that big idol there with the club." Terah fumed, "You know idols can't move or talk." Abram replied, "Well then, why do you worship them?"[7]

That story and this psalm are born from the same womb.

Some commentators say that 115:9–12 is the heart of the psalm. It is the summit of a chiasm, starting with 115:1–2 and concluding with 115:17–18. The psalmist addresses three groups of people: Israel, the house of Aaron, and those who fear God. Israel represents the entire family of Abraham. The house of Aaron is specifically the priests and Levites who offer sacrifices on behalf of the people. Ancient rabbis already speculated that those who fear the Lord are proselytes to Judaism (Alter 2007: 408). Christians can't hear that latter category and not think of those on the edges of Jewish life in the book of Acts who most quickly embraced the gospel (Acts 10:2, 22; 13:16, 26; 16:14; 18:7). A standard scholarly line has been something like this: Israel had often been admired by outsiders, and justly so, but Israel is difficult to join. Now, in Christ, Gentiles can worship Israel's God fully without having to be circumcised or keep kosher. This story line could be true. Jews have their own ways of saying that the yoke of Torah is blessed, whatever difficulties go with it. I suspect that God's intention for Gentiles—to draw close through the body of a crucified Messiah—is a good deal more difficult than the church has tended to think. A more frequent homiletical connection is to ask what our idols are today. We start in with our favorite lists—money, power, political parties, status (listeners don't perk up on such lists). Perhaps it may be better to construct one idol for the congregation's watching eyes, as the craftsman does in 115:4–8, before turning and praising the living God as the psalm does.

God blesses those "both small and great" (115:13). I confess my eye had missed that little line. Augustine's did not. The greatest ones in heaven take on the task of raising up, blessing, and forming little ones, he argues, with a glance at 1 Cor. 3:6 ("I planted, Apollos watered, but God gave the growth"). We might go further and say that in Christ, God becomes small so that sinners might become great. The form of the Christian life is one forged by the Word made flesh. The psalm continues to shower blessings in ways that echo God's original promise to Abram (Gen. 12:1–4). God's people's vocation is to scatter blessings much further abroad than we are accustomed to imagining. God's people suffer when we try to keep God's blessings to ourselves. We thrive, and become great and numerous, when

---

7. *Genesis Rabbah*, 38:13, 310–11. The story has been told and retold—one place is in Burton Visotzky, *Reading the Book: Making the Bible a Timeless Text* (Philadelphia: Jewish Publication Society, 2005), 66.

we remember God's blessings are not to us. They are *through* us, *for* other people, especially those our society despises.

"The heavens are the LORD's heavens," the psalm insists, "but the earth he has given to human beings" (115:16). Is the "heaven of heavens" a life with God beyond our imagining? Or is it the heavenly bodies farthest from our sight? The psalm could be interpreted either way. Either way it is important to note that heaven is a creation of God. Only God is uncreated. Religious people sometimes speak as though heaven is physically up, or is theologically all that matters. Conversely, modern scholars can speak as though heaven does not matter. Biblical scholars often tell us heaven is a Greek category, influenced by Platonism, foreign to the Hebraic mind-set of the Bible. There is some truth to that. Yet this psalm is shot through with talk of heaven (115:3, 16, also forming a chiasm). Heaven is where God lives, whence he does his gracious will, delegating his rule on earth to us (as in Ps. 8). Our stewardship and governance of earth, over the magnificence of creation with all our talents, is meant to reflect the way God blesses and governs the universe. We fail, of course. Only Christ is the human monarch God wants. But by his Spirit he restores us to rule alongside him. Very, very slowly.

"The dead do not praise the LORD," the psalm concludes, "nor do any that go down into silence" (115:17). This is a common reflection from a period in Israel without much fleshed-out content on the afterlife. Sheol was a shadowy underworld where there is no praise (a rather "Greek"-sounding notion, but never mind). Only later, perhaps in conversation with their Babylonian captors, did Jews start to think of opposing spiritual principles like God and Satan, heaven and hell. In Christian hands, verses about the dead not praising God came to refer to Jesus's resurrection. God would not let his holy one see decay, since the dead do not praise (Acts 13:35). What it means to be alive is to praise; therefore, God raised Jesus back into a life of worship (see, e.g., Acts 2:31). Given that we read the Old Testament through the New, we cannot *not* see the resurrection of Jesus in verses like Ps. 115:17. The concluding doxology of 115:18 is a sign that the one who raised Jesus will raise our mortal bodies also so that, fully alive at last, we can finally praise with every ounce of our being.

Heavenly? Otherworldly? Perhaps. So is this psalm. And yet its earthiness is indisputable. It is *earthly* bodies that Jesus inhabits, that God raises, that the Spirit will raise—God the Holy Trinity down in the dirt with us.

PSALM 116

For a Christian interpreter, three verses of Ps. 116 jump off the page. First, "Precious in the sight of the LORD is the death of his faithful ones" (116:15) is a verse that has long inspired theologies of martyrdom. Second, "I said in my consternation, 'Everyone is a liar'" (116:11) is a crucial verse for the church's doctrine of sin (see Rom. 3:4). Third, a verse that seems unpromising at first is "I kept my faith, even when I said . . ." (116:10). It sounds more demonstrative in its quotation in Paul: "I believed, and so I spoke" (2 Cor. 4:13). Paul sees in the psalm the pattern of death and resurrection, fleshed in Jesus, and re-created in the pattern of the church's life: "We know that the one who raised the Lord Jesus will raise us also with Jesus, and will bring us with you into his presence" (2 Cor. 4:14).

Imagine you make a promise to God when at the precipice of death. God delivers you. Now you must make good on that promise. How? In the Lord's house, with offerings of thanksgiving, and public praise (116:13–14, 17–19). Psalm 116 envisions death as the ultimate horror. Read in a Christian way, the psalm speaks of a deliverance even beyond death. The death of a faithful person is precious (not just painful) because it imitates and participates in Christ's victory over death. This loosing of bonds is not merely a temporary respite from a descent into Sheol, a pause in separation from life. It is instead unending deliverance that results in perpetual praise.

"I love the LORD, because he has heard my voice and my supplications" (116:1). Only one other psalm begins with a declaration of love for the Lord (Ps. 18: "I love you, O LORD, my strength"). Alter suggests 116:1 could read, "I love the Lord *when* he hears." Unabashed praise of love comes more easily from the Romantic nineteenth century than from our own cynical moment: it is "the sweetest of all graces and the surest of all evidences of salvation" to have love for God erupt in response to God's saving work (Spurgeon 1976: 496). Who has read the psalm well? Is it one who can say that this psalm represents an individual psalm of thanksgiving with a cultic background (Hossfeld and Zenger 2011: 215)? Or is it one who can say, with blessed naïveté, "I love the Lord"? Mays wisely sees the psalm as a description of what love does, and so what love is. Love calls the beloved by name (116:4), rests in the beloved (116:7), lives in the presence of the beloved (116:9), fulfills its vows in public (116:14), serves the beloved (116:16) (Mays 1994: 371). The theme of the whole psalm is the undoing of death. Its overturning by love reminds of the words of the Canticle, that "love is strong as death" (Song 8:6). Or stronger.

"Because he has inclined his ear to me, therefore I will call on him" (116:2). The anthropomorphic reference is compelling. The Lord has an ear and bends it profoundly toward us. For St. Basil the Great, the psalmist "signals his own weakness," and through it the Lord signals his kindness. "He inclined . . . as a kind physician" who leans in close to discern what ails the patient, Basil says (*Homilies on the Psalms* 22, in Wesselschmidt 2007: 285). The Lord doesn't just hear passively, the way we hear background noise. The Lord's hearing is operative. God acts on what God hears—the Lord's hearing is the same thing as granting (Richard Baker, in Spurgeon 1976: 496). The contours of the incarnation are clear—the Lord bends low, physically, to save.

"The snares of death encompassed me; the pangs of Sheol laid hold on me" (116:3). Kathryn Roberts compares this torment to Jonah's: "Waters closed in over me; the deep surrounded me; weeds were wrapped around my head" (Jonah 2:5, see also Ps. 18:5; Roberts, in Van Harn and Strawn 2009: 301). Sheol simply *is* death—a vague, shadowy underworld where no praise is given.[1] The place is best left unvisited. Yet the details are intentionally vague. Basil sees the specific pain of a mother in childbirth (*Homilies on the Psalms* 22, in Wesselschmidt 2007: 286). Alter (2007: 411) suggests that such language could refer to battle. Kraus (1993: 386) imagines more literally a dungeon or prison. The evil envisioned has a tentacle-like character, stretching up from below and entangling, dragging downward.

One problem for faith in the post-Christian West has been our inability to answer this question: Why do bad things happen to good people? If God were really God, surely God would race around stopping anything bad from happening. That the

---

1. Mays 1994: 370. This apt description from a leading modern scholar suggests that "Sheol" is not as far removed from traditional notions of hell as often thought. What else is hell other than a state beyond any possible relationship to God, from which praise cannot arise?

criticism has any purchase at all may be the result of lingering nontrinitarian theism. The God on the cross is no stranger to suffering. The people who chant psalms like this are not surprised when they are crushed. There is no "answer" to the "problem of evil." But prayers this gritty can make for a hardy people, unsurprised at suffering or at seeing God's goodness from the depths. This is not an answer to the problem of evil, but it is a presence in the midst of an insoluble problem. And a promise for evil's ultimate undoing. And a charge, in the meantime, to pray.

And . . . God answers (116:5–8). The psalmist is ecstatic to be alive. Precisely where we might expect an account of the psalmist's deliverance ("Then the LORD spoke to the fish, and it spewed Jonah out upon the dry land," Jonah 2:10), we have instead a description of the attributes of the Lord (Hossfeld, in Hossfeld and Zenger 2011: 217). It starts out a familiar formula: "Gracious is the LORD, and righteous" (116:5). Careful readers of scripture will expect here a reiteration of Exod. 34:6. Instead we get this: "The LORD protects the simple" (116:6). To be simple in scripture is not always a compliment (see Pss. 19:7; 119:130). The connotation is more "simpleton" than "guileless." God saves not just the clever. God's mercy sneaks up on the unsuspecting, the unlikely, with more stealth and surprise than the evil tentacles it lops off.

At the end of each section there is a self-exhortation (116:7, 13–14, 17–18). God has acted, so the psalmist will respond. This action and response shows us the fundamental form of the Christian life, which is not self-starting. The New Year's resolution is not a biblical thing. The promises in 116:7–9 come from one surprised and delighted to be alive. Yet there are tasks to be done. The love with which the psalm began has a form. Deuteronomy repeatedly suggests the inter-twining, the braiding, of the love of God with following God's Torah (Deut. 6:5; 10:12; 11:1; 19:9) (Kraus 1993: 386). Love is not a spontaneous emotion. It is a disciplined form of community life.

Religious faith has often been associated with a world-denying sort of escap-ism. The psalmist insists on the goodness of being alive. Death is the Bible's great enemy. And God's victory over death is complete—just not yet consummated. The upshot is that life is God's gift to be enjoyed. I'm reminded of Karl Barth's parable of salvation. A traveler arrives late at night at a house just beyond a vast snowy field to ask for lodging. The residents of the house are astonished that the visitor crossed the lake without breaking through and drowning. The traveler had no idea he was in such danger.[2] That's salvation: we had no idea what danger we

2. Karl Barth, *Deliverance to the Captives* (Eugene, OR: Wipf & Stock, 2010), 32.

were in until salvation came along. Having been given such an unsought gift and so narrowly avoided watery death, how will we live? Barth's parable doesn't fit the psalmist's crying out in 116:4! It does fit 116:7–9's promises after unexpected restoration of life (Kraus 1993: 387).

Psalm 116:10's celebration, "I kept my faith," is echoed in 2 Tim. 4:7's valedictory word, "I have fought the good fight, I have finished the race." The subsequent psalm verse, "I said in my consternation, 'Everyone is a liar'" (116:11), also does not fit well. Where did this come from? Is the psalmist the only truth-teller there is? But no one is above falsehood.[3] Dietrich Bonhoeffer repeatedly insists that Christ alone can pray these psalms truly (and we can only pray them in Christ).[4] Paul makes Ps. 116:11 a key verse among many others in his litany of human misery in Rom. 2–3. The statement is breathtaking in its comprehensiveness—*everyone* is a liar? What remedy can there be for such a terrible diagnosis?

Paul's "I believe, and so I spoke" is more declarative than 116:10 in most of our English translations. St. Augustine gives an example from elsewhere in the New Testament: when Zechariah does not believe the angel, he is struck dumb. He did not believe, and so he shall not speak (*Sermon* 290.4, in Wesselschmidt 2007: 290). When we believe, conversely, we ought to speak. God has not poured out goodness to us alone as a private treasure. God's grace is the sort of gift that we can only receive by giving away. One who has been miraculously delivered wants to tell that story. Second Corinthians' use of this verse helps us see the whole psalm transfigured. It is not just now about avoiding bodily death in this life. It is about Christ's pressing through death, his "trampling down death by death," as sung in Orthodox liturgy, in order to reinstitute life in the midst of death's reign. Bodily, this-worldly life is good and worthy of thanksgiving. Christ undoing death is goodness magnified. In 116:15, then, the death of the faithful is not just "costly" or bad, so that God should have prevented it. Death *has* happened to the most faithful one. And Christ has undone death itself. Now every death participates in his unending life. As Richard Baker notes, "death doth not damnify his saints, but his saints do dignify death" (quoted in Spurgeon 1976: 496).

The third part of the psalm, 116:13–18, piles on promises. But the psalmist is stuck. What can we give to God that isn't already a gift? Augustine describes the problem well: "I was nothing, and he made me; I had gotten lost, and he

3. It brings to mind the famous paradox referenced in Titus 1:12—if a Cretan says everyone is a liar, is he lying? I'm grateful to my colleague at Appalachian State, Davis Hankins, for pointing this out.
4. Dietrich Bonhoeffer, *Prayerbook of the Bible*, in *Life Together; Prayerbook of the Bible*, ed. Geffrey B. Kelly, trans. Daniel Bloesch, Dietrich Bonhoeffer Works 5 (Minneapolis: Fortress, 2004), 37, 59.

looked for me; looked for me and found me; I was a captive, and he redeemed me" (*Sermon* 254.6, in Wesselschmidt 2007: 292). Everything we have is already gift. What can we give back that God has not already given us? Alter (2007: 411) argues that we can't give anything back, but we can at least give thanks. The psalmist will lift up the cup of salvation, call on the name of the Lord, pay vows, offer thanksgiving, and give public testimony. These are small tokens, but small things matter to God.

The psalmist does what Israel is commanded to do: he offers up a drink offering (Exod. 29:40; Num. 28:7). A quarter of a hin of wine, or four-fifths of a liter by our measurement. The Mishnah stipulates that four cups will be blessed and drunk during the Passover celebration, and during the fourth cup Pss. 115–118 will be said. So Ps. 116:13 is recited as cups are being lifted, blessed, and drunk. Jesus chanted this psalm and lifted this cup on the day that became Maundy Thursday (Mark 14:26). Christ prays this psalm, and we learn what it means from him.[5] The cup of blessing is his blood, shed for us. Paul's sacramental note in 1 Cor. 10:16 originates here (Kraus 1993: 387). What a strange sort of banquet in which the host feeds us, his guests, with his own body and blood (Augustine, *Sermon* 329.1, in Wesselschmidt 2007: 294).

The vow poses a question (116:14, 18). Jesus commands his people not to swear oaths (Matt. 5:37). Yet some Christians take vows: Monastics make vows to poverty, chastity, obedience, and stability. Married people make a vow to one another as long as both shall live. Some single people have an unstated vow to chastity. These vows are difficult forms of disciplining our desires to reflect God's goodness to us in Christ. A recent popular news broadcast reported on causes for decline in hedge fund performance. Not surprisingly, when a hedge fund manager gets divorced, the funds under management decline. More surprisingly, when such a manager gets married, the funds decline as well. In other words, companies and investors should seek out celibate managers![6] Protestants generally reserve vow-making exclusively for married couples, but monastic and secular examples alike show that it can be part of discipleship more widely. The church has, somewhat surprisingly, taken the words of psalms like 116 more literally and Jesus's prohibition

---

5. I owe these last few sentences to Mays (1994: 369). I wish that Old Testament scholars would introduce their christological points at the beginning of their exposition rather than the end, so that their points can be debated, built on, argued over. To place them at the end makes them a sort of pious point of summation that a reader can take or leave.

6. Jonathan Marino, "For Hedge Fund Managers, the Only Thing Worse Than Divorce Is Marriage," *Business Insider*, February 27, 2015, http://www.businessinsider.com/hedge-fund-performance-around -marital-events-2015-2.

of oaths more figurally. We make vows and keep them to reflect the God who promises never to leave Israel.

"Precious in the sight of the LORD is the death of his faithful ones" (116:15). "Precious" should best be understood as "dear" or "costly." Such a death is grievous for God, since death would cost God "a true witness to his power" (Bernd Janowski, quoted in Hossfeld and Zenger 2011: 219). The psalmist offers praise precisely because the Lord has delivered from such a calamity. Life is a fundamental good, death a fundamental enemy. The constellation of God's witnesses dims a bit when one goes out. And yet the most precious death of all is the means by which God undoes death.

Islam's divergence from Christianity on Jesus's faith is instructive.[7] Some texts suggest that someone else was crucified instead of Christ. Another tradition suggests that he was taken down off the cross and died at an old age in Kashmir, where his grave can be seen today. He did not die on the cross, for that would be an unfitting end for a prophet of God. The church, of course, holds that Jesus did come to that end. And in that passing through death, he destroyed death itself. The martyrs' deaths participate in Christ's. While they are not raised bodily yet, waiting for bodily resurrection is an act of hope, not despair. God showed himself faithful in raising Jesus and will show himself faithful in raising the martyrs too.

Only because of Jesus's transformation of death can Christians see Ps. 116:15 in a new light. "Precious" here means beautiful, not just costly. The early church expressed triumphalism about martyrs. "The blood of the martyrs is the seed of the church," as Tertullian famously said.[8] This expression doesn't always hold true. Persecution has often reduced the church, even to the point of extinction.[9] Christianity is always a cross-bearing endeavor, but cross-bearing will not inevitably result in church growth. We can say with more confidence that Christ is nearest to those at the edges of life—especially those whose lives end like his incarnate one did.

7. Here I am entirely dependent on Kenneth Cragg, *The Call of the Minaret*, 3rd ed. (Oxford: Oneworld, 2000), 224–66. Surah 4.157: "They did not kill him, they did not crucify him, he was resembled to them." The Ahmadiyyah says that Jesus was on the cross, was taken down, revived in the tomb, escaped, and died at great age in Kashmir, near Srinagar, where the tomb is. Cragg summarizes, "Hostility to the prophets should not succeed in slaying them. Such a climax would be a divine failure to sustain them and corroborate their message" (*Call of the Minaret*, 266). Islam has its own resources for praising the deaths of its martyrs, of course.

8. Tertullian, *Apology* 50 (Pickerington, OH: Beloved, 2015), 83. The actual quote: "The oftener we are mown down by you, the more in number we grow."

9. Morgan Lee, "Sorry, Tertullian," *Christianity Today* 58, no. 10 (December 4, 2014), available at http://www.christianitytoday.com/ct/2014/december/sorry-tertullian.html.

Pay attention when scripture repeats itself: "I am your servant; I am your servant" (116:16), especially when the very next line seems a direct contradiction: "You have loosed my bonds." It is a strange sort of servant who thanks the master for release after doubly pledging fealty. The literal explanation would be that the bonds loosed were the snares of death (116:3). A figural one would be that at the moment of release, the psalmist longs to be bound again—to a master whose yoke is easy and whose burden is light (Spurgeon 1976: 496; Matt. 11:30).

PSALM 117

Psalm 117 is the shortest psalm and the shortest chapter in the Bible. Yet it tells who God is, with remarkable depth, in just seventeen Hebrew words. One doesn't have to speak at length to speak in depth.

Who are the people to whom God is faithful (117:2)? Exodus 34:6 proclaims that God is gracious and merciful, slow to anger and abounding in steadfast love. God is faithful to Israel first, and through Israel to all the rest of us.

But God's faithfulness extends in a certain order—the gospel is for the Jew first, and then for the Greek (Rom. 1:16). Paul wrestles with the question of God's faithfulness. Why should the Gentiles trust a God who would abandon his first love, the Jews? They should not. God has not abandoned his people Israel (Rom. 11:2). He has fulfilled his promises to Israel by raising Jesus from the dead and inviting the Gentiles to worship Israel's God. Psalm 117 appears in the climax of Rom. 15: "Christ has become a servant of the circumcised . . . in order that the Gentiles might glorify God for his mercy" (15:8–9; see also 15:11). This is the pattern of thought in Ps. 117:1—*all* nations should praise and *all* peoples extol— in a certain order. Psalm 117 helped St. Paul envision a church of all nations as a community through which God is making good on his promises to Abraham.

Psalm 117 has something to say on the miserably vexed question of race (Mays 1994: 372–73). Left to themselves, the Gentiles are a cacophonous assembly of warring rivalries. But with Israel and the church we have a chance to be healed, and through us God can heal the cosmos. The Jewish Jesus grafts us Gentiles into a tree against our nature to be part of his Jewish body (Rom. 11:11–24). In Western history, wealthy white males have thought and acted as though we are the tree, and have lopped off people we found lesser. But we are a branch—dependent for life and sap on the tree. How can branches go lopping off one another? Not to be sisters and brothers to all nations is not to be sisters and brothers to Christ, who saves us through Israel.

God is merciful, precisely when we don't deserve it. All nations, not just the good ones, are invited to praise.

PSALM 118

A friend now past his ninetieth birthday says the same thing at the beginning of each day: "Wow, I get another one of these." Scripture's way of putting it is, "This is the day that the LORD has made; let us rejoice and be glad in it" (Ps. 118:24).

Psalm 118 is tucked in between the Bible's shortest psalm and its longest (Harrelson 2003: 862). Between the brief, clear whistle reminding of God's fidelity in Ps. 117 and the long, moaning foghorn of God's wise word in Ps. 119 is this frenetic, celebratory incursion of God into human history in Ps. 118. It is the last of the Egyptian Hallel psalms, devoted to praising God at the Festival of Booths, when Israel reminds itself of its homelessness in the wilderness and its dire need for God from moment to moment. It is also a cornerstone psalm for the entire New Testament—remove it, and our Bible falls apart. The writers of the New Testament see the reversing action of God in history as supremely enacted in Jesus's resurrection. No wonder Christian communion liturgy includes this psalm's acclamation, "Blessed is the one who comes in the name of the LORD" (118:26). I'm grateful that Anglicans cross themselves at that moment—to emphasize that the reference is to the Crucified One. Psalm 118 also appears regularly in funeral liturgies. The one we mourn will share in the victory of the one who defeats death.

The nonagenarian's thanks is not just for another day of life, though scripture makes clear this is an unimaginable gift. It is thanks for the Lord's day of victory (118:15). In the Bible, creation is always understood through redemption. The new rise of every sun is a renewal of the celebration at the far banks of the Red Sea, of the women's bafflement and joy at an empty tomb.

Psalm 118 also poses a question to us. Are we able to be surprised by God? Robert Jenson says that the difference between a living God and a dead one is that a living God can still surprise you.[1] It is not obvious that this psalm should be read christologically. It is surprise enough that we Gentiles, not naturally part of God's people, find ourselves grafted into the people Israel. But we can domesticate this surprise into another sort of obvious. By contrast, the psalm says, every day can take our breath away. The only God there is, who gives this sun anew each day, intervenes in history personally—to liberate slaves.[2] God's ways astonish by undoing the ways of the powerful. All are invited to celebrate. The only requirement is to be willing to share celebration with the lowliest.

Psalm 118 starts as a thanksgiving after an unlikely escape (Mays 1994: 375). It is striking that the identity of the one giving thanks is left open. Whatever historical specificity caused its writing has been carefully omitted. Israel at any age should be able to step into this thanksgiving to the God who reverses fortunes ever anew. The powerful like to record their own specific triumph for all posterity—when *their* right hand was exalted (118:15–16). Scripture, by contrast, invites anyone who would pray into God's ongoing great reversal.

Psalm 118 begins and ends with the same words, inviting thanks to the Lord whose *hesed* endures forever (see also Ps. 136). How do we translate this rich Hebrew word? "Covenant faithfulness," "loyalty," "steadfast love," and "mercy" are common proposals. A North Carolina bluegrass band called FolkPsalm puts the psalms to bluegrass music, "just as the original Israelites intended," they joke. Their collaboration with Old Testament scholar Ellen Davis produces translations like this: *hesed* is "steady love."[3] Alter (2007: 418) translates it simply as "kindness." The best the preacher can do is note the feebleness of English-speakers' efforts and fill the word with biblical content: God will be faithful to the covenant however unfaithful we, God's human partners, may be.

Historical-critical interpretations have seen in Ps. 118 a script for three speakers: a festal party in procession to the temple, a group of temple priests, and one who has been healed or saved.[4] The surprising thing on this account would be that what was once a "purely private occasion" has been given broad political import, even cosmic significance. A military triumph has been added for good measure. And

1. William Willimon put it this way, quoting Jenson, during lectures at the Vancouver School of Theology, hosted by Christ Church Cathedral, in January 2016.
2. I take this formulation from Jonathan Sacks, who says a form of it often, for example in "What Is Faith?," lecture delivered February 26, 2000, available at http://rabbisacks.org/faith-lectures-what-is-faith.
3. For more on FolkPsalm and Davis, see Jessamyn Rubio, "Sing Praises to God," *Faith & Leadership*, January 30, 2011, https://www.faithandleadership.com/multimedia/sing-praises-god.
4. Hossfeld and Zenger (2011: 230) explain this in detail; Limburg (2000: 402) and Kraus (1993: 395) follow the same line.

perhaps a royal role as well (118:26).[5] Our speaker in Ps. 118 is "an individual . . . who also bears collective features" (Hossfeld and Zenger 2011: 232). Christians who seek to interpret christologically as often as possible can rush in too quickly. We need to be careful of a "god in the gaps" approach akin to apologists in science, who see every unexplained natural phenomenon as a reason to say, "Well, God must have done it." Not knowing how a text came together historically does not give us a blank check for christological interpretation.

We can more reliably say that Israel's scripture interprets Exodus's "graciousness formula" in a rich variety of ways. Psalm 118 repeatedly echoes Exod. 14–15's celebration of God's triumph over Pharaoh at the sea. It quotes Exod. 15:2 twice, it repeats motifs of the Lord's "right hand" and of the shattered enemy, and it emphasizes the uniqueness of the Lord among the gods as one who works wonders for Israel.[6] Psalm 118 represents then an "actualization and continuation of the exodus" (Hossfeld and Zenger 2011: 234). Isaiah is another text with which this psalm is intertwined. The celebration of the Lord at Isa. 12:2, the little apocalypse of chapters 24–27, and the cornerstone passage of 28:16 interpret the gathering of Israel out of its scattering in exile as another exodus, one that even includes Gentiles in a festal meal on Zion (Isa. 25:6–8; 43:1–21; Hossfeld and Zenger 2011: 235). Ezra 3:11 records the people's great shout when the foundation stone of the temple is laid: "For he is good, for his steadfast love endures forever toward Israel." These allusions show that the psalm—before we even have a New Testament appended to the Old—is already pointing toward the future, when the hope of Israel will be granted also to all nations.

Whatever the text's historical origins, it makes invitation to the sons of Israel, to the sons of Aaron (the priests), and to those who fear the Lord—that is, Gentiles who have lost trust in their former gods, having seen the works of the God of Israel (118:2–4; Hossfeld and Zenger 2011: 237). The three groups gather with the one who is giving thanks after repeatedly being delivered out of distress and back into the Lord's favor. They climb Mount Zion together to make sacrifice (118:27) amidst raucous cheering and celebration (118:15). Zenger (Hossfeld and Zenger 2011: 233) calls 118:19–28 "the feast of the saved"—not a bad description of the celebration for which Christians gather for worship. From our earliest days, the church has sung this song as an Easter celebration: the "day" that the Lord has made is an unending one, with no more night, in which Christ looks down on

5. The Gospel writers all interpret Ps. 118:26 in royal terms (Matt. 21:9; Mark 11:9–10; Luke 19:38; John 12:13).

6. I take all this from Hossfeld and Zenger (2011: 233–34).

all his foes (118:7). Psalm 118:1 can serve as a nutshell description of the entire biblical story. God is eternally good, as the creation stories in Genesis say. God's historical deeds show that his mercy is unending, as Exodus makes clear (Hossfeld and Zenger 2011: 237).

Next come several different accounts of crying out in distress and God's response of deliverance. Psalm 118:5–9 is the first, 118:10–18 the next. The image in 118:5 is graphic—the speaker is constrained, squeezed in. I remember a terrifying children's story about a spelunker who falls down into a narrow place, his arms wedged in underneath his body and his head in a crevice, with no way out except for someone *else* to come and pull him out by the legs (why do we read these things to children?!). So too here—God is the one who *gives room*, who sets Israel's feet in a broad and spacious place (see also Gen. 26:22; Pss. 4:1; 31:8; 66:12; Kraus 1993: 397). Christian interpreters, not surprisingly, hear an echo of St. Paul's triumphant exposition of the resurrection in Rom. 8:18–30 in Ps. 118:6, "What can mortals do to me?" (Limburg 2000: 403).

With the Lord at my right hand, what can mere mortals do against me? Quite a lot, one is tempted to say. But those against us are mere *adam*, 118:6 insists, mere flesh and blood. It is the sort of verse that has inspired martyrs and confessors not to be afraid. As Augustine says, most lovers lose what they love when they die, but the lover of God not only does not lose what he loves at death, but "in fact by dying he finds what he has loved" (*Sermon* 299E.1, in Wesselschmidt 2007: 302).

Psalm 118:9 offers a brief theology of politics: "It is better to take refuge in the LORD than to put confidence in princes." Scripture has a consistently low view of human authority, with the kings and rulers it depicts serving mostly as a rogues' gallery.[7] Princes are, as Spurgeon (1976: 505) puts it, "proverbially fickle"—their smiles fade faster than they arrive. St. Jerome imagines an interlocutor saying that pastors should cozy up to those in power to advocate on behalf of the poor: "I reply that a secular magistrate will defer more to a pastor who is self-denying than to one who is rich," he says. Pressed further, he doubles down: "Or if he is a man who will only listen to the clergy over a glass, I will readily forego his aid and will appeal to Christ, who can help more effectively than any judge" (*Letter* 52.11, in Wesselschmidt 2007: 301).

Psalm 118:10–18 is a longer reflection on praying during one's distress. The repetition hammers the point home: the psalmist was surrounded, and he cut them off. The verb for "cut" is akin to that used for circumcision but is also similar to the

7. Arthur Paul Boers, *Servants and Leaders* (Nashville: Abingdon, 2015).

word for snuffing out a light (Alter 2007: 415; Hossfeld and Zenger 2011: 239, citing Job 18:5). Both fire and thorns are dangerous (118:12), but a fire among thorns burns hot and then goes out quickly. Sin is self-immolating and consumes its flimsy fuel quickly. Nevertheless, these images are violent, and the triumph has a hint of the military in it (Mays 1994: 375). It is, however, a strange sort of military conquest that comes solely by the power of the Lord. As God commands Moses, the Lord will fight for him; Moses has only to stand still (Exod. 14:14).

The longer description of the praying one's distress comes in 118:13–18, which offers an "internal" reflection on persecution—how it felt to the one undergoing it (Hossfeld and Zenger 2011: 237). What is striking is that the Lord is credited not only with offering deliverance but also with causing the distress in the first place (118:13, 18).[8] It is God who pushes in 118:13, God who punishes in 118:18, and God who saves from death (118:21). There is here a mini-theodicy, one that attributes suffering finally to God, but not only suffering—also the defiance of death that is God's final word against suffering. When Christians speak 118:17 at funerals, it is either a patent absurdity or only made true by Christ's resurrection. This vision of suffering aligns well with the prophets, for whom distress is a strange and unwelcome sort of gift from God. Jonathan Sacks points out that the surprising newness in Israel's scripture is not that Israel's God fights for Israel's armies.[9] *All* people have some religious way of saying that their deity fights on their behalf. The key difference is that Israel's God fights for Israel's *enemies*. Jeremiah speaks often of the Lord's chastisement of Israel, to the point of using foreign armies to correct it (Jer. 5:3; 10:24; 30:11; 31:18; 32:33). The psalms speak of the distress that the Lord sends before the deliverance that the Lord also sends (Pss. 6:1; 66:10; 119:71). In the history of Christian spirituality, we have noticed that the ones who really have to worry are those whom God leaves alone. Those who struggle, who feel like they're in a fight, are the ones God is currently blessing. Those with no spiritual malady are those about whom the devil is not worried.[10]

As a pastor, I was surprised how often I felt unfairly attacked by parishioners. I came to see these attacks as strange gifts.[11] Certain parishioners may have had

---

8. The Tanakh's translation makes this divine agency clearer in 113:13: "You pressed me hard," although the editorial note suggests the "you" is "the enemy" (Berlin and Brettler 2014: 1401).

9. This comes in the context of an argument about the demythologizing present already in Israel's scriptures, offered in rebuke of the "new atheists," who think their demythologizing will somehow scandalize biblical people.

10. I take the description from David Steinmetz, who said it often, especially of Martin Luther.

11. I owe the language of "strange" or "unwelcome" gifts to my colleague Holly Taylor Coolman of Providence College.

no good at heart for me personally as they accused me of destroying our church. But that did not mean God had no good for me through them. There is, unfortunately, far more profit to be had in being criticized than in being praised. So I had to sit with parishioners' criticism, however unwarranted it seemed to me. There was in that criticism—perhaps despite the parishioners, certainly despite me—a blessing that had to be fought for. Augustine says something similar as he seizes on the image of bees in 118:12: the Lord's persecutors made him sweeter to us by causing him to suffer, "so that we may taste and see how delicious is the Lord" (2003: 336). Remember this when you feel "surrounded by bees," endangered, done in. Whatever the intention of those surrounding you, they are bees. Bees make sweet honey. They may not mean it for good, but God does. To attack Christ or his people is, in fact, only to hasten the day of entry to the land flowing with milk and honey; it is only to make Christ all the more sweet.

"I shall not die, but I shall live," the psalmist insists (118:17). The psalmist is not above trying to manipulate God by saying that if he dies, there will be one less voice to praise. This however is more of a declaration than a play to divine vanity. It announces the psalm's raison d'être—giving thanks for a startling recovery. One might demur, well, you will die eventually. No one gets out of this life alive. But the psalmist's insistence rings even more true than its writer may have known. God is the God who grants life far beyond death. Martin Luther took this verse as a sort of personal favorite after multiple deliveries from death (Limburg 2000: 402). And yet, after many close calls, Luther eventually died, as will the rest of us. The biblical hope of resurrection bleeds over from gratitude for surprising survival to survival *after* death's arrival, what N. T. Wright calls "life after life after death."[12] The purpose of such miraculous new life is "to recount the deeds of the Lord" (118:17), to offer continually the sort of praise that Ps. 118 is.

"Open to me the gates of righteousness, that I may enter through them and give thanks" (118:19). The assembly making its way up Zion to offer a sacrifice of thanksgiving stops at the closed doors and asks for entry. The doors to great houses of worship are still ceremonially important. The doors of the Baptistery of St. John in Florence tell the story of scripture as beautifully as anyone ever has. Some great cathedrals open their main doors only for rare and important occasions. Pope John Paul II once invited the Anglican Archbishop of Canterbury to open the doors of the Vatican with him as a sign of a unity of the church that isn't quite present yet. The Orthodox during the Easter Vigil shout out, "The doors!"

---

12. N. T. Wright, *Surprised by Hope: Rethinking Heaven, the Resurrection, and the Mission of the Church* (New York: HarperOne, 2008).

to signify that Christ is about to break down the doors of death and lift out Adam and Eve. At the climax of Jesus's own ministry, a different sort of door opens in God's house, the curtain of the temple being torn (Matt. 27:51). Christians pulled these emphases on the doors from passages like 118:19. In 118:19 "righteousness" is clearly God's own—only God can open these doors. The only way into God's presence is God's own righteousness shared with us by grace—grace available to us through such practices as pilgrimage, sacrifice, and singing psalms and having our world transfigured by them.

"The stone that the builders rejected has become the chief cornerstone" (118:22). A piece unfit for anything other than discarding now has the place of honor. Practically, this can happen—a builder can decide that a piece previously thought to be unusable is, in fact, perfect for completing the whole. One interpreter imagines the stone as more of a capstone—fitting in on top in a place that holds the building together (Hossfeld and Zenger 2011: 242). It would be architecturally difficult after all to find that a discarded stone can go *under* the nearly completed building.

But the psalm's language is one of pure astonishment, total reversal, bottom rail being on the top this time. Ancient Christians clearly saw Christ and the previously uninvited in this passage. The epistle writers marvel that Christ has not only broken down the dividing wall between Jews and Gentiles; he has also become the cornerstone of a new building, with the apostles and prophets as the foundation (Eph. 2:20). The First Epistle of Peter stretches the metaphor even further and adds a note of warning to it: we're to be "living stones" to whom he is "precious," but for those who don't believe, "the stone the builders rejected has become the very head of the corner" (1 Pet. 2:7). Peter's speech in Acts pushes this note of judgment still further, directing the italicized words at the chief priests: Jesus is "the stone that was rejected *by you*, the builders; it has become the cornerstone" (Acts 4:11). Jesus uses this verse in controversy polemics with the Pharisees after the parable of the vineyard: "Therefore I tell you, the kingdom of God will be taken away from you" (Matt. 21:42–43; see also Mark 12:12; Luke 20:19).

What once made for astonishment at God's world-upturning ways has quickly turned into blame of the Jews for what they've done to Jesus and approval of ourselves for being in the right. The problem with this sort of reading, of course, is that Ps. 118:22 is still true. God favors those who are most outside, and God overturns the presumption of the proud. The Christians who wrote these New Testament passages regarding the cornerstone, and Jesus who applied them to himself, were astonished. How do we regain that sort of astonishment? How do we reject those who are, by that very rejection, closest to God's heart? These sorts of verses, read centuries later, once Christians had far more civil power than the Jews in their midst, could make for bitterly anti-Jewish readings for which we still have to repent. But we have also to go a step further than repentance. How do we recapture the psalmist's shout of praise at God's world-reversing ways?

We might simply despair. Ephesians imagines a community of Jews and Gentiles who together make up the temple of God's body in the world—the Jews as Jews and the Gentiles as Gentiles worshiping the one God through one Lord, one faith, one baptism (Eph. 4:4). God's intention to knit humanity back together through Abraham's family is coming true in church. The most potent counter-witness to this good news is the Gentiles turning on God's original chosen people, the Jews, with jealousy and rage. The despair is that it's nearly impossible to imagine what Ephesians imagines. There are some Jews who try to continue as Jews while worshiping Jesus. They're mostly disliked by their fellow Jews. Most Gentiles are unaware that Jewishness still has any sort of positive valence in God's eyes, despite Rom. 11. To change this would take what Peter Ochs calls "another Reformation."[13]

But God is the one who gives life to the dead and takes what is rejected and restores it to honor. God always does more with less promising material.

The New Testament cites this psalm in another context with remarkable unanimity. "Blessed is the one who comes in the name of the LORD" (118:26) is what the crowds shout to Jesus as he makes his festal way up Zion at his triumphal entry (Matt. 21:9; Mark 11:9–10; Luke 19:38; John 12:13). They add notes of royal acclamation: "Hosanna to the Son of David," "blessed is the king who comes," "the King of Israel." What if the triumphal entry has in its background Ps. 118:26, a procession of folks wanting to make sacrifice for God's death-overturning provision? Then at the doors, upon the request for admission (118:19), Jesus is turned away. Or actually turns himself away ("Then he entered Jerusalem and went into the temple; and when he had looked around at everything, as it was already late, he went out to Bethany with the twelve," Mark 11:11). His conflict with the religious leaders of his own people is sharpest here at this point of his ministry—to the point that some of them, with the Romans, seek his death. The sacrifice Jesus had intended to offer in the temple (118:27) he ends up offering outside the city, not at the heart of God's own temple but in a place of refuse, for the execution of criminals (Heb. 13:12–13). The result tears open the space of the temple by an agency no human could muster (Mark 15:38). We are thus invited to link the

13. Peter Ochs, *Another Reformation: Post-liberal Christianity and the Jews* (Grand Rapids: Baker Academic, 2011).

branches binding the festal procession (Ps. 118:27) to those cut off and burned (118:12), to intermingle good religious folk and those rejected by such folk, as Jesus invites us outside the camp—the only place where the stone that the builders rejected can be found.[14]

But the one to whom he makes his offering of himself is the God who intervenes in history to liberate slaves (Exod. 15). It is the one who promises an eschatological feast for all peoples (Isa. 12). The right hand of the Lord that gives the psalmist victory (Ps. 118:16) now raises up Jesus (Acts 7:55–56). There are shouts of joy and victory indeed—not even the death of God's beloved can foil divine plans for creation. In fact, those divine plans are brought to fruition through the death of God's beloved. The despised and rejected one is now in the seat of all honor. Those who did the despising and rejecting—that is, all of us sinners—can do nothing but marvel.

Psalm 118 is one of the places in scripture where the mystery is thickest. It is an absolutely crucial passage for the New Testament. Yet let's be clear: it can and has been used in bitterly anti-Jewish ways, and the New Testament text itself has gone not a little way toward that misuse. We Christians cannot turn it into a barb at the Jews without hitting our own heart ("Do not boast. . . . Remember that it is not you that support the root, but the root that supports you," Rom. 11:18). We must look for whom we have despised and rejected—God is at work saving *us* through *them*. This is the God who gives honor to the lowliest, starting with his Son, then including all his Son's questionable friends—the poor, those on the fringes of society, the outcast. This is the Lord to whom we give the thanks of Ps. 118—the one who alone is good, whose steadfast love endures forever.

Every communion liturgy reminds us of the blessing proclaimed in Ps. 118: God always saves from the bottom up. We look in one direction, and God sneaks up and taps us on the shoulder from the other. We set our hearts and faces like stone, but God softens them into living stones. It is a demanding thing to be built into this building, made organically one with this sort of cornerstone. It is also raucously beautiful.

---

14. Again I am grateful to Davis Hankins for pointing out to me that Jesus's sacrifice outside the camp isn't just for us abstractly; we also have to imitate his move outside the camp.

PSALM 119

Psalm 119 is a peak this volume will not have to climb. Reinhard Hütter's stand-alone volume will comment on all 176 verses. This is appropriate in several ways. Psalm 119 is a microcosm of the entire Psalter. It deserves its own commentary not just for its sheer length but for its breathtaking scope. This is also appropriate because of our relationship. Reinhard was my Doktorvater at Duke. I so admire his concision and brilliance as a thinker that I look forward to him commenting on Ps. 119 rather than me. My other fellow writers on the psalms in this commentary series—Ellen Charry and Lauren Winner—are both Christians who were once Jews and who eschew christological interpretation for the most part. They are both elegant writers and brilliant theologians. Between the four of us, we offer a breadth of viewpoints on the praise of Israel. For my part I am applying the church fathers' and medievals' approach of finding Christ in a maximal sense—since he is already everywhere, and finding him is the church's constant delight.

I won't scale Ps. 119 here, but I will glance at it.

It is, famously, an acrostic poem. Each letter of the Hebrew alphabet, from *aleph* to *tav*, has a subsection of Ps. 119 with eight verses that start with that letter. The psalmist praises God's Torah from A to Zed, as we say in Canada. This suggests comprehensiveness, expansiveness—maximalism, if you will. Some interpreters have seen artifice rather than ingenuity. They're not wrong. Alter expresses particular annoyance with the *vav* section, in which each verse begins with the thoroughly uninspiring word "and" (*vav* not offering a lot by way of options). All art depends on boundaries, however, to put it in relief for the viewer. Alter notes moments of poetic success—119:83 compares the one praying to a wineskin in smoke. Psalm 119:54 describes the law as that which keeps me "in the house of my sojourning" (a phrase with much more life in it than the NRSV's "wherever I make my home") (Alter 2007: 419–20). The point isn't poetry alone. It's praise. And the praise has a narrow scope: praise of God's law, God's teaching, God's statutes, God's ordinances and precepts and ways. This immediately brings up anxiety for Christians, given our long and vexed history with the law. Psalm 119 suggests the law should first evoke delight. But there is nearly nothing about the content of the law in Ps. 119. It would be difficult to reconstruct the Ten Commandments, let alone Israel's other 613 commands, from this long psalm alone. The atmosphere in the psalm is ecstasy, jubilation, celebration. Before we Christians tie ourselves in knots over our theology of the law, we should dance with it, marry it.

Early Christian monks made it a practice to recite the entire Psalter weekly. Sometimes, in an allowance for the weakness of the flesh, they were allowed to chant the Psalter in two weeks. On whatever plan, they had to work hard to get in the entire Ps. 119. The monks at Trappist monasteries today live out this Benedictine (and earlier) tradition of chanting the psalms by reciting a bit of Ps. 119 every single day, like a one-a-day vitamin. This practice allows them to pray the whole Psalter over two weeks. It also allows some of the older monks to "know the whole David"—that is, not to have to open their Psalters anymore. The praise of Israel is imprinted on their hearts.

The content of that praise is love of the Torah of Israel. This concept has been contentious in the church since the time of the apostle Paul. In some places, Paul sounds like the law is positively harmful ("If justification comes through the law, then Christ died for nothing," Gal. 2:21). In other places he backtracks and insists the law is holy, righteous, and good ("Do we overthrow the law by this faith? By no means! On the contrary, we uphold the law," Rom. 3:31). In Protestant Christianity, we can see here the difference between the Reformers Martin Luther and John Calvin. For Luther, the enemies whom Christ defeats on the cross are sin, death, the devil, *and the law*. That's quite a rogue's gallery with which the law is associated! For Luther's younger colleague Calvin, Ps. 119's exuberant love of the law is something he can hymn in good faith: "O Lord how I love thy law" comes from his lips without qualification. Calvin not only thought the law had ongoing significance in shaping the church in holiness—he also lingered in the literal sense of passages like Ps. 119.

In the late twentieth century, we saw a massive shift in Christian interpretation of the New Testament with regard to the law. E. P. Sanders, N. T. Wright, and others showed that for Paul's Jewish contemporaries, their election by God is an act of grace. Jews in the first century are not Luther's sixteenth-century polemical opponents, attempting to earn their way into heaven by impressing God with spiritual résumés. Rather, they're chosen by God through no prior merit of their own and given the gift of the covenant that makes more of them than they ever could have made on their own. Even within this new perspective on Paul, there are great divergences over the ongoing significance of the law in general and the salvation of Israel according to the flesh in particular.[1] Wright analogizes between the law and a trip in a car—you get out of the car when you arrive, not because the car is bad, but because it's gotten you to where you needed to go. The language of Galatians about the law's temporary status over Israel means it is good but decidedly past tense (Gal. 3:23–25). Trying to use it for faith now is like trying to accumulate outdated currency—gather all you want, but it won't buy you anything.[2]

But Ps. 119 is still in the canon. And by virtue of its massive size, it stands out in the canon. Its purpose is to give endless variation on the praying community's love for the law. Its purpose is to create the "psychic condition" necessary for praise—so proposals to shorten it fail (Jon Levenson, cited in Hossfeld and Zenger 2011: 260). It wants you to pray until you can't stand the psalm anymore—and then to pray again. Jon Levenson compares the psalm to medieval *lectio divina*. We are to chew on this idea like a cow does her cud—swallow, throw it up, chew, swallow. . . . Some liturgies work in brevity. Some mean to be long (Hossfeld and Zenger 2011: 260). The psalm is simple enough to understand but hard to concentrate on enough to simply read it, let alone chant it or practice it. It intends not so much to instruct with endless content as to "enchant the imagination," evoking the sort of concentration and "submission" that Torah study requires (Mays 1994: 382). Whatever else we make of the law—and no doubt both Jesus and Paul played somewhat fast and loose with it—we are to love it, dance with it, and delight in it, as Ps. 119 proposes. We are to love the law because Christ is the purpose of the law (Rom. 10:4). He is the goal toward which it heads, not just its completion, and certainly not its disqualification. Stephen Farris makes this point unforgettably. He asks that we translate "law" and its various cognates in Ps. 119 with an existential rendering from Gerhard Ebeling, "O Lord, how I love thy *reality of fallen humankind*." It doesn't work. No one can pray that line, however helpful a paraphrase of Torah and "law" that it may be. But Farris suggests that we pray this instead: "O Lord how I love thy grace." Yes, we can pray

---

1. John Barclay, an adherent of the new perspective, has recently pushed further to ask what precisely we mean by "grace," and winds up in a more Reformation-friendly place in his interpretation of Paul. See Barclay, *Paul and the Gift* (Grand Rapids: Eerdmans, 2015).

2. Barclay, *Paul and the Gift*, 383.

that. And on the Reformed church's account, the law *is* grace. "O Lord, how I love thy Christ," in other words. Suddenly 176 verses become 176 ways to praise the gift not only of the law but of Christ, to whom the law constantly and joyfully points. For the law is hidden in the gospel like the tablets from Sinai are hidden in the ark of the covenant.[3]

3. It's Karl Barth's image, quoted in Stephen Farris, *Grace: A Preaching Commentary*, Great Texts (Nashville: Abingdon, 2003), 127.

PSALM 120

Psalm 120 begins the Psalms of Ascent (120–134) for pilgrims who go up to Zion. Imagine a long, perilous journey of groups unsure if they'll meet bandits or animals or angelic protection or all three, lightening the load of their journey by singing these psalms together. Now imagine longing to see a place so badly, to pray in God's unimaginably beautiful temple, to ignite your faith and others' on communal pilgrimage, badly enough to risk life and livelihood to do so, and you have this psalm and the ones to follow.

The ascent psalms are shorter than most (especially Ps. 119 just prior!). They refer repeatedly to Jerusalem, Zion, and Israel. They are filled with blessings and doxologies. And perhaps they have always been literal marching psalms (like twentieth-century freedom songs) *and also* figural songs of spiritual ascent. Meshech is as far north as Israel can imagine; Kedar as far south (120:5). The psalmist could not be in both places at once. And most Israelites, most Christians, have not been physically near Zion while chanting this or any other psalm. They form "a theological topography," as one modern scholar says (Hossfeld and Zenger 2011: 309). An ancient one concurs: "God arranges the ascent in his heart" (Augustine 2003: 498). Martin Luther writes that the psalms of ascent "deal with important teaching and almost all of the articles of our Christian faith, of preaching, forgiveness of sins, the cross, love, marriage, authorities, so that they set forth as it were a summary of all essential teachings" (quoted in Limburg 2000: 420).

The first verse (120:1) remembers when God has been faithful to answer prayer in the past. The second lifts up a new prayer—for "deliverance from a verbal net of lies, betrayal, intimidation, calumny and hostility" (Hossfeld and Zenger 2011: 306). As usual, the psalmist omits the specifics, allowing us to find ourselves and our particulars in it. I think here of the slander I suffered as a pastor, when gossip far outran truth (and now here I risk slandering them). Augustine finds a more universal application—anytime anyone starts to ascend toward God, others will discourage and hold them back. These others will be too clever to impugn Christ directly, and so will insist that being a Christian is admirable but impossible (Augustine 2003: 501). Ancient commentators generally praise the role of difficulty in discipleship. Without that theme of cross-bearing our faith deteriorates into so much prosperity pablum. If the psalmist experiences intense pain, and the written record of that agony is *holy scripture*, presumably we're to undergo something similar.

Psalm 120:3–4 reads like an invective against the liar's tongue, a mini-psalm of imprecation. In line with the Bible's *lex talionis*, "an eye for an eye," the psalmist asks for the same cutting and burning for the slanderer that the slanderer's words have caused. Broom coals were especially known for burning hot for a long time. The *lex talionis* was an effort in scripture to restrain violence, even though in popular culture it's a shorthand for biblically sanctioned violence. The Bible undoes its calls for violence as soon as it issues them: "I am for peace," as the NRSV has it, or more accurately, "I am peace," peace personified, in the midst of war (120:7; Alter 2007: 436). Luther notes how difficult it is to slander the slanderer. And this is just as well. Spiritually it is far better to be slandered than to slander (Luther, cited in Spurgeon 1976: 571). Augustine turns the images of arrows and coals around. The Lord's arrows (120:4), fired at us, seek to inspire "the arousal of love," he says. Then we, in turn, become arrows that God fires at others' hearts. A "live" coal, unlike a cold and dead one, gives off heat. It is an image for giving off the flame of the Holy Spirit. When they come across a live coal, Augustine's fellow worshipers at Hippo hear, they should "apply him [the personified live coal] to another who is dead, and set fire to her or him as well" (Augustine 2003: 504).

"Woe is me," the psalmist prays (120:5). They are, surprisingly, words of hope. Lament is powerful. It suggests the dismal present is not the only possibility.[1] A lament is powerful, Augustine says, "because the one who gives it has at least learned how to grieve" (2003: 505). The psalmist grieves for being as far from Zion as geographically possible, surrounded by warlike people who do not know the Lord's ways. Magog is the chief prince in warlike Meshech (Ezek. 38:2). The

---

1. See the work of Emmanuel Katongole for the hopefulness of lament, esp. Katongole and Jonathan Wilson-Hartgrove, *Mirror to the Church: Resurrecting Faith after Genocide in Rwanda* (Grand Rapids: Zondervan, 2009), and more recently Katongole, *Born from Lament: The Theology and Politics of Hope in Africa* (Grand Rapids: Eerdmans, 2017).

prophet promises that Kedar's arrows will one day be few—implying they are now plentiful (Isa. 21:16–17). The Bible has an inclination toward costly, self-sacrificial peace. Proclaiming peace can seem like hell to those bent on and benefitting from war. The best way to test your pacifist sensibilities is to announce them: people will immediately want to fight you. And precisely then you will learn how to pray this psalm.

The psalmist's declaration, "I am peace itself," is not the sort of thing any ordinary human being can say unashamedly (120:7). Only one of us can say he is the very presence of peace ("he is our peace," Eph. 2:14). Most readers and writers of commentary will not suffer the sort of calumny the psalmist refers to here. But our Lord did. And he responded to opprobrium with words of grace and forgiveness. Most who suffer, Chrysostom says, "gain ferocity." But the Lord's own example shows that "nothing is more powerful than gentleness" (Chrysostom 1998: 137). And he is no one-off virtuoso. In his church, he works to make us like him. Maybe this is why the church is so full of gossips and slanderers—all the more opportunity to practice holiness in return.

This is the first step in a series of steps up the way to Zion. These steps are the perfect companion to the seemingly endless Ps. 119—it proposes Torah as the way to be in God's presence, and then the ascent psalms propose the temple as the way to be in God's presence. When they are set side by side, we see both are true (Hossfeld and Zenger 2011: 119). We too might be as far removed from gentleness, from Zion's peace, as the north is from the south. But we can begin, as this psalm does, with a step in the right direction.

PSALM 121

There is a reason Ps. 121 is among the most beloved psalms. God is our helper, keeper, shader, non-sleeper—anyone who has ever felt endangered has reached for protection like this. Perhaps anyone who has ever climbed a hill, or lifted their eyes to the next rise on the horizon, or needed a bit of comfort—my Methodist church is not the only denomination in which this psalm appears in funeral liturgies. There is no going out or coming in that the Lord does not steward and safeguard.

The psalmist is heading out on a journey, perhaps originally leaving the sanctuary in Jerusalem to return home. I remember visiting Jerusalem and walking around the old city at night, fighting off jetlag, reciting a few psalms like this. I looked right to see how much farther the walk was and could not believe how steep the hill was, how dark it looked. I felt scared. This with the benefit of modern lighting and police for protection! How much more a faithful ancient pilgrim who wants to pray in God's house and has no help other than the God who hears prayer. Pilgrimage is about actual bodies that get tired, actual souls that get scared and soar, an actual God who creates ways to meet him in song, ascent, pilgrimage, and all creation. Furthermore, Christ has made a journey possible from his humanity to his divinity. The way is perilous, but the one who arranges the way is vigilant and near to help.

One key interpretive question is whether 121:1 poses a rhetorical question or one that is unanswered. Is the one praying reminded of the God of Israel by looking to the hills? Or are the hills rather the "high places" where idols are built and strange gods rule (e.g., 1 Kgs. 11:7–8; 13:33–34)? We should let the ambiguity stand. Sure, strange gods may claim the hills, but they, and everything else, ultimately belong to the only God there is (121:2). St. Augustine points out that hills are not lit from within. As with every piece of creation besides the sun, the hills reflect a derivative, received light. So it is with the saints, to whom all Christians look up in admiration, not for light that originates from them, but for light that reflects off of them (Augustine 2003: 515).

Several commentators imagine a pilgrim leaving the sanctuary of Jerusalem on the way home by dangerous roads (Kraus 1993: 426; Mays 1994: 389). They want the blessing of peace and safety that belongs to those who serve in the temple, and in their praise they receive it. St. Augustine points out that even pagans took refuge in Christian churches during the sack of Rome.[1] The church as a sanctuary—as a refuge from violence—is a venerable tradition. But it is not always true. The temple itself was destroyed several times. People who took refuge in churches in Rwanda were often slaughtered there. In what way could this psalm be literally true in this world?

Most of the second-person addressees in scripture are plural (as we say in the South, they're addressed to y'all). But in Ps. 121 these are singular: more intimate, personal even, like Ps. 23 (Mays 1994: 389). Since the psalm has unmoored itself from the specific circumstances of its authorship, we can see lots of its phrasing as general. So Augustine is reading with the grain of the psalm when he interprets it figurally—our foot slips by pride. Charity, by contrast, allows the pilgrim to make progress (note: the opposite of pride isn't humility but love!) (Augustine 2003: 515).

The triply negative reference to slumber recalls Elijah's mockery of the prophets of Baal (1 Kgs. 18:27). False gods sleep. The true God will never be caught napping but will always be vigilant. Of course, anyone who's actually *tried* prayer to YHWH has experienced God as unresponsive, and wondered whether God is, indeed, somnambulant. As Martin Luther insists, "Even though it appears that God is sleeping or snoring . . . this is certainly not so, despite the way we feel and think. God is surely awake and watching over us" (quoted in Limburg 2000: 423). But perhaps this anthropomorphic imagination of God isn't just a repudiation of paganism. Perhaps God *actually* sleeps. In Christ, God does every ordinary human thing we do, sleep included—even at some inopportune times! The disciples experience the God of the universe asleep and apparently doing nothing in their boat as a storm rages. They wake him in a panic. And he rebukes the wind and the waves. And they "feared a great fear" (Mark 4:41, Young's Literal Translation). A God in our flesh indeed sleeps. Yet at our urgent summons he awakes. Even beyond that, he sleeps when he dies our death. And he rises when we don't even think to try

---

1. Augustine, *City of God against the Pagans* 1.1, ed. R. W. Dyson, Cambridge Texts in the History of Political Thought (Cambridge: Cambridge University Press, 1998).

to summon him. Augustine riffs on the psalm that no mere human being can stay awake unendingly. And Christ is no mere human being (Augustine 2003: 515).

The key word in the latter part of this psalm is "keep," *shomer*, a reflection of the God who is mindful of us (121:3–5, 7–8). With the Lord as our keeper, our shade, we need not fear sun or moon or evil when we go out and come in. Augustine and Alter agree that the figure of going and coming suggests eternity (Augustine 2003: 519; Alter 2007: 437). They also disagree: Alter puzzlingly says "there is virtually no figurative language here," except for the reference to shade (as in, say, Ps. 17:8: "hide me in the shadow of your wings"). He must actually mean the figures are relatively transparent and biblically common. Augustine pushes farther: even quite faithful people can get sunburned. Many cultures fear the moon can make one crazy (as our word "lunatic" suggests) (Limburg 2000: 424). The psalm is full of figures. The question is what they mean. This question is heightened with even a modest amount of reflection on spiritual experience. If God is such a reliable "keeper," how do so many get so lost? Jesus's parables of God's maniacal effort to *find* suggest a keeper who is at least a little absentminded (Luke 15:8–10). Sure, she turns the house upside down looking for the lost coin. But why'd she lose it in the first place?

Christian interpreters trained in historical criticism are sometimes brave to make Christian moves at the end of their interpretation. For example, Limburg closes with a reference to Jesus's appeal to "come, follow me" in the blessing of our going and coming (Ps. 121:8). Coming at the end of an exegesis this can seem a pious bit of garnish. But what if we interpret christologically throughout? Augustine is, once again, a model. Sunburn is a reference to a heresy regarding the sun, who is Malachi's "sun of righteousness" (4:2), who is the light that the darkness cannot understand. But a false teaching regarding the church runs the risk of moonburn! The church is a derivative or reflection of God's light, not its source. Yet the incarnation brings together God and humanity, so that "the church is preached through the reality of Christ's flesh, for the very flesh of Christ is the head of the church" (Augustine 2003: 522). Some say allegory is world-abandoning and flesh-denying. Augustine shows otherwise. It is the Lord who keeps us from misinterpretation regarding Jesus, his church, and every other worldly thing. Because it is the Lord who keeps his people. Not perfectly—we do get lost from time to time. God has given us a terrible sort of freedom. But it is not ultimate freedom. God has filled the world with signs of his incarnation, and filled the scriptures with hope, and filled the life of discipleship with blazes on every trail, light by night and by day, and companions on the way. When we lift up our eyes, we are never left without guidance and hope.

PSALM 122

This commentary has often suggested figural readings of Israel's scripture. But let us start with the most literal reading of Ps. 122 possible: pray for the peace of Jerusalem. Now. Stop reading and ask God for the grace that the actual city be filled with peace that overflows to others. The psalm makes the "scandal of particularity" unmistakable. God lives at One Temple Way in Jerusalem, as Michael Wyschogrod puts it.[1] God wants this home full of peace that radiates out to others. And prayer is a matter of aligning our desire with God's. Jesus's tears over Jerusalem were his prayers (Luke 19:41–44). This psalm is God's smile over it.

This little psalm opens up a surprisingly broad array of issues: God's election of Israel, Jewish practices of pilgrimage, Jesus's own entering into those practices, Christians' continuity with our history, and the coming City of God. Modernity thought tribes inherently violent—nation-states are supposed to save us from tribal violence (122:4; Stephen Breck Reid, cited in Van Harn and Strawn 2009: 316–18). Postmodernity has observed more violence from nation-states than anything that preceded it—nation-states are just bigger, better-armed tribes. Christians have often insisted, over against Jewish interlocutors, that the psalm can't be about the actual geographic city. This is a mistake. Figural readings rest on literal ones. And the God who wants peace makes a home in Jerusalem. The great Abraham Joshua Heschel praised the physical city in similar terms to the psalm: "Here the trees, praise, the streets say grace, and my steps give thanks. The way of Jerusalem is a way of exaltation" (quoted in Limburg 2000: 429).

Yet Jesus's relationship with Jerusalem is testy. He is often in the city, as commanded by Israel's scripture (122:4). He loves God's house so much that he rebuked

1. Wyschogrod, "Incarnation," *Pro Ecclesia* 2 (1993): 208–15.

his parents for failing to realize that of course that was where he would be, teaching (Luke 2:41–52). Yet he laments the state of the city. It kills the prophets and those sent to it, and would eventually kill him (Luke 13:31–35). St. Paul is not above spiritualizing Jerusalem (Gal. 4:26). Christian reading attends to the words in light of the resurrection. What do we do then with this quite physical and specific city? We rejoice in it (122:1). We pray for it (122:6). And we give reasons why we do these things (122:3–9). These come straight from the psalm.

"I was glad when they said to me . . ." has opened many a Christian worship service, but the word doesn't appear often in scripture. Three times only Israel's scripture says, "I was glad" (Reid, in Van Harn and Strawn 2009: 315). A sermon on this text should be similarly glad. The Hebrew word translated "rejoice" has the same root as the festival Jews celebrate called Simchat Torah, in which folks rejoice over Torah. They dance with it, delight in it like a groom over a bride, like God over Israel (Limburg 2000: 429). Israel is often commanded to make festival and be joyous (Deut. 12:7; 16:11; 26:11). This is beyond how one personally feels. It's how God wants all of God's people to be on certain occasions.

Why is the psalmist so glad? Feet are within the gates (122:2). The city is intricate (122:3); it is the heart of Israel to which all tribes flow in procession (122:4); it has thrones set up for judgment (122:5); and for the sake of all whom I love, the psalmist says, I'll pray for and seek its peace (122:8). The emphasis is on the city's spiritual radiance more than its physical grandeur (as in Ps. 48)—the city is a refuge, a place of peace. Its emphasis on justice is significant: this is where those who have been wronged seek recourse (122:5). One thing Israel's scripture looks forward to from its Messiah is that he will be the ultimate arbiter of justice, which we have only ever approximated so far (see Isa. 11's "little apocalypse") (Kraus 1993: 433). The vision of the tribes streaming up to Zion is magnificent to imagine. The church has often seen itself in similar biblical glimpses of all people, Gentiles included, coming to worship Israel's God at the end of history (Isa. 2:1–4). Eventually, scripture hopes, the gravitational pull, the undertow in the water, from all Israel treading toward the temple will be so great that all people will join in. What's odd is that in the church Gentiles have begun this end-of-the-world procession. Many of God's own people Israel, "according to the flesh," as Paul puts it, think that time has not yet come. But with God an unexpected order of things is to be expected.

St. Augustine describes pilgrimage in his own day in North Africa, of the sort that modern people may only have approximated at sports events or rock concerts: "Call to mind a scene familiar to you. When some festival of the martyrs falls due, perhaps, and some holy place is named at which all are to assemble to celebrate the solemn rites, remember how the throngs incite one another, how people encourage each other, saying, 'Come on, let's go, let's go!' Others ask, 'Where are we going?' And they are told, 'To that place, to the holy site.' People talk to each other and catch fire with enthusiasm, and all the separate flames unite into a single flame" (Augustine 2004: 14).

Desire is contagious. It leaps from one person to the next. At a recent liturgy in a small church here in Vancouver, I saw the choir and priest robed for Pentecost. Tourists, robed quite differently, stopped on their bikes and asked what this parade was. "It's Pentecost," the priest said. "We'd love for you to join us." They waved and moved on. Desire didn't entirely take hold that time.

Augustine describes the contemporary feast beautifully and then subsumes it within a heavenly feast. How much more must the desire to go to heaven reorient our affections and rocket from one soul to the next? This can feel like the sort of spiritualization that's deadly to interpretation. Twentieth-century theology saw a great recovery of Israel and its particularity in Christian theology. Heaven talk is nearly entirely passé among modern Christians. But perhaps this loss is, surprisingly, a gift. St. John Chrysostom points out that the Jews who penned this psalm lost the ability to make this pilgrimage in the Babylonian exile. "This is the way God generally does things: when we do not appreciate the good things we have, he knocks them from our hands" (Chrysostom 1998: 147). Look at the psalmist's great desire for Jerusalem. The church says yes to this desire. And yet pilgrimage is about more than a long walk. It is about the soul in community with others and God. If this costly and dangerous journey to the navel of the world is this glorious, how much more glorious must be the costly and dangerous journey that is our entire life and afterlife toward the vision of God?

We are not there yet. Violence still marks our human life together. No glimpse of heaven is any good that doesn't launch us back into the world with a blessing of peace and pursuing it (122:9). The last generation or so has seen a remarkable recovery of urban theology and church planting among evangelicals. Inspired by stories like Redeemer Presbyterian Church in Manhattan, gifted seminary students now often want to plant churches in cities from which white middle-class people fled for generations (nonwhite Christians never lost this impetus for loving the city the way God does, of course).[2] God's scandalous love is incarnate first in Jerusalem. But then it teaches us how to love every city. Cities' compactness,

---

2. See Tim Stafford, "How Tim Keller Found Manhattan," *Christianity Today* 53, no. 6 (June 5, 2009): 20–26, available at http://www.christianitytoday.com/ct/2009/june/15.20.html; and Timothy Keller, *Center Church: Doing Balanced, Gospel-Centered Ministry in Your City* (Grand Rapids: Zondervan, 2012).

their inhabitants' efforts to approximate justice, their teeming life together are all beloved to God. This psalm can teach us anew how to love the city to which we're called in ministry now. For a new city is coming that will gather up all our efforts to love, do justice, pray, and bring peace, and will burn away their faults, crown what is good in them, and make this world the one God longs for (Rev. 21).

Thomas Merton once complained to his abbot about the Trappists' gathering seven times a day for the chanting of psalms (what did he think he was signing up for?!). The wise abbot suggested he contemplate Jesus on pilgrimage to Jerusalem chanting psalms like Ps. 122: "He said I should think of Jesus going up to Jerusalem with all the pilgrims roaring psalms out of their dusty throats."[3]

3. Merton, quoted in James Martin, SJ, *Jesus: A Pilgrimage* (New York: HarperOne, 2016), 332.

PSALM 123

We are in the middle of the Psalms of Ascent (Pss. 120–134). Yet this is the first time we have directly addressed God since Ps. 120 began our climb (Limburg 2000: 429). "I lift up my eyes," the psalmist prays (123:1), in a gesture parallel to the better-known Ps. 121:1. The Venerable Bede, early eighth-century English monk, points out that here the eyes are lifted beyond the hills, directly toward God (cited in Spurgeon 1976: 578).

God is enthroned in the heavens, and yet God is not disinterested in creation (123:1–2). God is full of power and the author of justice, and yet God also bends low, especially to the poor, whom God raises up (see also Ps. 113:5–9; Hossfeld and Zenger 2011: 346). However we envision God's might, it does not make God inaccessible to our pleas. Or perhaps better, God's might *is* God's accessibility to our pleas.

Psalm 123:2 puts us in the position of abject slaves. We are ever attentive to our master, whose "hand" is a sign not only of power but also of the ability to punish. Yet the biblical God is the one who redeems slaves. The slaves of Ps. 123 gaze intently upon God until he does what *they* want—God has mercy. That's the direction of this psalm—an intent gaze until God remembers God's nature is to alleviate suffering and cut down the scornful (Hossfeld and Zenger 2011: 349). An ultimate defeat of the Lord's servants would mean either that the Lord is impotent to deliver or too fickle to keep promises. This is an aggressive sort of prayer—eyes intently gazing at God, importuning God to have mercy (note the triple repetition of the plea for mercy in 123:2–3).

The second half of Ps. 123 groans that the praying community is sated with contempt. "A little contempt they could bear," Spurgeon says, but here they have had "a bellyful" (Spurgeon 1976: 578). Scripture often uses the language of contempt to describe those who lord over the poor, who "scoff and speak with malice," and who "loftily . . . threaten oppression" (Ps. 73:5, 8–9; Hossfeld and Zenger 2011: 348). Scripture's ultimate recipient of contempt is the suffering servant of Isaiah, who is "despised and rejected, a man of suffering acquainted with infirmity" (53:3). The church, of course, came to see this suffering servant as Jesus, the man of sorrows, who indeed had quite enough of contempt. And yet, remarkably, Jesus did not curse, but blessed, those who so treated him. This psalm names its opponents' contempt, and yet does so without belaboring the matter or promising revenge. The way of Jesus, which absorbs contempt rather than passing it on, meanders through this psalm.

Two reflections. One, Augustine has often been accused by modern critics of inflating the role of pride as a sin. But surely his elevation of pride to its status as our arch-vice can be defended with this psalm. It speaks of those at ease, contemptuous of those they scorn, and indeed they are proud (123:4). Two, the brief comparison of the Lord to a mistress keenly observed by a maid is a relatively rare yet straightforwardly feminine analogy for God (123:2).

The psalm is a "brief song, or rather a sigh" (Spurgeon 1976: 578). Martin Luther says its brevity points to something important about prayer, especially in the wake of the unending Ps. 119: we don't have to pray long to get God's attention, for "the force of prayer is not in many words" (quoted in Spurgeon 1976: 578).

PSALM 124

Somewhere between Pss. 123 and 124 God has answered a prayer. The prior psalm of ascent ended with scorn (123:4). Psalm 124 gives visceral voice to gratitude.

"Our thanksgiving needs a spur," Spurgeon said, and so the psalmist offers one by breaking the fourth wall: You! Look how lost we would be without the Lord (Spurgeon 1976: 580). The proposed list of historical references for this is nearly endless: The Assyrian invasion? The Babylonian exile? The rebuilding of the wall in Nehemiah? Perhaps the psalmist covers tracks because this is always true. Without the Lord on our side, we face disaster. One clear theological implication is that any victory by Israel is not due to its own skill but to the God who takes sides (Hossfeld and Zenger 2011: 355). Another, of course, is that God takes sides at all. God is not neutral, objective, or removed. God is unreservedly on the side of Israel, and God intervenes on behalf of the weak. This offends modern sensibilities in which we want to see ourselves at our best, and so too God in our image, as somehow unbiased (Reid, in Van Harn and Strawn 2009: 321). Another implication is that the danger we face is enormous. Chrysostom (1998: 157) points out that the devil was given just a little license to attack Job, and he wipes out his family, his health, his livelihood, every good thing in his life. It's dangerous out there. Finally this—the Lord's deliverance doesn't make for a life of ease. A parallel verse is Isa. 1:9, where the prophet says that without the Lord, Israel would have been like Sodom. As is, there is still a remnant. This is a severe deliverance indeed! Perhaps Augustine is right to see here the experience of the martyrs. This is not a deliverance *from* death but *through* it.

The NRSV's "when our enemies attacked us" (124:2) is laudably gender neutral, but the Hebrew says "when humanity (*adam*) rose up against us." Here the psalmist is already undoing the enemy's power. They are mere human beings, not gods, up against the power of the one true God who made heaven and earth (124:8).[1]

The ills averted are too terrible to contemplate: being eaten alive, burned, swept away by a flood, drowned (124:3–5). The first hints at the Babylonians, whose conquest indeed swallowed Israel alive (Nebuchadnezzar "swallowed me like a monster . . . [and] filled his belly with my delicacies," Jer. 51:34). Sheol itself is said to devour and fill its belly (Hossfeld and Zenger 2011: 356). The "raging" water could also be translated "boiling" (Reid, in Van Harn and Strawn 2009: 323). But the primary threat is to be washed away by a flood, with the image repeated for emphasis (124:4–5; Alter 2007: 433). Floods can be an image for a foreign military power overwhelming Israel (as in Isa. 8:7–8). But the floods can stretch back even further—past Noah even—to the primal chaos of the deep out of which God creates. As terrifying as an out-of-control flood is, it also points to God's creative saving work. God brought creation out of watery chaos. God brought his people out of slavery in Egypt through an impassable sea. The psalmist regularly recounts God's saving work as happening just before the water rises above the neck (e.g., Ps. 18:16, "he drew me out of the mighty waters"). Christians may perhaps be forgiven then for seeing an image of baptism here. The exodus is, for us, an image of the waters that drown our old person and birth the new one in Christ (1 Cor. 10:2). It is wise of the lectionary to pair this text with Jonah—the prophet who goes down into a watery grave, for whom the waters came up a good deal higher than the neck. Scripture's imagery for salvation through water goes beyond the last-second rescue into an impossible resurrection after death. Only a God who made creation in the first place could bring that about. Augustine thinks here of St. Peter's charge from God to "kill and eat" (Acts 10:13). The church doesn't eat people alive. It kills them first, and then eats them, makes them part of its body. The "killing" is baptism, and the body is the church (Augustine 2004: 46).

The image of raging water is not just terrifying. It is a reminder of salvation. High water subsides eventually (Chrysostom 1998: 159). Rage is brief. And it reminds us of God's creatively saving work. One of the legends of St. Francis has him say that when it rains, we should remember our baptism. Water is different now. It is a sign of the God who makes all things and then fills them all with reminders of God's saving work for us.

The psalmist blesses the Lord for not being given over to their teeth (124:6). But perhaps, as one commentator has it, we *were* given over into their *hands*

---

1. A point on which patristic commentators like Augustine and Chrysostom and modern ones are surprisingly in concert.

(Hossfeld and Zenger 2011: 356)! The water *was* up to and even over our necks. And as the next verse has it, we *were* in the snare (124:7). Yet we have escaped. This again emphasizes the depth of danger. The fowler knows how to lure prey (Spurgeon 1976: 582). The very fact that there is a trap laid suggests grave peril ("Does a bird fall into a snare on the earth, when there is no trap for it?" Amos 3:5). Historically this may suggest Babylon's conquest—and God's mighty deliverance of Israel back home and to peoplehood (Mays 1994: 397). Spiritually it suggests death. But we've seen what God can do with graves. Chrysostom's note is again instructive. He's nearly jubilant. The enemy is defeated: flat on his face, his weaponry shattered, his "power abolished, lodgings smashed, swords broken." We're only in danger at all if we sluggishly let ourselves go near an enemy bound, defenseless, weaponless, and toothless. And even then, we have the shield of faith, the sword of the Spirit, the cross in hand like a spear that won't bend, the nourishment of Christ's body and blood (Chrysostom 1998: 160).

For Augustine, now that we're free of the snare, we can make a din to keep other birds from falling into it. We can notice the bait set in the snare for us—the sweetness of life. And we can avoid it and warn others off from it.

The final note is one of doxology (124:8)—one that has fittingly found its way into worship in communities like Calvin's Geneva and monasteries in the Benedictine traditions (Mays 1994: 397). All these dangers—water, fire, snare, enemy armies—are undone by God. The maker of all things on earth and in heaven personally takes our side and is our helper, and we are right to praise.

PSALM 125

Some psalms, on their face, are not true. Barring an apocalypse.

Psalm 125, like much of the rest of scripture, promises vindication for the just and undoing for the wicked. The promises are impressive: to be like the holy mountain on which God's temple sits, never shaken. To be "sentineled" by the mountains round about Jerusalem (Spurgeon 1976: 583). The land will not just be unmoved—it'll not be unsettled (Alter 2007: 445). The problem is, the confidence in Zion's inviolability comes unraveled quickly. There *is* a scepter of wickedness on the land (125:3). Israel *has* been conquered in recent memory, Zion *is* shaken and unsettled, and the mountains did not protect the holy city (Alter 2007: 445). So whatever the psalm means, it can't mean what it seems to mean: that Israel cannot be conquered. There must be another Jerusalem to which this psalm refers (Gal. 4:26).[1] Or, as St. John Chrysostom says, those carried off into exile were not *actually* moved in the way that matters most: their virtue. Exile is not about zip codes. It is about proximity to God.

The psalm itself shakes simple confidence in its literal sense when it asks God to be good, to bring peace (125:4–5). The psalmist believes scripture's promises to vindicate the righteous but does not see their fruition. One common theme in the wisdom tradition in scripture is that the people should praise whatever its outward condition (Augustine 2004: 66). The word "allotted" (125:3) comes up in stories of Israel's tribes receiving their portion of the promised land (e.g., Num. 26:55). Inheritance also comes up in reference to unjust distribution of land in

---

1. It's Augustine's (2004: 58) point, somewhat spoiled by the anti-Jewish observation that there are now no Jews in the ruins of Jerusalem. In our day, over against him, there are blessedly so.

the prophets (Mic. 2:1–5). Christians think of the inheritance of the land for the meek, envisioned by Isaiah (57:13; 60:21; 65:9) and promised by Jesus, also not yet fulfilled (Matt. 5:5).[2]

God's list of unfulfilled promises is starting to stack up.

Both Sts. Augustine and John Chrysostom chide the wealthy people in their congregations for ignoring or looking down on the poor. Augustine laments that the rich never "stop there and at least reckon themselves human like the rest of us" (2004: 56)! Chrysostom calls the pursuit of a life of luxury for its own sake the "life of a worm" (1998: 164). This could be a case of turning the gospel into mere didactic moralism, but the psalm's final verses preserve us from that. The prayer in Ps. 125:4–5 is for God to deliver the righteous and to let the wicked go their own way.[3] In other words, it's for God to bring about the eschatological judgment that God promises. To listen to Jesus in, say, Matt. 25:31–46, we will be judged on our conduct toward the poor. These church fathers are helping their congregations get ready for that—which, arguably, is what preaching is for.

"Peace be upon Israel!" the psalmist prays (125:5). St. Paul likewise asks a blessing on "the Israel of God" at the end of a letter that has been a source of much of the church's anti-Judaism (Gal. 6:16). And indeed, one could see Jesus as leaning another direction than Ps. 125:1–2—for him, the temple will be thrown down, and great mountains can jump up and race into the sea (Mark 13:2; 11:23). For Paul, against Ps. 125:4, God is good to the *un*righteous (Rom. 4:5). Yet Paul blesses the same Israel that the psalmist does: Israel defeated, led away in exile, crushed, revived, birthing the Messiah, and yet mostly rejecting him. Israel ever protected by mountains and yet defeated; the church ever preached to by apostles (as Augustine glosses the mountains) and yet rejecting the gospel's full demands and promises.

There are no people except stubborn and stiff-necked ones like us. And there is no God except an endlessly merciful one. And for good people to be justified and the crooked led away, for there to be *anyone* on the side of the just, God is going to have to break in and make all things new.

Which is what God is promising to do. Which is a good thing, or else our praise would be full of lies.

---

2. Kraus 1993: 445 (though the point about not-yet fulfillment is mine).
3. Hossfeld and Zenger (2011: 267) point out there is asymmetry in the eschatological reward—the good are blessed with God's goodness, but the crooked are just left alone to go their own way.

PSALM 126

What is it like for a people to get what they most want, an end-of-the-world-sized desire fulfilled, and then not have history end?

Israel here remembers when God made good on divine promises and restored it from the grave, from Egypt, from exile (126:1–3). But now, more restoration is needed (126:4). Perhaps this is like contemporary South Africa, where a dream was realized with the ending of apartheid, but the story didn't end on that happy note. It is long, painstaking work to build a country. And a great deal more divine restoration work is needed.

The psalmist has layers and layers of biblical promise of restoration, direct from the mouths of the prophets (Jer. 29:14; Joel 3:1; Amos 9:13–15; Zeph. 2:7). The psalmist draws on a memory of God granting restoration, for Israel needs more of it (126:4–6). What it means to be a creature, a disciple, is to see God's past saving work and long for more of it—now, please. In biblical parlance, "those who dream" are those to whom God has made a promise, and made good on it (126:1; Gen. 37:5–11; Matt. 1:20–25).

But not yet, so Ps. 126 makes space for sorrow. The church with which I'm most familiar struggles with sorrow. Evangelical Protestants don't often draw on liturgical resources from Christ as the man of sorrows, acquainted with grief. We often try to engineer cheerfulness at every turn. Find me a praise chorus suitable for Lent—there aren't an abundance. And just so we've violated one tenet of what it means to be evangelical: we're not biblical. The psalms lament at every turn. Orthodox Christians speak of Lent, for example, as a "bright sadness." There is sorrow, to be sure. And there is coming glory. But the glory is not yet. Those with any practice in spirituality speak of the need for effort, sweat, tears: "God has made this way narrow and constrained," as St. John Chrysostom put it (1998: 170). Jesus himself blessed those who weep (Matt. 5:4). It is especially difficult to plant seeds in the ground that could feed one's hungry family now (Ps. 126:5–6). It is a wager on a future that will be abundant. But that future is not yet. This is a Holy Saturday psalm. It is in a place of sorrow. We remember divine trustworthiness. We just don't see it yet.

Many of Israel's neighbors had religious traditions around sowing and harvesting seed. To plant is to play undertaker, ushering a divinity into the underworld; to reap is to welcome that deity back.[1] There is a sort of divine power in seeds' death and rebirth—our ongoing life depends on it. Confessional Christian theology sometimes avoids these sorts of religious parallels. They could be seen to suggest that somehow paganism is original and Christianity only derivative. We should not fear. God is not stingy with signs of divine presence. God has left traces of God's self throughout creation, planting everywhere the longing for God that makes us human. Missionaries often felt they had to stamp out receiving people's religious practices for them to become Christian, with disastrous and sometimes genocidal results.[2] We need not have. Stories of death and rebirth, the fragile cycle of life and death and subsequent gratitude, are themselves witnesses to the gospel. Sometimes faint witnesses indeed! But if scripture could draw on other peoples' stories, so too can the church. They can be, as Justin Martyr said of Greek wisdom, like the Old Testament, witnessing in advance, sometimes unawares, often in need of correction, but always deserving of respect. Pious interpreters hear of sheaves and think of the story of Joseph, whose sheaves bowed down in a foreshadowing of Christ's reign (Gen. 37:5–8; Spurgeon 1976: 589). That is an obscure, but not ridiculous, reading. We should hunt for more, and more widely.

The psalm imagines laughter (126:2, 6). The desolation of current hunger is a sharp contrast to the promise of coming abundance. The prophet Amos imagines the harvester overtaking the sower. It's a joke—of the best sort, telling a truth we can't get at in normal speech. The greatest joke there is, is that a crucified Jew rules the cosmos. Those in on the knowledge rejoice. Those not must see it as grotesque or ridiculous. But they will eventually look on with admiration, even joy (126:2).

St. Papias in the ancient church spoke of an eschatological harvest of grapes: "The days will come in which vines shall grow, having each ten thousand branches

1. Harrelson 2003: 874; Kraus 1993: 449; Mays 1994: 399. Alter calls the interpretation "strained" (2007: 447).

2. I am drawing here on the history recounted in my colleague Ray Aldred's doctoral dissertation, "An Alternative Starting Place for an Indigenous Theology" (ThD diss., Wycliffe College, forthcoming), which offers Cree First Nation resources for a richer Christian anthropology.

and in each branch ten thousand twigs, and in each true twig ten thousand shoots, and in every one of the shoots ten thousand clusters, and on every one of the clusters ten thousand grapes, and every grape when pressed will give five-and-twenty metretes of wine."[3] A metrete is nine gallons. My calculator went on strike, refusing to calculate the amount of wine from each vine. It's supposed to be funny, joyous, beyond abundance, beyond imagination.

This moment in salvation history is like the blind man when he is partially healed by Jesus (Mark 8:23–24). He can see people, but they are like trees, shambling around. A fuller healing is yet to come. Its certainty is shown by the prior one. But our frustration is that the second, complete healing is not yet. It is coming. In the meantime, pray. And try to restrain that laughter, just a bit.

3. Papias, *Fragments* 4, in *The Ante-Nicene Fathers: Translations of the Writings of the Fathers down to A.D. 325*, ed. Alexander Roberts and James Donaldson (1885–1887; repr., Peabody, MA: Hendrickson, 1994), 1:153.

PSALM 127

My first financial advisor instructed me that the goal was to have my money make money "while you sleep." She was right about how to win at capitalism. The psalmist also has advice about what sleep means—it is a sign of God's faithfulness (127:2). We sleep some one-third of our lives. God apparently doesn't need our toil to direct the wise ordering of the cosmos.

The pilgrim ascending to Zion prays here for the household, the city, the family. Over against our age's spiritual individualism, there is no "me" except the one nestled in these relationships.

Psalm 127 has two distinct halves, perhaps originally separate (Hermann Gunkel, in Kraus 1993: 453). The second seems nearly atheistic—a proverb with no god (127:3–5). But these are all areas of life on which we spend most of our toil and so our worry, our prayer—the house and our work. And in both cases the psalm leans against the assumption that success is entirely dependent on our efforts (127:2; Limburg 2000: 438). These are parts of our lives we can treat atheistically, as if by our efforts alone the city will be built, the children born and raised well. The psalm says no. It assumes our contribution of work. But God's work is more important still.

The attribution to Solomon evokes the temple to which pilgrims ascend. It also calls to mind the scriptures' long tradition of wisdom. Wisdom is the blueprint according to which God makes the universe, the temple, the structures that govern our lives.[1] Christians see this wisdom as the Logos fleshed in Christ, who is the

---

1. Raymond Van Leeuwen, in Van Harn and Strawn 2009: 330, citing Prov. 3:19–20; 24:3–4; Exod. 31:1–3; 1 Kgs. 7:13–14.

pattern by which God makes everything there is (John 1). God's provision for his "beloved" in 127:2 is, as with the rest of the psalm, a reference to all Israel, not just the individual (Pss. 60:5; 108:6; Jer. 11:15). The Song of Solomon shows most vividly the way God delights in his beloved. The reference to sleep (Ps. 127:2) recalls for one of Spurgeon's interpreters the sleep of Adam during which God *provided* Eve (Gen. 2). Christians have long seen a figure here for the church's birth from the side of the dead Christ: so God "formed for Him, in His death . . . the church, the spiritual Eve, the Mother of all living; and gave her to Him as His bride." God gives the church when we aren't even there. Jesus is hardly *there* in death. When Christ sleeps, like Adam before him, God draws delight from his side, like a surgeon from an anesthetized patient (Spurgeon 1976: 592, drawing on Christopher Wordsworth).

The second part of Ps. 127 immediately alarms anyone with pastoral instincts. What of those who desperately want children? Are they somehow cursed by God, as they often report feeling? Perhaps we should not be so quick to apologize for the scripture. Children *are* indeed a blessing from God. But they are not a replacement *for* God. Having muscle at Israel's courtroom—the gate—is not the way to procure justice (127:5). Faithfulness is. Scripture is well aware that children can turn out badly and seem to be a curse even. The "children" here can be the virtues that all of us must bring to birth. Some evangelicals have taken verses like Ps. 127:3 as a reason to have as many physical children as possible. This is, indeed, a delight— who could argue? Yet it is not the case that those with the most children are most blessed, those without most cursed. Vowed religious have shown us otherwise. We can say this: children both physical and spiritual are a gift from God (127:3). The latter sort are especially helpful for bringing about the justice God longs for (127:5). And as we ascend and pray over family and work, we are told that their blessing comes from God alone—not from the effort we so strenuously put forth as we rise early, worry, climb the mountain, or try to reproduce and parent. God's way is uncertain, mysterious. But ultimately very, very good.

PSALM 128

As we continue to ascend this pilgrim psalter, we have to ask—have we taken a wrong turn? This psalm seeks the blessings of long life, children and children's children, a happy home, fruitful work, and the leisure to enjoy it.

Was Jesus of Nazareth then not a recipient of the Lord's blessings?

The promise is one of a domestic idyll (Alter 2007: 451). The table is full with the fruit of one's own hands. The blessed ones are also "happy" with what every human being wants, but which is often elusive. The Lord is the secret to happiness: "All the springs of happiness are in him. . . . It is his love gives a relish to all we taste, puts life and sweetness into all" (John Wesley, quoted in Spurgeon 1976: 595). The happy man's wife imaged as a vine recalls the pleasures of the Song of Songs, where the lovers meet beneath a fruitful vine (Song 7:12). The image can also suggest Israel itself, a vine brought out of Egypt, planted by God and towering over all others (Ps. 80). Domestic bliss includes children as plentiful as olive shoots, which have shoots of their own (128:6). God's gifts are shown here as two of Israel's traditional festal fruits: the grapevine and the olive plant (only poor figs left out!) (Hossfeld and Zenger 2011: 403). The overflowing table with family outnumbering the seats is a marvelous image for the home, and also for the church—the household of God.

As often in these ascent psalms, universal wisdom motifs are intertwined with Zion's specificity. The psalmist's good is bound up with Jerusalem's good (128:5). The prosperity gospel has seized on psalms like this, excising their specificity, to identify material blessings simply as God's favor.[1] If so, the Ferrari driver who pulled up beside my bicycle yesterday must be holier than any saint. But material blessings and holiness do not always come in tandem and often compete instead. Both in the ancient world and today, the holiest people's tables are often empty, their seats unoccupied by lost loved ones, their prayers of mourning prayed before meager meals.

What do we make of the psalm's extravagant blessings promised here?

First, we should let them stand. Every gift named here is indeed a blessing. Psalm 128:6 is appropriately and often used in wedding liturgies.[2] Even with proper pastoral concern that those without these gifts not imagine themselves cursed by God, we should name blessings for what they are and give thanks.

The prayer of blessing for children's children calls to mind a story about the Camp David peace accords worked out between Jimmy Carter, Anwar Sadat, and Menachem Begin. The talks nearly failed entirely. As the Israeli and Egyptian heads of state prepared to leave, Carter showed each leader photos of the other's grandchildren. He had asked for them beforehand for precisely this eventuality. As the men looked at the young faces of the grandchildren of their "enemy," they surrendered anger and agreed to go back to talks. They courageously made peace, and the world was blessed—because of a glimpse of the "children's children" of the other (128:6).[3]

Second, we must read all scripture in its broader canonical context. Jesus is the heart of the scriptures, and he received few of these blessings. The martyrs are the first readers of scripture, and they lost whatever of these blessings that they had. Christian priests, monks, and nuns foreswear many of these blessings (though not all). There are ways to read the blessings allegorically. The vine is Israel. The bride is the church; the bridegroom is Christ. The fruit of the vine is the Eucharist's wine; the fruit of the olive is the chrism that signals Christ's anointing and our baptisms. Children are the good works of faith; children's children are the fruit of those works.[4]

We should also let the text's literal sense stand. Fruitful labor, happiness, and a full house are all blessings. So is the church, imagined through these symbols. And yet the martyrs give up these genuine blessings for even greater blessings: a death

---

1. See Kate Bowler, *Blessed: A History of the American Prosperity Gospel* (New York: Oxford University Press, 2013).

2. Zenger suggests that might have been its origin (Hossfeld and Zenger 2011: 399).

3. Rabbi Dr. Gopin, director of the Center for World Religions, Diplomacy, and Conflict Resolution at George Mason University, told this story on a visit to the Vancouver School of Theology in May 2016.

4. The final reading is Augustine's (2004: 115).

that imitates the Lord's, even greater fruitfulness through prayer and sacrifice. Jesus fleshes this psalm most fully with his beloved wife, the church, his blessings that flow to the Gentile world from Zion, his countless spiritual progeny. Peace be upon Israel according to the flesh and Israel extended to include those who trust in Christ. There are multiple "ways" to walk with him—not just one (128:1).

PSALM 129

At a distance, the psalms blur together. But the closer you look, the more you see how unique each psalm is. For example, Ps. 129 has elements that are common elsewhere—a dash of Israel's history, a curse on its enemies. But it is hardly a prayer at all.[1] God is not addressed, or even really thanked for the history of deliverance in 129:1–4. The psalm is nearly unique in our last third of the Psalter for having even a soupçon of imprecation—the psalms get most of their cursing done early (though Ps. 137 is yet to come). One strong motif here unites the whole: that of plowing. The theological theme of God's own justice is propped up with two supports: a history of delivering Israel (129:1–4) and the observation that evil is its own dismal reward (129:5–8).

As in Ps. 124, here the psalmist repeats the opening line, as though to make sure of having the congregation's attention. The "I" is an individual speaker, and yet is also all of Israel—a certain "layering" of the first person is a common theme in the psalms. And the youth referred to is not likely any single individual but the whole people of God. Israel has been attacked by countless enemies, foundationally Egypt, but many more up to the present day. Midian in particular is remembered for making raids at harvest time that impoverish the people (Judg. 6:2–6), so that God's deliverance from the Midianites is especially praiseworthy (Isa. 9:3–4). The nearly unending list of hostile foes has not prevailed (Ps. 129:2). Rabbi Jonathan Sacks argues that empires tend to want to be rid of Jews because Jews abide by another set of laws and worship another Lawgiver. Jews signify difference; tyrants

---

1. I owe these observations to Zenger (Hossfeld and Zenger 2011: 408).

who seek uniformity would prefer not to have it. Yet those empires, from Egypt to the Nazis, are gone. And who is still there?

That failure is not for lack of trying. The image is of a plow grinding not through topsoil and humus and bumping the occasional rock but through the flesh of human backs. And these plowmen go all the way to the end of the field, to maximize their yield (129:3). When most oppressed, the Israelites themselves are treated like draft animals. That's bad enough, but here they are treated like dirt, with soft flesh flayed open. But God himself has cut the cord of the plowman, rendering the plow useless, and setting free those under the oppressor's yoke (129:4). This is a common biblical image for foreign oppression or even one's own tyrannical king (Lev. 26:3; Deut. 28:48; 1 Kgs. 12:3–4). God's delivery is forceful, with a chopping motion like that which severs limbs of enemies. The hope of Ps. 129:5 is also couched in military terms—as those put to shame and turned backward are enemies defeated in battle.[2]

"The history of Israel is one single passion narrative," Kraus says of this psalm and of the whole Bible (1993: 462). The only blessings God has to give are cross-shaped. God will be with his beloved people. And enemies will assail—often successfully. And God will show God's delivering character again. St. Augustine draws from this biblical theme of constant trouble and deliverance for his doctrine of the church. The church is always full of good and bad people, and should never try not to be. God will deliver eventually. In the meantime, the church will carry the bad people—all of us, that is—on its back (as his version of 129:3 has it). John Chrysostom is relatively quiet on this theme—enough so that his translator and editor on this psalm wishes he would pay attention to the mixed moral character of the church (1998: 190)! Israel's enemies have always been both external and internal. So have the church's. And the Lord is the one who breaks the yoke and turns them back in shame—in God's own time.

Haters of Zion are, the psalmist hopes, to be like grass in the roof that sprouts up and withers quickly. No harvest is needed or possible here. The weeds need not even be pulled—they will just blow away (as I write, I see the weeds in my neighbor's gutter—and wonder what lurks in my own!). Evil is insubstantial. It is ugly, but it is not lasting, and to choose it is to become nothing, as it is. Grass on roofs is conspicuous, easy to see, and so a good sign for vanity and rootlessness. A crop planted in a field is deeply rooted—an association for charity in St. Augustine's mind (2004: 124). Another church father, Cassiodorus, says the grass

---

2. It is hard to see a sentence in this paragraph not thoroughly indebted to Zenger's remarkable commentary (Hossfeld and Zenger 2011: 408–18).

should have been humbly planted in the humus, and it would have grown strong (*Expositions of the Psalms* 128.6, in Wesselschmidt 2007: 359).

The ultimate curse pronounced here is not to be included in the exchange of blessing at harvest time. As workers gather in the fruit of their hands (Ps. 128:2), they sing out in liturgical greeting, blessing one another. We see this in the Ruth: "Just then Boaz came from Bethlehem. He said to the reapers, 'The LORD be with you.' They answered, 'The LORD bless you'" (Ruth 2:4). To love Zion is to take part in its blessings, from hard work with the plow in rich soil and a bountiful yield all the way up the ascent to blessing one another in the name of the Lord who gives soil and plow and seed and yield and steps to ascend and Zion and the whole world.

If the history of Israel is one great passion narrative, then the creativity of God is one great resurrection. As much as the aggressors may plow Israel's backs, God simply brings good fruit out of their harm. Likewise, the church is only "increased by the losses it sustains," Cassiodorus says (*Expositions of the Psalms* 128.2, in Wesselschmidt 2007: 360). These are the perfect biblical curses. They simply say what is. Evil disintegrates on its own. And the ultimate evil is not to participate in the exchange of blessings between God's people. The ultimate good is to bless one another in the name of the God of Zion. Attackers meant their violent work with the plow simply to destroy. Instead it has born much fruit. All things cannot help but bear witness to God eventually: good by its lively creativity and power; evil by its futility and frailty; we creatures by praising this God with psalms like this.

PSALM 130

I can't think of Ps. 130 without singing it. This is because of two sung versions, neither widely famous. One is by Chris Miner and is well known in some campus ministries and based on Martin Luther's translation. The other is by Charles Pettee and FolkPsalm, who set the psalms to bluegrass. Both illustrate how song and scripture work. I needed each mournful song at a different sad period of my life. Now I sing the songs as a sort of memorial to when I was in the depths and God met me there through these communities of song.

There's a lot of "me" and "my" in that paragraph. Blame the psalmist. The psalmist's capacious "I" often succeeds in drawing its singers in.

The psalmist is in the depths—a place of dire danger. Yet it can't be a place of death quite yet, since the dead cannot praise.[1] The depths conjure fear of praiseless Sheol, and even the mythic chaos out of which God summoned creation (Hossfeld and Zenger 2011: 428, citing Ps. 88:4–7). Yet the waters are also a memorial of God's prior creating and saving work: "Was it not you who dried up the sea . . . ?" (Isa. 51:10). Spurgeon (1976: 600) remembers the ancestors who plunge into the depths—Joseph in the well, Daniel in the den, the three Hebrews in the furnace, Jonah in the fish. That theme could yield a theology of optimism—"whatever doesn't kill you makes you stronger," as the cheerful saying misquotes Nietzsche. But for Christians, all these images conjure Jesus's tomb. He didn't escape death. Its depths consumed him.

The genre here is elusive. The psalmist doesn't blame anyone or even ask for anything. Instead the psalmist seems to wait (130:5–6). It is an ascent psalm,

---

1. Alter calls Ps. 130:1 an "image of the realm of death" (2007: 445).

though it begins with descent. The prior psalm attended to Israel's vulnerability before its enemies; this one attends instead to Israel's "moral fragility" (Van Harn and Strawn 2009: 336). Augustine (2004: 127) says humanity could fall on its own but cannot save itself on its own. There is a reason Ps. 130 has been ranked since ancient times as one of the seven great penitential psalms of the church (with Pss. 6, 32, 38, 51, 102, and 143). Martin Luther called it the whole of the gospel, and it inspired John Wesley the day before his Aldersgate conversion experience.[2]

The psalm neither lauds nor encourages any initiative or agency on our own (130:5–6). All we do is wait and pray. The psalmist reaches for God's "ears" (130:2), implying that God does not seem to be listening at the moment (Limburg 2000: 446). From a neighboring culture, Egyptian artists often render the human ear as a sign that prayers are being heard—one stela from Memphis portrays 376 such ears (Hossfeld and Zenger 2011: 429). The psalmist asks for one or two. And then the psalmist implicitly hopes they'll be occasionally blocked (130:3–4). If God remembers sins, who can stand? Anne Lamott satirizes the common conception of God as a cranky principal in a school, fussily searching our files to see what we've done wrong this time.[3] A Christian doctrine of original sin holds that Christ's saving work is so magnificent that our prior predicament must have been dire indeed (Rom. 3:3, 23). The universality of sin is not only a New Testament idea: Job hits this theme often (4:17; 15:14; 25:4), and the historical books echo it (1 Kgs. 8:46; Ezra 9:9–15). Psalm 130:3 puts it more poetically: Who can stand before God?

Yet God's very nature is unending mercy. Prayer is a matter of "reminding" God to be again who God eternally is. The psalmist doesn't claim innocence or even ask for mercy or claim it for himself. The psalmist is barely there in 130:3–4. God is the one who has both the authority and the disposition to forgive (Mays 1994: 406). So then the Lord should be feared. Some interpreters see this as a sort of appeal to divine vanity—God "has to" forgive so there'll still be a people who fear. That theme resounds in other passages but seems a stretch here. I see instead an echo of the wisdom theme of fear of the Lord as the beginning of wisdom, and the ethical theme that meeting the true God yields ethical action—a people who live in fear of the Lord—in the world (Hossfeld and Zenger 2011: 435–36).

The next verses (130:5–6) repeat the psalmist's admonition to "watch" and "wait" for the Lord several different ways. Scripture often sees God's people

---

2. All from Mays 1994: 405. Luther says of the psalm that it is one of "the most precious and important psalms because it deals with justification, that article of faith of which it can truly be said: if you stand, the church stands; if you fall, the church falls!" (in Hossfeld and Zenger 2011: 442).

3. Anne Lamott, *Bird by Bird: Some Instructions on Writing and Life* (New York: Pantheon, 1994), 30.

reminding themselves and teaching others to wait and hope (Pss. 27:14; 31:24; Isa. 8:17; 25:9; 26:8; 33:2; 40:31; 49:23; 60:9). Watchers seek the first light of the dawn and the end of their sleepy vigilance. And in scripture hope often comes in the morning (Hossfeld and Zenger 2011: 436). Augustine (2004: 135) interprets this in light of the resurrection, which the gospels place first thing in the morning. The church is now perched on the edge of its seat, watching for the first glimpse of the dawn of the general resurrection and God's renewal of all creation. Waiting is a surprisingly pacific stance for one caught in the depths. Those close to death more ordinarily thrash about, desperate to survive. The psalm says in several different ways: Don't do something. Just stand there. The Lord will act.

And that action is always redeeming. By the final verses of the psalm, the "I cry" with which we began has been subsumed into the "O Israel, hope in the LORD!" of the gathered community in 130:7–8 (Limburg 2000: 449). Zenger hears an echo of the psalm in Matthew's Gospel (2011: 441). Jesus's very name is explained to Mary this way: "he will save his people from their sins" (1:21). The language recurs in Jesus's institution of the Lord's Supper: "for this is my blood of the covenant, which is poured out for many for the forgiveness of sins" (26:28). Jesus is Israel incarnate—the one in the depths of Sheol who is miraculously raised and admonishes the rest of us to wait for his coming, when he will save all people and transfigure the world.

Those who pray these psalms ought never again to be afraid of the depths. They're where God does his best saving work.

PSALM 131

Interpreters compete with one another to praise this psalm. It is "a pearl in the psalter." "A sigh." "The loveliest little whole lyric composition we have received."[1] It is the second-shortest psalm, after 117. And yet, as Spurgeon says, its few words take a lifetime to learn.

Psalms of lament often begin with trust before their complaints. Here the note of trust has become the whole (Limburg 2000: 450). Three times the psalmist foreswears great things. This is surprising, since God is the one who works marvels. So our talk of God is necessarily taken up with things too great for us (131:1)![2] There is here a refusal of ambition for what is greater than God intends for us (Jer. 45:5) (Van Harn and Strawn 2009: 338). The psalmist is in the position of Job, having come face-to-face with a God whose wonders we can't fathom (Hossfeld and Zenger 2011: 450). In the New Testament, Jesus will bless this posture and call it "meekness" (Matt. 5:5). Christian tradition has long equated pride with the apex of sin. Our culture has reversed that entirely, making it a positive virtue. And over against such desperate grasping for significance, "I acquire, therefore I am," Jesus commends a child. The little one's eyes are not too high—except to look to his mother.[3]

---

1. The references are all from Zenger: "exegetes as a rule accord it the highest praise" (Hossfeld and Zenger 2011: 446).
2. I base this on Ross Wagner's commentary in Van Harn and Strawn 2009: 337–40. See here Exod. 3:20; Deut. 10:21; Jer. 32:17.
3. These last few lines borrow from Eugene Peterson's marvelous sermon "My Eyes Are Not Raised Too High," in *A Chorus of Witnesses*, ed. Thomas G. Long and Cornelius Plantinga Jr. (Grand Rapids: Eerdmans, 1994), 179–88.

Contemporary liberal interpreters often appreciate this psalm's maternal imagery for God, which is nearly unique in the Psalter (131:2). There is some linguistic ambiguity as to whether the psalmist is like a nursing child with its mother or a weaned child. If the former, the image is one of intimacy, dependence, and contentment. If the latter, the image is one of having grown up a bit, not throwing a tantrum for what one doesn't have, and being with the mother for her own sake rather than for the meeting of needs.[4] Either way, God is imaged in feminine terms, with believers portrayed as childlike (Matt. 18:3). Peterson points to the necessity of growing up, of not needing to rush back to mom for reassurance at every moment, of the child knowing it is loved and moving toward maturity—as believers must do.[5]

The final verse (131:3) reminds us of 130:7 as its speaker turns toward all Israel and implores us to wait on the Lord forever. In this portion of the Psalter, the ascending pilgrims are about to enter the temple (Ps. 132). As we do, our soul is entirely contented, like the child still with milk on her lips. There is no playing or protesting or pleading (Kraus 1993: 471). Just contentment with our Mother and even with ourselves. And a wish for that same contentment for Israel and all flesh.

4. Most interpreters think linguistically the terms favor "weaned," though Zenger has arguments for "nursing" (Hossfeld and Zenger 2011: 448).
5. Peterson, "My Eyes Are Not Raised."

PSALM 132

The psalms of ascent are not usually this long. And they do not usually focus this extensively on the person of David or the place of Zion. "Remember," the psalmist instructs, as if God could forget (132:1). But of course asking God to remember is a way of asking God to summon up the same sort of power anew. The *Jewish Study Bible* notes the psalmist's hope that retelling the events of Zion's establishment will "foreshadow the replaying" of those events in the rebuilding of the temple and reestablishment of the monarchy (Berlin and Brettler 2014: 1419). Kraus (1993: 472) has tried to remember in a different way—insisting that historically this psalm originates in a "royal festival of Zion," re-creating the discovery of the ark in Kiriath-Jearim and processing it anew into the temple to renew the people's worship. Other scholars are less sure we can re-create the prehistory so precisely. Such historical-critical re-creation is itself a way of creatively remembering—trying to piece back together from shreds of evidence what "actually happened." Both Israel and the church do something similar in our regular worship of the God of Israel. But we don't usually concentrate on filling in gaps in the historical record—our knowledge is not antiquarian alone. We try to engineer anew the encounter with God attested to in the text and promised when God meets God's people in worship.

This memory of the worship at Zion is a little unconventional. Solomon is the builder of the temple, but he goes unmentioned here. The origins of the temple are attributed entirely to David—to the point of filling in an oath from David's lips nowhere else recorded in scripture (132:3–5). God is asked specifically to remember David's "hardships"—a word with connotations that include misery, being bowed down, and suffering (Hossfeld and Zenger 2011: 460). Spurgeon

(1976: 607) notes that the psalm starts with affliction and ends with a crown (132:18)—like the life of discipleship generally. The hardships could refer to David's "tireless zeal," with which he prepared for the temple's building (1 Chr. 22:14 describes the "millions" of talents of precious metals and building material he gathered) (Ross Wagner, in Van Harn and Strawn 2009: 340). The translation of *unnot* in front of St. Augustine (2004: 155) is *mansuetudo*, which can mean weakness, humility, gentleness, forbearance. David, Israel's greatest conquering king, actually rules during hardship, suffering. The New Testament learned well to hymn a king who reigns by suffering (Phil. 2:6–11; Mays 1994: 412).

The rest of the psalm consists of mutual vows made by David and by God. We don't ordinarily get this clear of a response to prayer as we do in 132:11–18! The psalmist asks that God remember Zion for David's sake, and God promises to do just that. Jesus, of course, has harsh things to say about making vows (Matt. 5:33–37). And yet Jesus's people, among others, still do so—especially at places like weddings, ordinations, baptisms. We might take the psalm as a model for how to pray generally. Other accounts of the origin of the temple start with David's initiative but then minimize his role in its construction—God is the builder, not David. David is a man of war, so his son will build the house instead (1 Chr. 22:8; 28:3). But there is no disparagement of David in this psalm. David's passionate, intense promise is held out before God: Couldn't God show a little passionate intensity in return?

David's vow in 132:3–5 is, of course, a figure of speech, "just" a way of saying the temple is important to him. But of course in scripture nothing is "just" anything. Israel is that odd people for whom a house for the Lord is more important than a house for the king. St. Augustine, the champion of the sort of allegory we've been employing in this commentary, reads the verses more literally than any modern interpreter I've found. For him David's vow is a condemnation of private property. The apostolic church had power when the first believers held all their material possessions in common. Augustine's parishioners won't do it. They have children for whom to provide. He asks aloud why we're surprised our gospel lacks power (Augustine 2004: 159). A vow of dubious historicity, haggled over as a sign of postexilic liturgy for this or that invested party, leaps off the page and into our faces: Is the state of God's house more important to us than our own family's comfort?

The speakers in the psalm heard about the ark in Ephrathah—that is, Bethlehem (Gen. 35:19; 48:7; Mic. 5:2). Jaar is in Kiriath-Jearim, west of Jerusalem, where the ark was with Israel's enemies for two sorrowful decades (1 Sam. 7:1–2). But then David retrieved it and restored it to Jerusalem, amidst singing and dancing and general celebration (2 Sam. 6–7). And now, the psalmist exhorts, let us go and do likewise. "Rise up," the petition in 132:8, reminds us of the ark's status as a sacred sign under which the Israelites marched into war. And yet the verse immediately undercuts any bellicose purpose as it asks God to rise up . . . and go to a resting place (132:8). This is no procession to battle—it is a procession to praise. The priests' clothes are ones of righteousness, not armor; and the shouts are those not of violence but of joy (132:9).

The petition of 132:8–10 is repeated verbatim in 2 Chr. 6:40–42. Solomon's prayer there shows his dedication of the temple to be, in the Chronicler's view, a faithful fulfillment of Psalm 132's prayer. Heaven agrees, as fire falls and consumes the burnt offering and sacrifices (2 Chr. 7:1). "Rise up, O LORD, and go to your dwelling place" is a perfect psalm verse for the feast of Christ's ascension, when God indeed went up—physically enough to make even the staunchest literalist a little uncomfortable (Acts 1:9). We pilgrims go up because God already has. Even a cursory reading of these verses shows the chief problem with most of our Sunday assemblies: they're boring. Perhaps we have lost what the psalmist takes for granted: God is dwelling with his people (132:13–14). The one praying hopes for a renewed monarchy and restored temple worship (132:8–9).

But do we hope for much of anything from God as we pray?

The ark was a physical instantiation of God's presence. Its mobility befitted a nomadic people, before the building of the temple, the restoration of which this psalmist seeks. Some Christians have seen in the ark a sign of the indwelling of God in Christ.[1] Others, more promisingly to my mind, see it as a sign of the Virgin Mary—an empty space in which God deigns to dwell by grace. The ark is also a sign of the fearsomeness of a God in physical space—conquering enemies, killing even allies who approach the wrong way (poor Uzzah! 2 Sam. 6:3–7). These typologies can sit lightly—no single one has to be chosen at the expense of the others. The ark and the temple are physical places where God dwells with his people. God will dwell most fully with his people through his Son—whom we can't even imagine without these prior images. But a people of the incarnation will delight in the specificity here: God's desire for a *place*. This is no abstraction or idea being worshiped. It is a God with an address. Mount Zion is where God lives.

Most of us don't notice an explicit, detailed response from God when we pray. Psalm 132:11–18 offers one to the prayer of 132:1–10. The Lord responds precisely

---

1. Augustine refers to "another interpretation proposed by some," whom Maria Boulding identifies as Hilary of Poitiers (2004: 165).

to the prayed vow of 132:3–5 (Hossfeld and Zenger 2011: 463). A son of David's body will continue on the throne (132:11; Augustine's translation says "a son from David's womb"!)—*if* his descendants keep the covenant and its decrees. The hinge of the psalm is highly conditional: if. Any reader of the Bible knows that the kings after David (and indeed including David) kept the covenant minimally at best. They're a rogue's gallery of miserable rulers. Readers of the Bible know the rest of the story to which the psalmist alludes: they do not keep the covenant, and the monarchy comes to an end. The "if" is thrown into the lap of those praying the psalm: if *they*, or really *we*, keep the covenant, God will restore a monarch with a seat in Zion's temple. But of course previous peoples who heard that "if" did no such thing.

The "if" sits poorly with the rest of the psalm. God promises a throne in Zion "forever" (132:12, 14). It will be God's resting place, for he has "desired" it (132:14). God *hungers* for Israel. He longs for Israel. In light of such a devouring love for his people, can the sins of Israel's kings really undo God's eternal promise of devotion?[2] The "if" suggests a desire to see Israel live in the way outlined in God's law. But God's strong affection and devotion here and elsewhere in scripture undercut the "if." "Forever" has no conditions on it. A people grafted into Israel in Christ hang on by the strength of this "forever."

The Lord's effusion of love for Israel is the heart of the second vow, 132:13–18. God's hunger and thirst for Israel will yield the fruit of bread for the hungry (132:15). We live in a time when the word "blessing" has become nearly synonymous with material provision. The psalm makes a similar equation, only this is provision by God for the poor, not for those who already have enough. The restoration of Zion envisioned here sees a table spread and enough to eat for everyone. Unlike some psalms about Zion and worship in the temple, the emphasis here is not on the offerings being brought to God. Rather, it is on God, who is the generous host, and on those most vulnerable, who are the most blessed (!) guests (132:15). The Lord promises to vest priests with salvation—just as the priests and people were vested with salvation when the ark made its procession back to the temple in David's day (132:9, 16 are nearly perfectly parallel). And the Lord will clothe Israel's enemies with disgrace (132:18). The image is of a divine clothier dispensing glorious raiment for his people and doleful ones for their enemies.[3] The New Testament too

2. Ross Wagner also argues for the unconditional nature of the covenant vow of the Lord in this psalm (Van Harn and Strawn 2009: 340). See also Ps. 78:68, "he chose the tribe of Judah, Mount Zion, which he loves," and 87:2, "the LORD loves the gates of Zion more than all the dwellings of Jacob."

3. Lauren Winner has made the biblical image unforgettable with her *Wearing God: Clothing, Laughter, Fire, and Other Overlooked Ways of Meeting God* (New York: HarperOne, 2016).

speaks of God's provision of clothing. Baptism is a matter of "putting on" Christ, and so joining those who shout praises (Gal. 3:27; Rom. 13:14).

Three royal images conclude the psalm—a horn, a lamp, and a crown. First a horn, which will sprout up for David (132:17). It is a sign of power, a restoration of might. But horns don't start out that way. J. G. Wood imagines the smooth head on a young stag that becomes two lumps that soon become a magnificent display of antlers (in Spurgeon 1976: 611). The horn signals power but also patience. Second, God has prepared a lamp for the anointed one, on whom God will not turn back (132:10). As in Kings, where God will preserve one tribe, Judah, despite the desecrations of King Jeroboam and others like him, so here God lights a lamp that will not go out (1 Kgs. 11:36; Hossfeld and Zenger 2011: 467). And finally, the gleaming crown (132:18). Spurgeon notes that the psalm begins in affliction and ends with a crown, like our lives. A more literal translation would have that crown "bloom" rather than "gleam." Eschatological images of restoration often involve a branch growing out of the stump of Israel, life to a tree once cut off, now grown glorious.[4]

It is striking how easily Christians use words like "messiah," "king," or even "Christ" without attention to the matrix from which these words are born. The Bible's prototypical king obsesses over the health of God's house and the worship therein (132:3–5). He leads the procession of God's very presence from faraway places back home (132:6–10). The king's strength is rooted in God's frighteningly committed passion for Israel (132:13–16). And God, the true King of Israel, distributes to the poor generously, unendingly. The New Testament connects such messianic scriptures to Jesus's reign (Acts 2:30–32; 7:46). The church has often negatively contrasted this rule with that of Israel's kings—as if Israel has to be without monarch or temple for Christ to be our king and temple. But we would do better to find ourselves in the position of Ps. 132: longing for a monarch and for liturgy that are not yet here in full.

---

4. Wagner in Van Harn and Strawn 2009: 342, citing Isa. 11:1 ("a shoot shall come out from the stump of Jesse, and a branch shall grow out of his roots"), Isa. 4:2 ("the branch of the Lord shall be beautiful and glorious"), Jer. 23:5 ("I will raise up for David a righteous branch, and he shall reign as king"), and Jer. 33:15 ("I will cause a righteous branch to spring up for David, and he shall execute justice").

PSALM 133

A friend of mine says that whenever a church's name has a word like "united" in it, watch out: it means the members are mean, and they tried to make nice at some point. Don't believe them. The unity of which the scriptures speak is difficult and hard won, with no papering over of differences but rather what Ephraim Radner calls "a brutal unity." It is the sort of unity that comes when Joseph, condemned by his brothers to death and slavery, is elevated by God to power over all Egypt and offers mercy, not vengeance; for what they intended for evil, God intended for good (Gen. 50:20).[1]

Unity, Christians believe, is a gift given in Christ, not something we earn (Eph. 4:5). Yet Jesus himself prays for it (John 17:21), and scripture like Ps. 133 longs for it, suggesting it is more elusive than we think. The twentieth century saw a great effort at reuniting broken shards of Christendom. This process may have reversed in the early twenty-first century with churches dividing anew. Western cultures once held together by at least a tepid embrace of Christianity, then democracy and human rights, are now fraying in the absence of any social cohesion. Whatever "unity" the church has to give the wider world is not our own. We cannot even pull ourselves together, let alone anybody else. It is oil cascading down the head and beard and robes of Aaron. That is, it is dumped all over God's priest, who prays for the rest of us, as we pray for the whole world. Such prayers are powerful and will be answered eventually. As Peter Leithart argues, "The Father loves the Son

---

1. Ephraim Radner, *A Brutal Unity: The Spiritual Politics of the Christian Church* (Waco: Baylor University Press, 2012). This psalm is paired with the reveal in the Joseph story in the Revised Common Lectionary, Year A, Proper 15 (Gen. 45:1–15).

and will give him what he asks. . . . The Father will give the Son a unified church, and the Son will unify the church by his Spirit. This is what the church will be."[2]

The version of unity delighted in here is not necessarily what we would think of as "religious." An original referent of Ps. 133 may have been that "brothers" live in unity rather than divide their father's land and the family's affections.[3] Others see here a desire for the reunion of the northern (Hermon) and southern (Zion) kingdoms and a restoration of temple worship (133:2–3; Berlin and Brettler 2014: 1420–21). Some historians despair of discovering any "original" meaning.[4] But of course texts birth new meanings—they don't just camouflage lost ones. St. Augustine (2004: 175) speaks of the inspiration from this psalm to men and women to renounce the world and join monasteries. St. Aelred of Rievaulx (d. 1167) said, "When I was walking around the monastery cloister . . . I found not one brother in that whole multitude whom I did not love, and by whom I did not think I was loved in turn. . . . It surpassed all the delights of this world. . . . I could say with the Prophet, 'Behold, how good and pleasant it is, when brothers dwell together in unity.'"[5]

Preachers should relish images as sensual as that of the oil (Ps. 133:2). There is an extravagance here, a tidal wave of oil when a smidgen would suffice. Dew from Hermon cascading all the way to Zion doesn't make a lot of sense geographically, but it makes plenty theologically. Oil doesn't just smell good. It's also good for anointing prophets, priests, and kings. And God doesn't withhold God's blessings. Life eternal is chief among them, a blessing that unites us with those we can't stand on our own but with whom we are covered with the same oil.

2. Peter J. Leithart, *The End of Protestantism: Pursuing Unity in a Fragmented Church* (Grand Rapids: Brazos, 2016), 8, with gratitude to James Howell, whose longing for unity in our United Methodist Church is inspiring.

3. Kraus (1993: 484–86), for whom there is nothing religious in the original before interpolations.

4. "Its true meaning unfortunately remains closed to us." Willi Staerk, quoted in Hossfeld and Zenger 2011: 472.

5. Aelred of Rievaulx, *Spiritual Friendship*, trans. Mark F. Williams (Scranton, PA: University of Scranton Press, 1994), 3:82, quoted in Stanley Hauerwas and Laura Yordy, "Captured in Time: Friendship and Aging," in *Growing Old in Christ*, ed. Stanley Hauerwas, Carole Bailey Stoneking, Keith G. Meador, and David Cloutier (Grand Rapids: Eerdmans, 2003), 184.

PSALM 134

At the end of the ascent psalms (Pss. 120–134), as at the end of our lives, there is reciprocal, mutual blessing. The people bless the Lord's house one last time (134:2). Then, in turn, the Lord blesses the people (134:3), with all the power of one who flung stars into space and all the attentive care of one who knows us in every intricate detail.

There is some scholarly discussion over who precisely the "servants" of the Lord are, who serve "by night" in the house of the Lord. It is not clear historically how often worship took place at night in the temple.[1] The Levites are given a sort of guard duty in the temple (1 Chr. 9:27; Berlin and Brettler 2014: 1421). The psalm may have had an original address to priests, whereas the previous psalm suggested blessing in everyday life (Hossfeld and Zenger 2011: 487). I imagine the praying pilgrims on their way home exhorting those in the temple to keep on praising—even by night, when official duties are over (1 Thess. 5:17). Even as we go home to our lives, *someone* is praising in God's house.

Night can be an image for death. Monks and nuns contemplate death on their beds with psalms like Pss. 4 and 91. Night invites trust. Death is not unencumbered by God's reign.

The gesture of lifting hands is a common one of blessing in many cultures (Hossfeld and Zenger 2011: 487). It is a regular posture of prayer in scripture. Catacomb drawings of ancient Christians have their hands out, palms up, like priests at Mass or Pentecostals anytime.[2] We may overly spiritualize the blessings

---

1. Hossfeld and Zenger (2011: 486) are more circumspect about the precise historical background.
2. So Pss. 28:2; 63:4; and often elsewhere (NRSV).

of which scripture speaks. It depicts a bounty—full crops, full households, full breasts, land at peace, abundance of clothing, good sleep, the kind face of another (Hossfeld and Zenger 2011: 486, citing Othmar Keel and Silvia Schroer). As a pastor I often stand with arms outstretched to offer a benediction and wonder what I'm really doing. Will my parishioners' homes be more full of bounty for this moment? They seem to think so. Heads bow expectantly. I sometimes wonder if this is the whole reason they turn up—to bless the Lord, and now in this final, tender moment, to be blessed by the Lord in return.

The closing benediction of this psalm, and the ascent psalms generally, presents a remarkable juxtaposition: the maker of heaven and earth, bless you *from Zion* (Berlin and Brettler 2014: 1421). The universal and matchless Creator grants blessings from one specific, tangible, historical place. This blessing is as universal and as Jewish as it can be. This same God would later contain the power that contains the cosmos inside the womb of one Jewish teenager—a blessing yet more universal and peculiar still.

PSALM 135

After an interval for praise of the law (Ps. 119) and the ascent up Mount Zion (Pss. 120–134), the Psalter returns to its imperative to praise (Mays 1994: 415). Psalm 135 is nestled in tightly with those around it, with opening words similar to 134 and so many similarities to 136 that they can be called "twins" (Hossfeld and Zenger 2011: 493). With its twin, Ps. 135 is part of the Great Hallel (from its repetition of "hallelujah"), analogous to the Egyptian Hallel of Pss. 113–118. This psalm takes up the same polemic against idols offered in its twin (135:15–18; cf. 136:10–22) and elsewhere (115:4–8). In fact, Ps. 135 consists of so many quotations and intertextual ties to other portions of scripture it's almost a pastiche, a quilt, a recycling of existing materials to make something new.[1] I've noticed that pastors who reach new people well are not afraid to repeat themselves—longtimers are annoyed, but new people have a chance to hear something unfamiliar, consider it, slowly soak it in. So too the psalmist is not afraid to repeat the important things. And the result has been fruitful—this psalm is used in the introduction to morning liturgy in Sabbath and festival services in synagogues (Berlin and Brettler 2014: 1422). Originality is overrated.

There are, however, unique notes sounded here. The speaker sounds praises from the temple, which is not unusual. But those in the "courts" of the temple are invited to praise also (135:2). The psalm quotes Jethro's affirmation of faith to Moses, "Now I know that the LORD is greater than other gods," folding into Israel's praise the voice of a Midianite priest (135:5; see Exod. 18:11). Those who "fear" the Lord are exhorted to join in (135:20). This psalm's cohortative reach

---

1. Hossfeld and Zenger 2011: 493, where Zenger cites dozens of intertextual references.

extends slightly beyond Israel to include those on the edges of its life, whom the book of Acts describes as being among the first Gentiles to join in the praise of Israel's God in Christ (Acts 10:2; 13:16; 16:14; Limburg 2000: 460). Andrew Walls describes Christianity as something that dies in the middle and renews itself at its edges—where the church gives its faith away in mission and in turn is revitalized by receiving cultures bringing their gifts.[2]

At this moment where the church has fancied itself our most original, we're actually being the most Jewish, according to Ps. 135.

"Hymn His name, for it is sweet," Alter (2007: 465) translates 135:3. We hear the psalmist describe God as "good" so often it can fail to lodge in the ear. But to say it is pleasant to praise strikes a newer note. St. John Chrysostom (1998: 216) noticed the unusual language as well, arguing that it is not only useful and holiness-inducing to praise, but it is also "charming." We praise as "servants" (135:1), as the psalms say here and often elsewhere. How much more delightful is it to be transfigured from mere servants into sons and daughters of the one we praise (Rom. 8:17)?[3]

There are two primary strands of praise braided into this one psalm (Mays 1994: 415). One is specific—God has chosen Israel to be his beloved and has vindicated the nation throughout its history (135:4, 8–14). The other is general—the Lord is God of all creation, and all other gods are imposters (135:5–7, 15–18).

First, the specific: God is not God in the abstract, in the realm merely of bloodless ideas. Spurgeon (1976: 615) begs that we study the "name" of the Lord (135:1)—that is, that we study God's unique character—via scriptures like this. And it is a common patristic theme that God accommodates to our human weakness, ignorance, and inability to understand: God has "tempered his praise," so we can join in.[4] Lots of peoples claim their god is great. The Bible's God is so great as to become lowly enough to make even us great.

Israel is God's *segullah*—that is, treasure. Sometimes the term refers to treasures of silver and gold (Eccl. 2:8; 1 Chr. 29:3). Sometimes it refers to Israel in particular as God's own most-prized possession (Exod. 19:5–6; Deut. 7:6). The psalmist's primary reason to praise God is for God's election, the singling out and delighting in of God's beloved Israel (Limburg 2000: 459–60). Augustine argues

2. See Andrew Walls, *The Cross-Cultural Process in Christian History: Studies in the Transmission and Appropriation of Faith* (Maryknoll, NY: Orbis, 2002), part 1.
3. Augustine 2004: 190, riffing off of Paul's theme of adoption into sonship in Rom. 8:15–17 and Gal. 4:6–7.
4. The quote is from Augustine (2004: 195).

that God has assigned a guardian angel to every nation, to bless and watch over them. But God has not assigned a lieutenant to care for Israel—God watches over Jacob personally (135:4; Augustine 2004: 197).

As the particular strand continues, the psalm singles out the final plague in Egypt as an example of God's exquisite care for Israel (135:8; Berlin and Brettler 2014: 1421). This is the plague that finally "worked," forcing Pharaoh to let Israel go. It is also, of course, the most morally troubling, with every firstborn struck down from the palace to the lowliest, including Egypt's animals. One can allegorize the text, as Augustine does (the firstborn signifies our old life, which must die in Christ; Augustine 2004: 205). But Israel's scripture suggests the relentless historicity of this story: Israel's deliverance from slavery came as a result of God killing Egypt's firstborn. The exodus itself is unmentioned here in the psalm. Only God's deathly strike is highlighted (Hossfeld and Zenger 2011: 498). The language goes down deep into the bedrock of biblical language (Gen. 22). Egypt, of course, killed more than Israel's firstborn—it sought to kill every male child, and so the entire nation (Exod. 1:22). This is, in a sense, just retribution (Spurgeon 1976: 618). But God's nature is merciful, not retributive. The next verses emphasize God's action against pagan kings—Sihon of the Amorites and Og of Bashan—both notches in Israel's belt (135:11). Unlike the telling of these stories in Numbers and Deuteronomy and Joshua, the emphasis here is not on Moses's and Joshua's and Israel's might but on the "signs and wonders" of God alone (135:10–11).

What do we do with this monument to violence at the heart of Israel's scripture?

Scripture itself has some hints for us. The story of Israel's conquest of the Amorites and Bashan in Num. 21 emphasizes that Israel had no interest in fighting. It merely wished to pass through Sihon's territory. The Israelites promised they would not even turn aside into a field or vineyard or even drink from a well (Num. 21:22). It was Sihon who mustered for battle—to his and his people's doom. Then King Og mustered for battle. He is a giant in Israel's memory (Deut. 3:11—his bed is thirteen feet by six feet!).[5] This also turned out poorly for him. Israel in every case is the people under duress. They are enslaved, then in a foreign land and in need of hospitality. They meet instead with coldhearted cruelty and war. God delivers them. The battle plan here is that of Exod. 14:4—"The LORD will fight for you, and you have only to stand still"—one not commonly taught in military academies then or now. God acts on behalf of the oppressed and takes up their cause, and God delivers, not by their might (they have none) nor by their clever tactics against a more

5. Alter (2007: 466) points out the Deuteronomy passage and translates the size.

powerful enemy (none are mentioned here), but by God's own power (135:10). The text is not pacifist with regard to God. But it could be read in a way that discourages violence done by God's people. We won't fight. But God may fight for us.[6]

God's delivering power is not remembered in a vacuum. Even though the precise historical circumstances are not obvious, praying a psalm like this implies that times are difficult once more (135:14). Israel's scripture reminds those praying that God has been faithful before. The summary in Ps. 135:14 even quotes Deut. 32:36 verbatim: "The LORD will vindicate his people, and have compassion on his servants." Israel is often surrounded by hostile foreign adversaries. This may seem like so much bellicose commotion among strange peoples in long-ago Palestine, but for the church, "on the fate of one of these nations of Palestine the happiness of the human race depended" (Spurgeon 1976: 619). This is the scandal of particularity. The church views itself in similar terms, as God's elect, singled out, treasured, and also harassed on every side, in need of a deliverance we cannot arrange for ourselves (1 Pet. 2:9; Titus 2:14; Mays 1994: 418). God has delivered before. Does God still do that sort of thing? Psalm 135:13 restates the Lord's promise from the burning bush, to be faithful to himself: "This is my name forever" (Exod. 3:15; Mays 1994: 418). Don't just remember that, Israel. Don't just trust it. But also praise, like Ps. 135 does.

The more general strand of Ps. 135, with which the specific is braided together, begins with a strong statement of faith, "I *know* the Lord is great" (135:5). The psalmist "is no agnostic," as one preacher says (Spurgeon 1976: 617). Scripture speaks with more hesitation, ambivalence, and doubt elsewhere. Why so certain here? Because "whatever the LORD pleases he does" (135:6). This strong statement of omnipotence opens up questions best addressed elsewhere about the existence of evil. The language of omnipotence has been important in Christian theology about creation. God brings the worlds into existence through no toil or external coercion, but out of sheer, unnecessary delight (Augustine 2004: 199). God says, "Why not?" and there's a universe. What a contrast to us, who, as Paul makes clear in Rom. 7, cannot even do what we want to *within our own selves* (Augustine 2004: 199). God creates and saves in sheer freedom—a freedom we creatures often only know by its absence. But when we are in the presence of this God, we know and celebrate his greatness, as the psalms often do (e.g., Pss. 95:3; 96:4–5; 97:7, 9; Mays 1994: 417).

---

6. John Bowlin notes the moral fervor with which critics of just war theory denounce Augustine, even while they themselves are not committed to nonviolence in all circumstances. Bowlin, "Augustine on Justifying Coercion," *Annual Society of Christian Ethics* 17 (1997): 49–70.

The Lord makes the clouds rise, makes lightning for the rainstorms, and brings the wind from his storehouse (Ps. 135:7; Jer. 10:13; 51:16 make similar claims). No Baal is in charge of the weather, contrary to the teachings of Israel's neighbors (Kraus 1993: 491–92). It is the Lord of Israel who controls nature—all other claimants to such power are imposters. The Lord does what he wishes even in the deep. Israel is not overly enamored with the sea—it is a place of chaos and unknown monsters and death. Yet the Lord does what he wishes even there. These natural phenomena can and should all be read spiritually as well. Augustine sees the deeps as the hidden places in the human heart, which we cannot change, but God, miraculously, can and often does (Augustine 2004: 204). Or, in a more contemporary spiritual reading, the depths suggest that God's working is beyond our imagining or comprehension (Hossfeld and Zenger 2011: 497). Lightning is often terrifying, rain comforting, and likewise God only sends difficulty in order to get our attention, and then God couples such difficulty with mercy (Chrysostom 1998: 225; George Horne, cited in Spurgeon 1976: 617). The winds and the clouds are both preachers for Augustine, who cites Isa. 5:6 (he could have also used 1 Cor. 3:6). It is God who sends the Word to whomever God wants and who, strangely, at times withholds it.[7]

Unlike this mighty world-making God, idols are made by human hands and can make nothing, except that they make their makers as lifeless as they are (135:15–18). We have seen this sort of polemic before and will see it again (115:4–8; 136:10–22). Apparently, Israel, and we, need reminding. It would be less ridiculous to worship our own hands than the things our hands make, one preacher says (Spurgeon 1976: 619). Our hands are, like the rest of us, made in the image of God. When we make images, however, these are mute and powerless. And so we become like that. We become like what we worship. This is why scripture repeats its insistence so regularly that we are to worship the one true God and no one else. Worship does not add to God, Augustine says. It adds to us, makes us like the one we praise, full of life and goodness and love. It takes a bit of imagination to see our own idols—the things we make, and worship, that take life from us (it is far easier to identify others' idolatry than our own!). It is no groundbreaking observation to note that our age is obsessed with celebrity. Our media entrances us with images of superficial beauty, wealth, and power. Then social media allows us each to treat ourselves like celebrities. It has become common for people in a

---

7. Augustine 2004: 204–5. Augustine couples this insight with the observation that "the end of the earth" in 135:7 is a link to Christ's mission field in places like Acts 1:8, where apostles are sent "to the ends of the earth."

digital age to ignore the human beings nearby and attend to faux people far away who appear close on the screen of their devices. Here a flesh-and-blood image of God is discarded, and the images manufactured by others for consumption are preferred. And so we become what we make—flat, two-dimensional, glossy, empty. Meanwhile the sorts of virtues that the Lord loves go neglected. By contrast, the psalmist insists, everyone should praise: the house of Aaron (the priests), the house of Levi (the singers), the whole house of Israel, anybody who fears the Lord (all the rest of us) should offer praise.

To do so tastes delicious.

PSALM 136

There are those who say we can never properly translate a word from one language to another.[1] When we look at the translations for the biblically crucial word *hesed*, we can see why. The NRSV has "steadfast love." Alter has "kindness" (2007: 469). The word has connotations of "loyalty." Another is "steady love."[2] A note in the *Jewish Study Bible* describes *hesed* as a "favor done out of loyalty" (Berlin and Brettler 2014: 1422). Most premodern Christians, working from the Septuagint or the King James, read "mercy." One scholar has a translation that may be too piously Christian: "amazing grace" (Limburg 2000: 463). But he fills in the portrait well with the book of Hosea. The prophet Hosea is commanded to marry the prostitute "in steadfast love," *hesed* (2:19). He is to love her the way the Lord loves Israel, "though they turn to other gods" (3:1). Marital love is a distant reflection of the love God has for humanity—though less distant than other analogies. However disparate these translations of *hesed* are, marital love includes all of them and more. And the story from Hosea includes an element of incomprehensibility, even to the point of offensiveness. What sort of love suffers this kind of unfaithfulness and yet continues on "forever" (Hos. 2:19)? The proper response to such unimaginable love from God despite our unfaithfulness is, of course, worship, of the sort outlined in Ps. 136 (Limburg 2000: 463).

1. Alasdair MacIntyre lays out this argument in his *After Virtue*, 3rd ed. (Notre Dame, IN: University of Notre Dame, 2007). He sets the bar high for carrying meaning from one language to another—rather than translate, one has to learn a "second first language."
2. As expressed in the sung version of this psalm by Charles Pettee and FolkPsalm. Pettee draws on Old Testament scholar Ellen Davis for help in translation.

The genre of a psalm is sometimes difficult to discern. Here there is no difficulty discerning that this is a liturgy, and so an "imperatival hymn" as the scholarship has it—a hymn that invites, or even commands, others to join in (arguably all hymns, as well as all biblical faith, are imperatival). The precise historical origin can't be pinned down, as usual with the Bible, especially the psalms. But a glance at some biblical stories in which such worship takes place is instructive. In 2 Chronicles' depiction of Solomon's dedication of the temple, the king prays, fire comes down and consumes the burnt offering, the priests can't enter the temple because the glory of the Lord is so thick, and all the people, seeing all of this, bow down on the pavement with their faces to the ground and offer the words repeated in Ps. 136:1, "for he is good, for his steadfast love endures forever" (2 Chr. 7:3, 6) (Kraus 1993: 496). The same line goes up when the ark is brought into the new temple (2 Chr. 5:13), and when the foundation of the new temple is laid, the priests and the Levites sing the line responsively (Ezra 3:11) (Mays 1994: 418). These texts are likely all written after the exile, though of course the Chronicler is describing the first temple. In other words, Israel remembers God's faithfulness after centuries of foreign conquest, the destruction of Jerusalem, being carried off in exile and restored piecemeal, and building a new temple that is scarcely a shadow of the old. Yet God is good; God's mercy is unending. All the people sing, and their legacy invites us to join them in song, whatever depth we have likewise suffered. Or, in the case of most North American readers, we have to imagine the scope of this sort of suffering among others in order to learn how to praise with the depth and height of a psalm like Ps. 136.

The superlatives of 136:2–3 suggest to modern scholars a prehistory of a pantheon of gods, from among which YHWH eventually stood out (Kraus 1993: 497). Israel, like most ancient peoples, was at one time henotheistic, meaning it had its god, fully cognizant that other people had theirs. Over time Israel came to be more properly monotheistic, insisting by the time of the middle portion of Isaiah and psalms like this one that the God of Israel is the only God there is, and other peoples' purported gods are no more than fantasy. Historians may, of course, be right about the historical progression, but the question remains how to interpret the words now, in light of the full biblical revelation culminating in Christ. What are we to make of these so-called gods and lords? St. John Chrysostom (1998: 234) argues that they are demons. The demons sought freedom in their rebellion against God but ended up slaves, subject to evil, with no freedom at all. Any other god than the one true God of Israel has no proper being or existence. Yet we sinners treat other gods as though they do and are. St. Paul insists that whatever is claimed for the status of other gods, the church must recognize that they do not exist in the proper sense (1 Cor. 8:6). The demons have only the shadow existence of fallen angels—reaching for greater existence, falling out of it altogether. Martin Luther famously said, "Whatever your heart clings to and confides in, that is really your God."[3] It is a near-perfect description of false worship. We do indeed genuinely worship something not worthy of worship, on its way to nonexistence, that sends us on our way there as well.

St. Augustine sees the "gods" here very differently—not as demons, but as human beings, honorifically called "gods" by virtue of the divinity bestowed on them by Christ. Psalm 82 may also have originally imagined a pantheon of gods (82:1). By its conclusion, these so-called gods are as mortal as any human being (82:7). Augustine thinks of Ps. 82 so often because none other than Jesus quotes it in a christological debate with his opponents (2004: 214). If scripture can say that mere creatures are gods, "and the scripture cannot be annulled," what objection should anyone have that Jesus calls himself God's "son" (John 10:35–36)? It may not be the most convincing argument for an exclusively high Christology (the bar to be called "god" is so low any creature can clear it—even Jesus!). But it comes for Augustine, and for John, in a context of a specific understanding of salvation. Jesus is not the Son of God in any exclusive sense. He is the Son of God in an abundant sense—he desires to share his divinity with others. Here then the valence of "gods" is quite a bit different than the language of "imposter" I've used elsewhere. It suggests *theosis*, or human divinization, by virtue of becoming fellow sons and daughters of God, siblings of Jesus, receiving divinity by grace that Jesus is by nature. In Augustine's words, "Thanks to his mercy that we who were unjust will be righteous, we who were sick will be whole, we who were dead will live, we who were mortal will be immortal, and we who were miserable will be blessed" (2004: 214).

"Who alone does great wonders" (136:4)—the psalm itself cures us of any notion that any other god can do anything good. Only the God of Israel can act at all.[4] And the wonder this God is always doing is his choice of Israel, his ongoing mercy despite human infidelity. God only has sinners to work with. These verses suggest that all God *is* is unending mercy. The Lord does not exercise mercy at one time and arbitrarily revoke it another (Chrysostom 1998: 234; Spurgeon

3. Martin Luther, *Luther's Large Catechism: God's Call to Repentance, Faith and Prayer*, trans. John Nicholas Lenker (Minneapolis: Luther Press, 1908), 44.
4. The *Jewish Study Bible* notes this verse revokes any place for any other god (Berlin and Brettler 2014: 1422).

1976: 623). There is no God other than the one who is an unending source of *hesed*. And that God has no other face than kindness.[5]

It is by his "understanding" that God made the heavens (136:5). Another English term for the Hebrew behind this is that God made all things by his "wisdom" (see also Jer. 10:12; 51:15; Prov. 3:19) (Harrelson 2003: 880). The New Testament picks up this Old Testament wisdom terminology for one of its key descriptions of Jesus (e.g., 1 Cor. 1:24). The sketch, or blueprint, or schema according to which God made everything that is, is Christ. The rest of the psalm describes the way God's natural wonders and God's supernatural works on behalf of Israel invite the people's praise. For the Talmud, this psalm shows that the ordinary, mundane gifts of God and the otherworldly miraculous works of God are actually one and the same: "The provision of daily sustenance is as significant as the splitting of the sea" (Talmud, quoted in Limburg 2000: 462). As a pastor I have often had folks ask why they don't see the sorts of marvels described in the Bible. Sometimes they ask this because they are anxiously praying for a miracle; other times they ask out of more idle curiosity. Either way the answer is the same—we do see marvels all the time. We just don't notice them. Every bite of food, breath of air, face of another person is a miracle, usually unrecognized. Occasionally God does something more obviously stupendous, suspending the normal "laws" of how things work, to give us a glimpse of how God intends to transfigure all creation one day. This isn't frequent. Biblical books like Esther show a very different understanding of the miraculous than, say, Exodus, for not a single naturally inexplicable thing happens.[6] Scripture itself may have been written for those who have not seen a miracle themselves but have heard stories about them and want to see those stories replicated. The psalmist insists that God will be faithful. God cannot be otherwise than loyally merciful. The question is just how God will be merciful this time.

There is a modernist answer to why we don't see miracles: they don't happen. Scripture describes spiritual realities that take place in us, but not historical events that take place in ordinary time and space. Where I work in Vancouver, there is great theological enthusiasm for various forms of process theology that object to "interventionist" portraits of God. Thinkers in this tradition want us to be reasonable—God doesn't turn up and do magic tricks. God can be sought for

5. Augustine is troubled slightly by the word "alone" in Ps. 136:4. Doesn't God the Father share his creative work with God the Son and so not work "alone" at all but in concert? Yes, Augustine answers, yet the three persons of the Trinity work indivisibly, so that we can call them "one" and say they work "alone" in creation and salvation (2004: 218–19).

6. Samuel Wells and George Sumner, *Esther & Daniel*, Brazos Theological Commentary on the Bible (Grand Rapids: Brazos, 2013), 5.

solace, comfort, spiritual growth. But the premodern people who wrote down the Bible can't be trusted as guides for how things happen in time and space. Or maybe the Bible's authors were very clever indeed but wrote down these spiritual things under the guise of something else, not expecting their readers to be so gullible as to think they're describing actual events. These are all parts of modernist apologetics that I regard as a failed strategy.[7] It tries to draw the circle of what has to be believed to be Christian ever more narrowly. The Virgin Birth? Nah. The Resurrection? No way. Miracles? Of course not. We can see the appeal of such a modernist strategy even in looking at this psalm. Are there *really* waters below the earth and above the heavens (135:6; Gen. 7:11)? The problem, of course, is that as this circle narrows, we realize that there is nothing left within it. Nothing of what we believe about God and the Bible is rational on modernist grounds. None of it can be easily swallowed by our fellow citizens of modern nation-states who use cell phones and watch movies streamed on the web. It's all incredible. A better strategy is to marvel at all the wonderful things we get to believe. Do we understand them? Can we give an apologetic by which a skeptical person can believe it? Of course not! And yet all of it is delightful; all of it teaches spiritually, as modernists are wont to agree. And as for whether such things take place in time and space—who knows? The marvel that any one of us is alive is no greater than the marvel of the parting of the Red Sea. As Spurgeon puts this point, "He who causes the waters of the sea ordinarily to remain as one mass can with equal readiness divide them" (1976: 625). Are we so sure that wonders natural and supernatural somehow *can't* have happened? If we believe in a God who makes everything and redeems it in Christ, it is no great leap to believe that God may show up among creatures and act in love. As for the term "interventionist," it is no intervention for God to act in his creation any more than it is a crime for a person to enter her own office, to cook in his own kitchen. It is not even "supernatural" for God to act *according to his nature* to create the cosmos or save it. That's what it means for God to be God.

The psalmist doesn't understand any of this either. Neither do we. So we offer praise instead.

And the waters below the earth and above the heavens? They're a sign of the mystery of God. God can destroy, as God does in Gen. 7. And God can have mercy, as God promises after that flood (Gen. 9:13, 16). All water is a sign of God's mercy. That's why Christians baptize, and why we remember our baptism

---

7. I am borrowing here from Stanley Hauerwas's observations in lectures and seminars at Duke Divinity School, 1997–2000.

whenever it rains.[8] There really is water below and above everything that is. Because that water is the unending mercy of God.

There is another problem at a slight remove from the text, and so not always engaged by commentaries: What do we make of the tradition of the conquest and the inheritance of the land, for which here the psalmist gives praise (136:17–22)? Israel doesn't just conquer great kings and inherit their land, as attested here. Israel also commits what we moderns call genocide, down to destroying all the animals, and it takes land that isn't its own (e.g., 1 Sam. 15; Deut. 6:11). These are, as one interpreter puts it, "psalms of violence": even if recounted amidst memory of violence done to Israel, they celebrate violence by which Israel benefits (Hossfeld and Zenger 2011: 509). They still serve to legitimate troubling political policies in the world today. Why shouldn't some people attack, subdue, destroy, and plunder others if *God's* people in the Bible did the same? The answer, of course, is that those tempted to plunder now are not biblical Israel. And this is not the same time. God made those commands in a specific time and place, and the definitive revelation of God in Christ includes the clear command to love enemies and not harm them. Still, isn't God the sort of God who, having commanded such things at one time, might again? The psalm presents, above all, a God who "strikes" (136:10, 17).[9] Sometimes this criticism is offered by critics of religion who don't realize that what it means to *be* a religion is to have tradition-steeped reading strategies for *not* doing what scripture seems to allow. Scripture itself already includes apologetics around these matters—as when Num. 21 argues that Og and Sihon chose battles with Israel that it would have rather avoided, and that the land handed over was not originally *theirs* anyway (how do you steal from a thief?). Ancient Christians followed the lead of ancient Jews in reading the conquest stories figurally for the sort of conquest of our vices that has to take place in the life of faith. I am sympathetic to such readings. But I must admit that the sort of hermeneutic described in the paragraph above, by which God could work the miraculous, leaves open the charge discussed in this paragraph, that God could command what we regard as immoral. God is free to be God, and we are not free to circumscribe how God can or cannot act. And yet even here the letter of scripture cuts the other way. The psalm insists that it is God's *mercy* that is forever. We may not circumscribe God, but God may, and has, in Christ.

The psalm concludes with a summary statement of who God is and how God acts toward God's people (136:23–24). Some historians have tried to specify

8. The tradition dates to St. Francis.
9. The "God who strikes" is Zenger's terminology (Hossfeld and Zenger 2011: 504).

when it is that God acts this way. Is it in the restoration after the exile? Or is it a farther back memory, of the time of the judges (Kraus 1993: 498)? Of course, what it means to be a biblical people is to learn from scripture how God has been merciful in the past, on the way to seeing how God will be merciful again now (Hossfeld and Zenger 2011: 510). The psalm's intertwining of themes of God's miraculous deliverance and of God's quotidian provision is also helpful for our time. Several generations now have criticized Christian theology for its inattention to matters of environmental stewardship, creation care, and more recently climate change and even ecocatastrophe. This psalm offers a refrain as appropriate for a prayer over a humble meal as it is over the cutting up of the sea and the shaking of Pharaoh; as apt for marveling at the stars in the sky as at the miracle in the mirror or in rags on the street corner.

Historians are wont to try to reconstruct things lost to us—that's their specific gift, and it is much needed. What is even more needed is people to live the scriptures out.[10] The psalmist has adroitly hidden the specific historical tracks. There is no precise reconstruction of when Ps. 136 was written, though terminology like "God of heaven" may suggest Persian influence and so a later dating for that line (136:26).[11] But what the psalm really wants us to do is to act it out, to live into it. We treasure and cultivate and pass on liturgies so they can be celebrated anew. One way to get to know the psalm is simply to recite it. Have each person gathered say one line, and everyone together say the refrain, "for his steadfast love endures forever." Eventually the repetition allows the point to sink in, not unlike the nearly unending repetition of Ps. 119—God's mercy really is forever.

---

10. I am borrowing here from Nicholas Lash, "What Might Martyrdom Mean" and "Performing the Scriptures," in *Theology on the Way to Emmaus* (London: SCM, 1986).

11. Hossfeld and Zenger 2011: 505. I find this sort of observation fascinating, but I always wonder whether it is merely antiquarian interest. Here Israel's borrowing from its neighbors is fruitful: something doesn't have to have come from "us" to be true; God has sprinkled truth liberally throughout creation and among peoples, and wherever we find truth, it is God's.

PSALM 137

Each of the three sections of this psalm would be worthy of renown were they independent psalms. I have heard Ps. 137:1–3 used to describe the "multiple overwhelmings" of the twentieth century, which saw the coinage of the word "genocide" and too many instantiations of it to list them all.[1] The middle portion describes Jerusalem as the psalmist's highest joy—which is one explanation for the custom at Jewish weddings of the couple smashing a glass. It is a reminder, at the pinnacle of human joy, of the destruction of Zion (Berlin and Brettler 2014: 1422). Yet Ps. 137 is an indissoluble unit, so the horror of 137:7–9 is what is most commonly remembered here, a "parade example" of the Bible's purported brutality (Van Harn and Strawn 2009: 346). There are other descriptions of the brutality of ancient warfare that do not burrow into the memory the way this one does (e.g., 2 Kgs. 8:12; Hos. 10:14; Nah. 3:10; Mays 1994: 423). But this psalm has a *blessing* for those who smash children's heads—in a psalm that is meant for singing in praise of God in communal worship. What do we do with those final verses?

One common response in today's churches is to ignore it as simply too ugly to be prayed or preached in a service. The problem is that people know it's there. Even those ignorant of much of scripture know there is brutality on display someplace.[2] Not to preach a text like this is to refuse resources to God's people for responding to an appropriate protest from faith's critics. Some have responded, with a passion similar to Ps. 137 itself: "Let those find fault with it who have never seen their

---

1. I heard this language at David Ford's sermon at Greg Jones's induction as dean of Duke Divinity School in 1997. The language appeared in Ford, *The Shape of Living: Spiritual Directions for Everyday Life* (Grand Rapids: Baker Books, 2004), 15, 20.
2. Strawn makes similar arguments (Van Harn and Strawn 2009: 346).

temple burned, their city ruined, their wives ravished, and their children slain; they might not, perhaps, be quite so velvet-mouthed if they had suffered after this fashion" (Spurgeon 1976: 627).

Point taken. And yet the worry is real. What people has ever harmed another without a background story of prior monstrous harm done to it? One apologetic strategy for psalms like this is to say that the psalmist speaks hate in order *not* to act on it.[3] Anger is given vent here in words so it does not take up arms. There may be something to that: "Vengeance is mine, I will repay," Paul quotes Deuteronomy as saying (Rom. 12:19; Deut. 32:35). The problem is that people are always dehumanized in language before they are harmed less metaphorically. We need something more than that lest this volatile psalm erupt from speech to action.

The first section of Ps. 137 shows its historical origins with a clarity that historians wish for all the psalms. The Jews are in exile. The "rivers" of the opening verse are either Babylon's famous irrigation streams or its great rivers (Alter 2007: 473). The temple singers hang up their harps because they will not comply with their captors' cruel demands for entertainment (137:2). Israel has become like the dead in Sheol who cannot praise (Berlin and Brettler 2014: 1422). The curse sworn on oath in 137:5 has, in effect, taken place—the musician's hand is as good as withered; his tongue may as well be severed (Van Harn and Strawn 2009: 347).

The preacher's job, on liberal Protestant accounts, is to build a bridge between this ancient text and modern people out there listening. And one bridge would be to use recent times of calamity. So perhaps there is an analogy between the September 11, 2001, terror attacks and the destruction of Jerusalem. If the destruction that befell the Twin Towers hit every single building in one's hometown, then perhaps we could understand Ps. 137. The great difference is that the anguish in Ps. 137 is also specifically theological. *God's* promises appear to have failed. The God so great that other gods are imposters, the God who chose Israel and swore to protect Zion, has failed (Limburg 2000: 466). Marduk has defeated him (Hossfeld and Zenger 2011: 516). God has not swept in at the last possible moment and prevented a calamitous defeat. Calamity has come instead of rescue.

And Israel will remember. Its neighbor Edom stood by during Jerusalem's fall. No—Edom joined in, with taunts (137:7), with collaboration attested to elsewhere (Obadiah). How could Israel forget?

---

3. Patrick Miller offers this with as much skill as anyone I've seen: the psalmist manages with his anger both to "let it go" and "hold it back." Speaking it keeps one from acting on it (quoted in Van Harn and Strawn 2009: 349).

And finally, the spasm of vitriol at Babylon itself (Ps. 137:8–9). Commentators point out that this is poetry, not dogma (Hossfeld and Zenger 2011: 513). It is to be read, offered in praise, studied, but there is here no "go thou and do likewise." It is a curse aimed at Babylon, not one pronounced by God or even aimed at God, but pronounced by the violated psalmist. Biblically speaking, it is an articulation of the *lex talionis*, the law of reparation. The psalmist is asking for repair of the cosmos. What has happened to Israel should also happen to its oppressor, not more.

And yet there it is, an open wound, not yet a scar, in the letter of our scripture, through which, we believe, God speaks words meant to mend the world. How can Ps. 137 be part of God's work to make right everything we have made wrong?

David Steinmetz focused on this psalm to make his unforgettable argument for reading scripture in ways other than narrowly historicist:

> How was a French priest in 1150 to understand Psalm 137, which bemoans captivity in Babylon, makes rude remarks about Edomites, expresses an ineradicable longing for a glimpse of Jerusalem, and pronounces a blessing on anyone who avenges the destruction of the temple by dashing Babylonian children against a rock? The priest lives in Concale, not Babylon, has no personal quarrel with Edomites, cherishes no ambitions to visit Jerusalem (though he might fancy a holiday in Paris), and is expressly forbidden by Jesus to avenge himself on his enemies. Unless Psalm 137 has more than one possible meaning, it cannot be used as a prayer by the church and must be rejected as a lament belonging exclusively to the piety of ancient Israel.[4]

We can read the text spiritually, with regard to the struggles we have to conform our desires with God's desires. Origen reads the little ones as "troublesome spiritual thoughts," which should be rooted out of our minds "even at their birth" (*Against Celsus* 7.22, in Wesselschmidt 2007: 379–80). C. S. Lewis thinks of the whiny voice in us that seeks recognition, begrudges its withholding, and envies its extension to those we deem unworthy of it. We should be ruthless to the vices of entitlement and resentment: "Knock the little bastards' brains out."[5] This reading strategy is, of course, quite far from the original context of conquered exiles. And yet, of course, when you canonize a text, you open it up to countless future contexts. This sort of spiritual reading aimed at cultivating the life of faith is what

---

4. Steinmetz, "The Superiority of Pre-critical Exegesis," *Theology Today* 37, no. 1 (1980): 27–38, here 29–30.

5. C. S. Lewis, *Reflections on the Psalms* (New York: Harcourt, 1958), 136.

communities of faith do—objectionable in principle only if ongoing communities of faith are objectionable in principle.

St. Augustine famously compares Babylon to this world and Jerusalem to the City of God. They are intermingled currently, only to be disentangled eschatologically. There are texts that make relative peace with Babylon (Jer. 29:4–9). Others remember the hot pain of displacement and betrayal and ruin. Later interpretive tradition would speak of this as an anagogical reading, focused on hope. And, of course, hope focuses our political action now. What are we doing today that will last after this world? Here the psalmist's bitterness can be harnessed for good communal work in the world now. We might worry at this point. Too escapist! Too otherworldly! Yet we should levy our protest also against the book of Revelation, which already begins this interpretive trajectory by equating Rome with Babylon and the coming City of God with Jerusalem (e.g., Rev. 14:18; 18:2).

I am an advocate for these reading strategies, as this book has made clear. Yet we are still left with the plain fact of the letter, which can never be effaced as we read more deeply. And here the observation that this is a prayer determines everything else. Prayer leaves the outcome in the hands of God, life's ultimate judge, still and ever the only source of the unending mercy praised in Ps. 136. The prayer, in Ellen Davis's words, demands "that our enemies be driven into God's hands."[6] And those hands, later fleshed in Jesus of Nazareth and driven through with nails, dispense mercy to all of God's enemies.

Even, we hope, to us.

---

6. Ellen Davis, *Getting Involved with God: Rediscovering the Old Testament* (Cambridge, MA: Cowley, 2001), 27, quoted in Van Harn and Strawn 2009: 353.

PSALM 138

All of scripture is prayer—inspired by God, passed down to be a means for later generations to approach God. But the psalms are prayers in a double sense. The one reading is not only reading. She is also actually praying—addressing herself to God directly, whether she intended to or not.[1] A passage in the Talmud tells of an angel whose purpose is to "fashion crowns for the almighty from the prayers of Israel."[2]

Psalm 138 opens a section of psalms attributed to David. It is similar to Ps. 145, the opposite bookend of this last set of psalms attributed to David (Limburg 2000: 468). The prayers in between, 139–144, are each individual psalms of lament. The structure of this mini-section makes an argument: that life is bookended with praise, opening and concluding with hallelujah. Lament crops up with regularity in between. It is not hushed, but it is contextualized. Sorrow is not the first or last word. That belongs to hallelujah.

The psalmist opens with a promise to acclaim the Lord with a "whole heart" (138:1). This is a pledge to obey the Bible's central command in Deut. 6:5, and a reciprocation of God's wholehearted love for Israel ("I will plant them in this land in faithfulness, with all my heart and all my soul," Jer. 32:41), the spouse's "I do" in response to the beloved's initial "I do" (Hossfeld and Zenger 2011: 528). But that picture of religious monogamy is interrupted by the next clause, "Before the gods I sing your praise" (138:1).

---

1. This reflection sounds Augustinian, perhaps from the *Confessions*, but I remember learning it from Amy Laura Hall's seminar at Duke Divinity School, 1998.

2. Adin Steinsaltz, *A Guide to Jewish Prayer* (New York: Schocken, 2000), 6. Thanks to Rabbi Jay Gutovich for putting me on to this introduction to the Siddur.

Wait—isn't there only one of those?

This reference to "gods" could, of course, be a leftover fossil of a previous faith that had place for more than one deity (Alter 2007: 476). It could be a polemic against any purported foreign gods, which "exist" only insofar as confused people acclaim them, but there is not an obvious polemic here (Hossfeld and Zenger 2011: 528). The Septuagint solves the problem by translating "gods" as "angels," or those closest to God in praise (Augustine 2004: 244). The Septuagint rendering turns up in St. Paul's cryptic comment that women should cover their heads when they speak in church (1 Cor. 11:2–16), "because of the angels" (11:10). The Venerable Bede sees a connection between this symbol of humility and the posture of the women at the tomb of Jesus, where they bow in the presence of the angels. So too ought we to bow in the presence of the Risen One at the Lord's table (*Homilies on the Gospels* 2.10, in Wesselschmidt 2007: 381). Bede manages to take what seems a piece of cultural custom in Paul, which over time reinforced sexism, and make it a reminder of how we should all be in God's presence.

The one praying bows down and gives thanks to God's "name"—that is, to the specific way the transcendent God has turned *toward* us (138:2; Hossfeld and Zenger 2011: 529). And the psalmist praises God for his "steadfast love and faithfulness." That pair of attributes characterizes God's "ways" (138:5) throughout the scriptures (Exod. 34:6–7). This "graciousness formula" has come up often in this portion of the Psalter and informs such New Testament formulations as John's description of the Messiah as one "full of grace and truth" (John 1:14).[3] But then the next formulation appears nowhere else and makes far less sense. Alter renders the cumbersome Hebrew into cumbersome English this way: "You have made your word greater than all your name" (Alter 2007: 476). He smooths it out with a textual variant, "greater than your heavens," but of course in text criticism the more cumbersome rendering is the more likely original. Other translators, like the NRSV, have the Lord's name and word exalted "above everything," which makes a sort of anodyne sense. One interpreter makes a riskier move, letting the text stand, with its claim that somehow God's word is "greater" than God's name, arguing that God "would sooner allow his perfections to fail than for his faithfulness to come to naught" (Joseph Philpot, quoted in Spurgeon 1976: 630).

The psalmist gives thanks for the Lord's delivery in a way that's rather more perfunctory than the powerful poetry of the neighboring psalms 137 and 139. And yet the brief prayer is instructive. The psalmist is teaching us how to pray.

---

3. Hossfeld and Zenger 2011: 529. See Pss. 111:4; 112:4; 115:1; 116:5; 130:4, 7; 145:8.

What does he pray for? Not material acquisitions, not fame, not even delivery from danger, but rather "increased strength of soul" (138:3). This is a prayer for virtue—for a stretchier, more elastic soul that can accommodate more of the divine presence (Augustine 2004: 248). God promises no free pass from trouble, but rather God's own crucified presence amidst whatever trouble (Chrysostom 1998: 251).

The middle portion of the psalm speaks of kings of the earth coming and worshiping Israel's God. It is the same dream as that of the latter portions of Isaiah and elsewhere in the prophets—that at the end of the world even Gentiles would stream to Zion. In one way, the mention of kings makes sense (138:4–5)—this is a royal psalm ("of David"), and kings have made appearances in neighboring psalms (see Pss. 135–136). In another way, it is odd that the delivery of one Israelite, however noble, would get the attention of foreign kings, let alone *change the way they worship*. The previous poor kings in the Psalter, Og and Sihon, are remembered only for being killed (135:10–11; 136:18–20). One Jewish interpretation argues that foreign kings praise because they come to see the beauty of Torah.[4] Christian interpreters tend to see the conversion of the nations upon seeing Jesus's coming prophesied and then fulfilled. Either reading works, or both. Christians might add that the only one whose delivery has converted pagan nations and their kings is the resurrected Christ, who is God's transcendence turned toward us (138:2, 6).

The psalmist describes God as high, and yet attentive to the lowly, and regarding the haughty from afar (138:6). This is the kenotic way in which God deals with creation. God bends low (Phil. 2:5–11). God is tender and intimate with Israel and then in Christ. Kings can only approach by bending low, where God is. Yet why are the haughty only regarded from afar (138:6)? Surely God is no farther physically from the proud than God is from the poor or holy. The claim is not a metaphysical one. Yet those who hold their heads high God only regards from far off, like a stranger, one who hardly commands interest. The parallel in Matthew's Gospel is terrifying: "I never knew you" (7:23).

The final portion of the psalm brings the action into the present, with the psalmist praying for God's ongoing preserving and delivering presence (138:7–8). Psalm 138:7 recalls the praise in Ps. 23 for the Lord's protection amidst enemies. And both final verses (138:7–8) speak of the Lord's "hands," as the next psalm will too (139:10). The verb in 138:8 suggests a loosening of the hands to drop a

4. Berlin and Brettler 2014: 1424. Zenger weighs in on the side of this interpretation, citing the parallels between Pss. 138 and 119 (Hossfeld and Zenger 2011: 529).

treasure.[5] But scripture regularly promises that God would never drop his treasured people, any more than he would drop the garland of Israel's prayers (Deut. 4:31; 31:6, 8; Josh. 1:5; Hossfeld and Zenger 2011: 530). The Psalter is astonishingly anthropomorphic, speaking of God in the only way we human beings can speak of anything—by analogy with our own life and experience. But these anthropomorphisms are more than literary techniques. They are, Christians hold, glimpses of the incarnation beforehand. The Lord's "hand" in poetry becomes the Lord's hand in flesh. Now those of us with weak hands, who betray and forsake, those in the midst of danger, and even the haughty who hold our heads high, have hope. For God has hands like ours and also greater than ours, and they do not let go.

5. Alter on the verb *hirpah*, to "relax the muscles of the hand" (2007: 477).

PSALM 139

"Have you accepted Jesus as your personal Lord and savior?"

There is much that is nonsensical in this question. "Accepting" is not particularly a biblical notion. The church fathers, medievals, and Reformers don't ask it: it's a way of describing salvation that is barely more than a century old. Jesus's lordship is not merely personal, as though he could be reduced to the tiny confines of my individual wants and needs. His saving work is cosmic—his resurrection defeats the powers of evil and sets the entire creation to rights. And Christianity is not a one-time transaction, contrary to the consumerist tinges in the question. We must take up our cross daily.

And yet, for all that, Ps. 139 suggests there may be something to the question.

Psalm 139 is a remarkably intimate portrait of the believer and God. The question above is a way of asking whether someone knows God intimately, entirely, the way we are known by God. The psalm's response may be that we don't so much know God as we are known by God. Fearfully so. And lovingly. This most intimate of psalms shows a God who knows us minutely, and who wants to be known back with similar depth and delight.

Commentators stumble over themselves to sing the psalm's praises. Spurgeon uses apocalyptic praise, likening it to "a sapphire stone," or Ezekiel's "terrible crystal" on the heads of the living creature (the King James Version of Ezek. 1:22). The psalm flashes out light so bright that it could turn night into day (Spurgeon 1976: 634). Gerhard von Rad calls the psalm a "paradigm of intermingling faith and knowledge," as it wonders after the way that the Bible braids faith and knowledge together (quoted in Kraus 1993: 519).

Psalm 139 may belong to the tradition of testing in Israel. The psalmist wants God to shine a light in every dark corner and see that he is, in fact, innocent and deserves deliverance from the foe. This genre would make sense of the otherwise surprising turn at 139:19–22. The curses there would fit perfectly if the psalmist is, in fact, unjustly oppressed and seeking deliverance. But unlike other psalms of testing, there is no real theodicy here (Hossfeld and Zenger 2011: 545). The psalmist is not now worried about the disconnect between the wealth of God's promises and the poverty of his present status. He is simply exulting in God's intimate knowledge.

There are similar theological notes in the prophet Jeremiah, who praises how God judges righteously and tries the mind and heart (11:20). The prophet exults that God knows, remembers, and visits us, and asks that God would bring down retribution on persecutors (15:15). Their plotting is not unknown to God, so the prophet prays that God would not blot out their sin and would deal with them *while* God is still angry—don't walk away, don't count to ten, but strike while hot. Jeremiah also has the theme of God's foreknowledge before our birth, the testing of our inner person, and our longed-for separation from nihilistic ways (Hossfeld and Zenger 2011: 545).

The psalmist and the prophet connect God's knowledge and judgment with God setting some people apart to be slaughtered like sheep.[1] "You, O LORD, know me; You see me and test me. . . . Pull them out like sheep for the slaughter, and set them apart for the day of slaughter" (Jer. 12:3). That curse is directed at Israel's enemies. The psalmist's observation is about Israel's own fate: "You have rejected us and abased us. . . . You have made us like sheep for the slaughter" (Ps. 44:9, 11). In the Christian imagination, these remarkable passages intertwine with a God with flesh on. Rather than slaughtering Israel's enemies, or slaughtering Israel, the God of the Bible becomes Israel, and *is* slaughtered. God's intimate and exacting knowledge of us is not lobbed from afar or from the safety of the judge's bench. God himself was knit together in a mother's womb. The fearful and wonderful inner workings of God's own body were destroyed. By and for us.

The danger of a testing psalm like this can be its insistence on its own innocence. On Christian grounds, there is no one who is fully innocent. This is why Bonhoeffer counseled reading such psalms as spoken by Jesus alone. Only he can speak of himself as innocently as this psalmist does. Any of the rest of us who

---

1. Kraus (1993: 513) set me to thinking along the lines of this paragraph, though I take matters further than he does there.

think ourselves innocent are a hair's breadth away from slaying the wicked for God. Worse, we're lying.

I once heard a prominent American pulpiteer take to the media to boast proudly that "I have always lived a chaste and moral life." The claim may be true—he may have slept with no one other than with one wife (though Jesus's more exacting demands against even lust in Matt. 5:28 make that claim more dubious). And it is also dangerous. To stand and insist on one's own purity is to stand and insist on one's need for no savior. Which is an odd thing for an evangelical to insist on.

The psalm starts like any good preacher, warming up to the idea, but without shouting yet. God's knowledge of us is searching (139:1). It is aware of seemingly mundane things (139:2). Not a word is spoken that God doesn't know in advance (139:4). God's knowledge of the psalmist proceeds from outer to inner (Hossfeld and Zenger 2011: 540). The first four verses suggest God's distance (esp. 139:2). The latter part of the psalm suggests a God more interior than we are to ourselves (esp. 139:15; Limburg 2000: 472).

The note about God's foreknowledge of our deepest selves opens up greater questions about divine omniscience and human freedom (139:15–16). Twentieth-century interpreters are quick to insist that such verses do *not* suggest predestination or omniscience. Limburg (2000: 473) is one of many who insists that the psalm does not assert divine foreknowledge but rather trust in God's present knowledge of the person praying. These two are not mutually exclusive. The claim is part of modern theology's effort to divide supposedly Greek philosophical concepts (all the "omnis") from supposedly Hebraic and biblical affirmations, with the former as cold and abstract, the latter as lively, flesh-affirming and rooted in creation. But the dichotomy is a false one. Ancient Christians picked up categories like the omnis and filled them with biblical character. Whatever we mean by saying God is omniscient, we mean what this psalm means, not what some philosopher may have meant. Patrick Miller gets at the point well. Predestination, he says, "has always been a theological claim that works better as a personal conviction about one's own destiny being set in the purpose of God than it does as an effort to work out logically the mystery of God's purpose for others" (Limburg 2000: 473, quoting Miller, *Interpreting the Psalms*, 147). And divine truths are better when prayed or preached over than when disputed over (Spurgeon 1976: 635). The psalm is not a polemical one (139:19–22 notwithstanding). Nor should its commentators be.

Perhaps a more promising line of inquiry is pursued by St. Augustine. In response to interlocutors who demand to understand more about the Trinity,

Augustine (*On the Trinity* 15.7.13, in Wesselschmidt 2007: 384) thickens the mystery. We can't even understand ourselves fully. Who can remember what they felt yesterday, when they sat down or rose last week, what words they said a month ago, let alone *how* this intricate combination of flesh and bone can sit, speak, or do those things? *And we want to understand God?!*

What we can know of ourselves is not altogether flattering, contrary to a superficial reading of Ps. 139. With this sort of deep, searching light on, we might want to hide. Better not to be known than to be pitied or loathed. The psalmist has pushed through this and is willing to stand naked before God and all, unveiled by God's piercing eye. There is a moral lesson here: "Live innocently. God is present" (Spurgeon 1976: 636).

"You hem me in, behind and before, and lay your hand upon me" (139:5). I have always read this devotionally as a comfort. But the psalmist may mean something more menacing. You hem something in that you don't want escaping (Hossfeld and Zenger 2011: 540). Could the psalmist wish to run away, like Jonah? One similar affirmation is also in Job, who describes Sheol itself as naked before God (Job 26:6). The image is one of vulnerability, exposure, frailty. The prophet Amos makes this theme starker—the swift try to run, but their swiftness flees them (2:14). You might successfully flee a lion but run right into a bear (5:19), for no one escapes God's slaughter (9:1) (Kraus 1993: 516). Other interpreters keep the line's interpretation as comfort. The gesture of hemming in, Alter (2007: 480) insists, is not menacing but rather the act of a potter. You also hem in something you want to defend. Hossfeld gets the balance right when he proposes subtitling this section "Exposed to God's Knowledge," with its hint of menace overwhelmed in grace (Hossfeld and Zenger 2011: 541, citing Christoph Buysch). For the psalmist says in the very next verse: "Such knowledge is too wonderful for me; it is so high I cannot attain it" (139:6).

"Where can I go from your Spirit? Or where can I flee from your presence?" Psalm 139:7–12 ratchets up the emotional intensity on the claim for divine omnipresence—there is no place however far, nor darkness however thick, that God is absent. God is not absent in the heavens (139:8). God is not absent in the depths, in Sheol, in hell. This latter claim is especially interesting. Sheol is sometimes spoken of as a place of divine absence. This psalm insists there is no such thing. If Sheol is a place, it is full of God, and no one can hide from God even there. Those dwelling in darkness, those languishing in their own hells, also should know they are not absent, cut off, forgotten by God. Christ's descent into hell was a descent into a place that God already held in existence and where he already reigns. Christ's liberation of the damned is here prefigured. Orthodox iconography depicts Christ as breaking down the gate of hell with his cross and lifting out Adam and Eve.

The psalmist uses every point on the compass to illumine divine omnipresence. The wings of the morning suggest the east; the sea in Israel's geography is to the west (139:9). Every direction is then marked as resplendent with God's presence (Kraus 1993: 515). Ancient Christian interpreters were impressed with the way the cross stretches in all directions (Eph. 3:18). Christ points one way and another with his nailed-down hands, signaling the extent of his global reign.

Not even darkness can hide God. The night is as bright as the day (139:12). Dark and light are among the most primal "things" there are. Their opposition reminds of creation's first day, of Christ's death darkening the heavens, of a celestial city in which the sun never sets. Thomas Merton sees in Genesis's division of light and dark the first hint that Christ will be crucified (Gen. 1:3–5).[2] The rending of his flesh reminds of the original rending in creation, as God divides that which will be put back together for his beloved creation's sake. The book of Sirach says that God's eyes are ten thousand times brighter than the sun (Sir. 28:19). It is very hard to speak of light and dark without speaking in poetic terms. That must be why God put them there.

St. Augustine attests, from firsthand experience, how hard it is to flee the Lord (*Homilies on 1 John* 6.3.2, in Wesselschmidt 2007: 386). As the psalmist has made clear, there is nowhere where God is not. So the only way to flee God is to flee . . . toward him. With confession. Having realized there is no escape, we can come to God and receive forgiveness. This omnipresence is not ominous. It makes us luminous.

God does some of the best divine work in the dark. "For it was you who formed my inward parts," the psalmist exults (139:13). The more literal Hebrew rendering states that God made our kidneys, and by extension all our guts. All the parts that make you who you are, were knit together by God, a master weaver. I think immediately here of two friends who have had kidney diseases. Is it a word of comfort that God has made their kidneys, which would end up unhealthy to the point of death? Perhaps—all their days were written in God's book also (139:16). We fixate on our end, but actually no moment in our life is owed to us by right. It is all a gift. Hebrew language has the seat of the self physically deeper (in the bowels) than we normally do (the heart). Whether "we" are our kidneys or our

2. From a CD of Merton's sermons at the Abbey of Gethsemani, this one on the passion. *Thomas Merton's Great Sermons*, ed. Anthony Ciorra (Chevy Chase, MD: Now You Know Media, 2012).

heart or, as I suspect more commonly now since modernity, our "mind," we are an intricate splendor.

Here is something more splendid still: God is fearfully and wonderfully made. Jesus himself was moved in his bowels, the Greek often says; when he is angry, he snorts with his nostrils (*splanchnistheis* in Mark 1:41; *enebrimēsato* in John 11:33). These are more fully embodied descriptions than most anthropologies allow. They are not mere poetry. They are fully fleshy descriptions of the Word made flesh.

The word "body" always has a threefold resonance, at least in Christian speech. The body of Christ is the man Jesus, fully human and fully God, born of Mary. The body of Christ is also the body of the church, with many members, spread through time and space. The body of Christ is also the bread of life on the table through which Jesus becomes part of our mortal bodies and makes us part of his immortal one. Unlike other food, this food digests *us*, and transforms us into the body of Christ.[3] These three bodies are one—no one can be understood without the other. And each is a miracle, a wonder. The psalm suggests each human person is God's best work of art. How much more so the one human person who fully is God? God made by God (Jesus), God made by the Spirit (church), and God in simple elements (Eucharist) (Spurgeon 1976: 640).

Why "fearfully" (139:14)? I have especially had church folks ask about this. We have worked so hard to make God seem cuddly and friendly that this crucial biblical theme falls on the ear with a clunk. Being in the presence of any sort of genuine beauty is frightening. It calls us out from ourselves, makes us literally ecstatic, and demands something better from us. Divine beauty is one that can incinerate. Moses can only see God's backside without disintegrating (Exod. 33:18–23). An Israelite who reaches out a hand to steady the ark is demolished (2 Sam. 6:7). The disciples are right to cower in God's transfigured presence on Tabor (Matt. 17). The angels who appear to people always have to say, "Fear not," because they are so terrifyingly beautiful. No one can say God is pretty. God is beautiful—and fearful. St. John Chrysostom says that God is beautiful from afar, from a safe distance, like the ocean. But also like the ocean, once we're in it, without safety or sight of shore, God is fearful and remains wonderful (*Against the Anomoeans* 1.24–25, in Wesselschmidt 2007: 385).

Psalm 139:16's "unformed substance" is the origin of ancient Jewish mythology about the *golem*, the Hebrew word there.[4] If non-Jews know anything about the

3. Augustine, *Confessions*, trans. Henry Chadwick (New York: Oxford, 1991), 124.
4. William Brown, *Seeing the Psalms: A Theology of Metaphor* (Louisville: Westminster John Knox, 2003), 211.

golem, it likely comes from J. R. R. Tolkien's character by that name in *The Hobbit* and *The Lord of the Rings* and the movies based on them. Tolkien's Christianized and Platonized version of the golem is that he is descended from a hobbit; he is a shadow creature, made hollow by evil and self-regard. It is an image of us when we clasp anything other than the living God, thinking it will make us live. The psalm's word is that even our golem self, our not-formed-in-holiness self, is not unknown to God. God treasures us at our worst. So much Christian mythology suggests that faith is some sort of plan for self-improvement, that God likes the good kids and puts the bad ones in the corner. We have to use scripture's contrary story constantly: God extends his neck for the worst of us and will not forget to transform any of us from unformed, badly formed, into fully formed holy and human beings.

To say that God's thoughts of us are more than the sand (Ps. 139:18) is the sort of poetry that cannot be improved on. Spurgeon notes that sins, like tiny grains of sand, can become a mass, like a beach or desert. But tiny acts of kindness can pile up too and become an overwhelming mass of virtue. God forgets the one mass but not the other (Spurgeon 1976: 640).

To what does "the end" refer in 139:18? It is suddenly introduced and without context. Is the psalmist's effort to count the grains of sand ended, with the psalmist exhausted (Kraus 1993: 482)? Another translation has "I awake, I am still with you"—perhaps from exhausted sleep (Kraus 1993: 482). Hegel once noted that ancient people used to awake and say their prayers. But by Hegel's day folks would awake and read the newspaper. In our day, we awake and check our social media feeds. We go from awaking with God to awaking with the dismal litany of the news to awaking reading others' narcissistic self-obsession and adding our own. The psalm suggests another sort of bookend for the day.

The end could refer to death, in which case the psalm would be promising that God's presence is not endangered by death the way other creatures' presence is (Hossfeld and Zenger 2011: 543). The psalmist's note of God's intricate care for our pre-birth being extends to our post-death being. Patrick Miller puts the point this way: "In our death we are caught up in the memory of God, remembered by God, held forever in the hand and mind of God. . . . Most of us do not have any basic anxiety about our prebirth nonbeing, but we tend to have that about our postdeath nonbeing. The psalmist, however, calls us to look at both states in the same way" (quoted in Van Harn and Strawn 2009: 360).

The psalm's turn to cursing enemies feels like a violation of all the tenderness that has come before (139:19–22). Contemporary uses of the psalm often skip such lines. And not only in liberal ecclesial settings—the monastery at which I worship regularly has a pencil mark by lines such as these, and the chanting monks simply skip over them. Men so devoted to the Psalter that they chant it seven times a day will not chant these lines. Why? Their whole lives are formed after the image of Christ, who commands us to love enemies. This is not squeamishness about morally difficult scripture. It is costly seriousness about another part of scripture. These verses come from "a heart that has not heard the Sermon on the Mount" (H. Schmidt, quoted in Kraus 1993: 517)! Such a reading seems supersessionist[5]—our (Christian) scripture is better than your (Jewish) scripture. But is it wrong?

Interpreters often see in these verses the reason for the psalm's existence in the first place (Kraus 1993: 517–18). This is the first real petition in Ps. 139—the sort of prayer that usually comes at a psalm's beginning (Mays 1994: 429). Perhaps there were even specific rituals of testing sought here, to discern who was in the right before God and who not. The psalmist looks forward to all witnesses knowing his innocence and their hypocrisy (Kraus 1993: 518). He has been accused of misdoing and insists the accusation is false—it is actually his opponents, outwardly religious as they are, who are in the wrong. They break the third commandment by taking the Lord's name in vain and accusing falsely (Alter 2007: 483). God should test *their* kidneys and show them full of wickedness (Hossfeld and Zenger 2011: 543).

Some of our best contemporary interpreters try to pass between an overt Christianization of the psalm and its plain sense cursing of enemies. This move does not require leaving off the letter of the psalm itself. The move from 139:22 to 139:23 shows the psalmist is aware that wickedness might not just be "out there," in someone else. It might be "in here," in the one praying, who needs God's searching forgiveness (Mays 1994: 426). The final prayer leaves us with not even a "murmur of self-righteousness" (426). The cry for vengeance is left behind as the psalm concludes with praise.[6] And the psalm's certainty that God alone is judge is what keeps the psalmist from simply projecting his enemies as God's own enemies (Brueggemann 2014: 584). Anne Lamott writes that we can be pretty sure we have remade God in our image when God has all the same enemies we do.[7] This sentiment, gospel-filled

5. Note that using one part of scripture to object to another is not an intrinsically supersessionist move. Israel has its own abundant resources for turning a word of scripture that would seem violent on its face into one that discourages any violence on our part.

6. Brown, *Seeing the Psalms*, 215.

7. Lamott, *Traveling Mercies: Some Thoughts on Faith* (New Work: Anchor, 2000), 22.

and wise as it is, seems hard to square entirely with the raison d'être of the psalm being a condemnation of the enemy and a desire to be vindicated.

We do well to let the letter of the imprecatory psalms stand—even to chant it in choir. It undoes the sentimentality that hides beneath much of our piety, one that says religion, whatever else it should do, must be nice. And these words are not nice. They show that the world is full of evil—a reality more palpable in places where the church is hard-pressed by enemies with actual weapons, as in Nigeria and Iraq and Syria as of this writing. God is the one before whom "all hearts are open, all desires known, from whom no secrets are hidden," as the *Book of Common Prayer* prays. God as judge will leave no sin unrecorded, unnoticed, unpunished. God's word to sin is not "don't worry about it." God will not tolerate the harm we do to one another and to God's creation, and God will deliver the powerless and crushed.

How precisely does God deliver the powerless and the crushed? By becoming powerless and crushed himself. This prayer against wickedness can, in Christ, be transformed from a prayer against others into a prayer against the wickedness and waywardness in us. It is then a prayer that is prayed against ourselves. The cross that Christ commands his people to bear signifies the painful process of being transfigured out of our sins and into holiness. That is costly, painful, lifelong, and saving. This psalm asks that the psalmist and those who chant and live into the psalms be found on God's side. In Israel, in Christ, God has already declared God's self on our side. There is work to be done—painful, difficult, costly work. God will slay evil in the end. That slaying will include the evil present in ourselves. To pray this prayer will then feel like a cross. And to pray it will have us come out on the other end, cross-shaped and glorified, with friends and enemies alike at our side, all made new by the one who transfigures all things into himself.

"Have you accepted Jesus as your personal Lord and savior?" is a question with more biblical support than usually thought by mainline Christians who come from traditions that only know who they are by *not* being evangelical. Yet Psalm 139 does not stay in the limited confines of an individual heart. It ends up as expansive and cosmic as the Christ through whom God makes all things new.

PSALM 140

If you are not poor yourself, you know the discomfort when a needier person approaches you on the street. You look away, you try to get away, you'll even give them something to be left alone. There is an irrational anxiety that overtakes us when strangers' neediness is unavoidably and publicly made visible.[1]

I confess to similar irrational anxiety with Ps. 140. Does the psalmist really have to spleen so loudly about somebody speaking ill of him or her? The psalmist feels hunted here, like a wild animal. The prayer is for God's powerful intervention *on behalf of the poor* (140:12; note: not on behalf of us who feel discomfited by the poor). The anxiety is more raw than most white, Western religious folks and our respectable lives tend to allow. How do we read it then?

First, we must read Ps. 140 literally and put ourselves in the position of the one praying "Deliver us from evil." That phrase in the Lord's Prayer has a deep biblical history. We often race right past it. This psalm can help us slow down and contemplate what we pray. St. Paul includes a line from Ps. 140 in his litany against sinful humanity in Rom. 3:13. While the psalmist aims vituperation against enemies, Paul directs it again the entire human race: there is no one without the venom of vipers on their lips (140:3)—what hope could we possibly have (see here Rom. 7:25)? Second, the closing verses of this psalm articulate the character of God as one who acts on behalf of the marginalized. The twentieth century in theology saw the coinage of the phrase "God's preferential option for the poor," inspired by scripture like this. Finally, there is a potential spiritual danger here.

1. Kelly Johnson, *The Fear of Beggars*: *Stewardship and Poverty in Christian Ethics* (Grand Rapids: Eerdmans, 2007), 1–11.

The one praying can imagine herself righteous, and her opponents as simply God's adversaries. St. Paul sets us on a reading trajectory in another direction—the psalm indicts all of us. St. Augustine takes this one step further—no one can tell who is among God's elect. One who mistreats us now may eventually become a sister or brother in Christ. We are bound to love all.

How does praying this psalm help us do that? How *do* we get this venom off our lips?

The first prayer for delivery makes clear the psalmist's opponents are attacking primarily with slander (140:3). Folk wisdom tries to downplay the effects of slander ("sticks and stones may break my bones . . ."), but slander precedes mob action and murder. For the Hutus to attempt genocide against their Tutsi neighbors in Rwanda, it was necessary first to slander them, call them cockroaches, accuse them of being recent interlopers at the behest of colonizers into that part of Africa (racist disdain that was learned well from Belgian colonizers).[2] Necessary, but not sufficient. Jesus famously tightens the screws on Israel's commandments. His disciples must not just avoid murder—they also must not hate in their hearts or be angry or curse (Matt. 5:43–47). Here Jesus is just reading his Bible well. The psalmist speaks as one being hunted, targeted, for violence. The present reality may be words. That's a necessary step to violence.

Ancient commentators seize on Ps. 140:2's description that slanderers plan evil "in their minds." Jesus echoes this same teaching (Luke 6:45). There is no evil that does not originate in the imagination—the "Could it be?" of contemplation that precedes the "Come, let us" of action. In a way, Augustine says, it is easier to respond to open hostility. Calumnious talk is a "secret enemy," harder to detect, and so harder to engage (Augustine 2004: 286–87). Chrysostom notes the dangerous critters of 140:3 (the Septuagint adds scorpions to the list). We know to recoil from a dangerous animal. Human beings look safer but in fact act worse (Chrysostom 1998: 264). And interpreters throughout church history note that God's people throughout the length of the Bible have bitter enemies. Virtuous Mordecai has his Haman. Jesus, the best of us, faced the worst opposition. Ancient Christians were persecuted for perceived incest, cannibalism, and murder (Spurgeon 1976: 645, citing George Horne). As the old ladies in churches I serve used to say at prayer meeting, "When God gets busy, the devil gets busy too." And here I'm struck that premodern readers of Ps. 140 approach it with more energy, more first-person experience, than more removed modern and postmodern

2. Emmanuel Katongole and Jonathan Wilson-Hartgrove, *Mirror to the Church: Resurrecting Faith after Genocide in Rwanda* (Grand Rapids: Zondervan, 2009), 10–90.

interpreters. They're willing to let the psalm narrate the difficulty of the life of faith. In medieval Christians' terms, they read it on the tropological level—having to do with the spiritual and moral progress of the soul. And in that register, the best good news is that one faces opposition. Martin Luther taught that the devil can leave a soul alone who is totally within his grasp. Struggle, opposition, pain—these are signs that one is making progress.[3] And here ancient Christians see a way forward as well: resist. Fight. St. Athanasius insists that devils will flee at the slightest opposition (the sign of the cross is enough in most cases; *Life of St. Anthony* 23.1–6, in Wesselschmidt 2007: 391). St. Augustine notes that the psalmist responds to a smear campaign of gossip with a remedy no more violent than prayer (140:4; Augustine 2004: 287).

The litany of complaints in Ps. 140 cuts against two common and incompatible views of evil in our culture. One comes more frequently from the political and cultural left. It tends to deemphasize the agency of evil. The problem with evildoers is that they lack education, or economic opportunity, or the chance to become as enlightened as "we" are. The psalm offers no such superficial explanation of evil. It just laments it, and denounces it, and asks for protection from it, for it lays snares, and digs pits, and sets out traps, and lies to sully others' reputation. The view that evil is simply a lack of information may be as old as Plato, but its appearance today is especially naïve. Not to overly link these comments with contemporary political goings on, but some recent events around the refugee crisis in Syria and elsewhere have reinforced my faith in the evil of humanity. We have heard reports of people selling "life jackets" actually stuffed with paper products. When those fleeing for their lives on the Mediterranean end up in the water, their dearly bought life jackets drag them and their loved ones down rather than bear them up. It's good to have one's confidence in a judging God and a coming hell reaffirmed.

Another approach to evil, perhaps more common in "conservative" settings, is to see it in Manichaean terms—it is someone else's fault, but we will heroically defeat it. That is, evil is "over there," in those bad people, and what we need to do is destroy it, so arm yourselves and fire away. This purported "realist" view of evil uses slander and stirs up gossip against people of other races or religions or political parties, insists that "we" are innocent over against an alien "they," and is happy to propose extraordinary measures like war to deal with such problems. But the Bible insists it is sin to "stir up wars" (140:2; see also Pss. 56:7; 59:4). Violence

3. I take this from David Steinmetz's church history lectures and seminars at Duke Divinity School, 1997–2000.

is no virtue with God. Some in bellicose Western countries seem to view it as a Christian duty to send soldiers somewhere to fight against someone, all the while insisting that those who oppose violence are soft, unpatriotic, sub-Christian. The Bible itself says stirring up wars is a sin and laments and denounces it.

Psalm 140 suggests another approach to evil: it is self-defeating. Evil sets out a trap and falls in it; it lays a snare to capture someone else and ends up capturing itself (140:9–11). Evil is like Haman, hanged on his own gallows (Esth. 7:10); it is, as one interpreter says, like the hunter torn apart by his own hounds (Spurgeon 1976: 647). God doesn't have to punish us when we do evil. God just "gives us up" to the faux gods and the rebellious ways that we ourselves have chosen (so Rom. 1–3).

There are some vivid images and details here. God is the one who covers our head, the psalmist says (140:7). This sounds either like a literal helmet or a crown worn by a king, or perhaps simply like a description of divine protection (Kraus 1993: 522). The hope for burning coals may be a prayer for destruction like that of Sodom and Gomorrah (Gen. 19). Or it could be a prayer for a trial by fire, to determine who is innocent and who is not. Augustine (2004: 294) sees the flames as a more positive image—they burn up dross, purify gold, cauterize wounds, and ignite others with similar beneficent illumination. And of course St. Paul uses burning coals in a way that is both punitive and magnanimous in his own unforgettable way (Rom. 12:20, quoting Prov. 25:21–22).

The psalm is more detailed in its imprecations than it is in its praise. But its praise does matter. God is unmistakably on the side of the poor. In Christian tradition, we have often spiritualized this poverty ("poor in spirit," Matt. 5:3). The poor are the contrite, who sigh over their own sins (Augustine 2004: 299; Chrysostom 1998: 272). That's not wrong. But it contradicts the letter with the spirit of scripture when we don't have to. Jesus says both that the poor are blessed and that the poor *in spirit* are blessed (Luke 6:20).[4] This psalm can say both as well.

God is not only for the poor. God becomes poor in Christ (2 Cor. 8:9). And the church is commanded to meet Christ in his poor now.

This is one of the few psalms in the last third of the Psalter that uses the musical measure "Selah" (140:3, 5, 8). At least we think it's a musical measure. Historians

---

4. Limburg (2000: 476) gives an impressive litany of the scriptures' insistence on God's bias in favor of the (quite unmistakably materially) poor: Pss. 146:7–9; 147:6; legal texts like Exod. 22:21–24; Lev. 19:9–10; 25:35–38; Deut. 24:14–22; wisdom texts like Prov. 14:21; 22:22–23; 23:10–11; 29:14; prophetic ones like Isa. 1:16–17, 23; Amos 4:1; 5:12; 8:4–6; New Testament ones like Jas. 1:27–2:7. God's rule is a just one for the sake of the poor (Ps. 76:9–10), and God will make just judgments on their behalf (Ps. 82) (Hossfeld and Zenger 2011: 551).

say the term is still "untranslatable."[5] Alter writes that even his translation of all of 140:9–12 here is an educated guess—the text as we have inherited it shows "numerous signs of mangling" (Alter 2007: 484). In one way this is sad—that there are words from God to which we do not have access. In another it is exhilarating. Wendell Berry writes of animal species that we humans, with all our avarice and rapaciousness, have not yet discovered. He hopes, even prays, that there will forever remain animals unknown to us. His hope is that something of "nature" remains wild, undomesticated, untamable, unseen, unknown. So too with God and God's words. Something of them will always elude our grasp.[6]

Selah.

5. For Hossfeld the term is "still uninterpreted" (Hossfeld and Zenger 2011: 549).

6. I learned this from Belden Lane, *Solace of Fierce Landscapes* (New York: Oxford University Press, 1998), where the quote precisely is this, attributed to Berry's daughter: "I hope there's an animal somewhere that nobody has ever seen. And I hope nobody ever sees it" (85).

PSALM 141

It is often assumed that faith is a matter of believing in certain propositions—that there is a God, that the world is made good, that Christ redeems, and so on. That's not wrong, of course; it's just too narrow. Faith goes far beyond mere mental assent. Here in Ps. 141 faith is a full-bodied experience (Limburg 2000: 479). It involves God's "ear," and of course the ears of those praying (141:1). It involves the rich smell of incense—burnt offering, rising up and pleasing God (141:2). It involves the tongue—not only tasting here (141:4) but also blessing and cursing (hopefully more of the former; 141:3). Faith also involves oil on the head for anointing, which makes for mutual company and friendship (141:5). And faith involves the eyes with which one looks to God rather than elsewhere (141:8). Biblical faith is full-bodied and sensuous. Our intellect is part of our embodied faith, but only a part. As this psalm makes clear, "faith" in Israel is an embodied, communal way of life. And the God of Israel not only made us bodily creatures—God *is* a bodily creature.

Many Protestant churches invest little energy in how worship *smells*. Scripture, however, suggests we should care. The psalmist speaks of the sacrifice offered at the end of each day, which Aaron and his sons are to burn nightly forever (Exod. 30:7–8; Hossfeld and Zenger 2011: 558). The mention of the evening is likely what has made this psalm a standard one for evening prayer. St. John Chrysostom tells his congregation they all know it—they chant it every day. Yet for them it is like an unopened treasure, for they don't consider its depths. To ponder it is to undo the sin committed during the day, to scrub clean from the many stains incurred (Chrysostom 1998: 276). For him, the lifting up of the hands is an offering to God of the limbs with which we commit all kinds of sins, from robbery to assault to fraud (Chrysostom's congregation was more interesting than the ones I have served apparently!). This prayer asks that those limbs be consecrated to God instead (141:2–3).

The lifting up of the hands is a potent image for prayer. At least since the rise of the modern Pentecostal movement, Protestants have been divided into those who lift their hands to pray and those who keep their hands stodgily at our sides. Ancient catacomb paintings suggest that the first Christians were more Pentecostal in their approach, perhaps inspired by psalms like this one. The *orans* gesture of hands uplifted is also one mandated for priests presiding at altar in communions like the Catholic, Anglican, and Orthodox, in imitation of Jesus, whose raised hands make for our salvation. Mainline Protestants like me, then, are in the vast minority of those who never pray with hands upraised. This psalm suggests we enter into prayer with that full-bodied gesture.

For Augustine, it is always Christ who prays first. And the hands upraised suggests for him Christ on the cross. The evening is not the time of day; it is rather when the sun ceased to shine, out of mourning for the death of its maker (Mark 15:33). And Christ "confesses" sin here (as 141:1 has it in the Septuagint) not for his own sake but for ours. The one with no sin confesses sin to show us sinners how to do likewise. And Christ is crucified in us as we slowly and painfully unlearn sin and grow into grace (Rom. 6:6; Augustine 2004: 303–9).

There is a slight inner-Protestant polemic relating to this verse. Is it an argument against literal sacrifice and for a spiritual one—an "intrusion of rational thinking into the patriarchal cultic world"?[1] Or is there no internal critique of physical sacrifice here (Hossfeld and Zenger 2011: 558)? The former seems the sort of thing Protestant interpreters used to say as we hunted the scriptures for anti-Catholic ammunition. And faith communities who have abandoned any *actual* sacrifice, with knife and blood and smell, often also lose the metaphor of sacrifice in our spiritual lives as well. There is no opposition between word and sacrament here, just as there is not between belief and embodiment (Mays 1994: 431).

The psalmist asks for a guard over his mouth—that tiny member responsible for so much harm in our lives and world (141:3). Wisdom literature often speaks of the difficulty of mastering the tongue. It is capable of no small amount of havoc, as Jas. 3:1–12 makes clear. Here the psalmist laments trouble coming not from others, outsiders, enemies, but from within, against which she is surprisingly defenseless (as in Rom. 7). The psalmist hopes not to be like the ones condemned

---

1. Kraus 1993: 527, quoting Gerhard von Rad, pointing to such "spiritualizing" interpretations as Isa. 1:13.

elsewhere in Pss. 140–141. The hope is not just for a closed mouth—that can also do harm. It is for a judiciousness about when to open and when to close, like a guard zealously defending the city.

The psalmist prays for the correction of the righteous—their corporal punishment in fact (141:5). Better the wounds of a friend than the kisses of an enemy, Proverbs agrees (27:6). As one commentator puts it, the desire for a box on the ear is not a gentle one; it is an invitation for authoritarian punishment (Hossfeld and Zenger 2011: 558). Spurgeon suggests that those who offer such correction can grow too fond of it. We should only correct others' sins like a person who moves a patient with rheumatoid gout. It hurts the patient. We should move and correct as gently as possible, with as much love expressed as we can muster (Spurgeon 1976: 651). Overlook much, correct a little, as Pope John XXIII famously counseled.[2]

The textual clarity and translation become very difficult in Ps. 141:6–8.[3] That the imagery is violent is clear enough (141:7). It suggests an earthquake, a breaking apart of the very ground under one's feet, the exposure of the bones of the dead and judgment for the living. The Old Testament uses such imagery elsewhere, as when Korah and his uprising are swallowed up (Num. 16:31–32) and when Isaiah prophesies destruction by the enlarged mouth and ravenous appetite of Sheol (Isa. 5:14; Kraus 1993: 527). The rock (Ps. 141:7) is suggestive of Christ in Christian imagination. Those who falter beside the rock, for Augustine, are pagan authorities like Aristotle and Pythagoras, who now "tremble in the underworld," and about whose prospects at the resurrection Augustine does not "wish to inquire."[4] Augustine offers a somber reflection on the bones: they are not the church's enemies but rather its beloved martyrs. Their bones fertilize the earth, their blood irrigates the world, and new crops of faithfulness sprout and rise up (Augustine 2004: 320–22).

The psalmist concludes with more prayers for evil's self-inflicted undoing. The theodicy of this portion of the Psalter is one in which evil always defeats itself. I wonder whether it is because I am an *American* Christian that I find the impulse too quietist. Surely we can do more than wait? But the psalmist insists again—those who set traps fall into them, and we escape (141:9). At the least, the charge to wait resembles the promise of the Hippocratic oath, or the Wesleyan societies'

2. Pope John XXIII, *Overlook Much, Correct a Little: 99 Sayings by Pope John XXIII* (Hyde Park, NY: New City, 2007).

3. Alter: "Everything in this section of the text is doubtful" (2007: 488).

4. The NRSV translation differs from the one in front of Augustine—it has that the rock *is* smashed, not that it smashes others, and so perhaps witnesses to Christ crucified.

first rule, that we first "do no harm." The impulse to fight evil often makes things worse. Remember the evening prayer to see evil undo itself while those praying escape its snare. Evil thought it had done its worst when it crucified Christ. All it did was cause an earthquake, wake the dead, lose its grip on all its hostages, and bring about the victory of God's coming kingdom. The Gospel of Matthew alludes to this psalm when in it Christ promises that the angels will one day collect "all evildoers" (Matt. 13:41, echoing Ps. 141:4). It is Christ who eventually will right the wrongs in his beloved creation. In the meantime, we pray psalms like this nightly, hands raised, and ask for a seal on our tongues, so that they offer praise and not cursing.

PSALM 142

Psalm 142 opens and closes in darkness. Its superscription links it to David in the caves, hiding from Saul's efforts to kill him (e.g., 1 Sam. 24). The psalm closes with a desire to be brought up out of prison by the God who raised Israel from Egypt.[1] God does his best saving work in the dark.

The psalm does not specify which story of David in the cave to which it refers. I prefer the story in 1 Sam. 22, in which all of those in "distress," "debt," and "discontent" gather in the cave at Adullam (22:1–5). Hardly an inspiring congregation. But apparently Ps. 142 has more in common with the cave of En-Gedi, where David spares Saul's life, rebukes himself for cutting off a corner of his cloak, and rebukes his men for saying God has delivered David's enemy into his hands (1 Sam. 24:4–7). In both that story and in this psalm, David is praised for his mercy to his enemy the king (1 Sam. 24:11, 18–19), a voice cries out (24:16), enemies lurk (24:19), and David is in danger (24:12) (Hossfeld and Zenger 2011: 565). The psalmist prays to be brought up from darkness, and the scribe who appended the superscription remembered the story of David and linked the two. The Bible unfolds in patterns. And its master pattern is one of mercy (1 Sam. 24:17).

Commentators often note that this prayer is not particularly original.[2] The psalms often are not. Unoriginality may bore us commentators but should instruct

1. It's Robert Jenson's description of God. Commentators divide over whether this is an image for Sheol, the pit, where the dead cannot praise God, or whether the psalmist is in custody awaiting a legal verdict, or whether some other dungeon is meant. We need not choose between metaphor and the letter of course.

2. Berlin and Brettler 2014: 1428. Hossfeld and Zenger (2011: 568) note all the other psalms that "influenced" this petitioner, ones "employed" but not necessarily quoted in Ps. 142: Pss. 16:5; 77:2–4; 107:5, 6, 10–16, 19, 28; 116:6, 9.

those who pray. T. S. Eliot's adage fits here: immature poets borrow, mature poets steal.[3] Those who pray find themselves in the same place over and over, as if walking only in circles. But God meets us precisely there, not impatiently scolding, but with another version of the same prayer. The circles spiral toward God.

The psalmist emphasizes that the cry is "with my voice," repeating it twice (both in 142:1). God is not summoned with polite indirection here but is rather addressed directly, strenuously, from distress, more like a woman in labor than a supplicant with hat in hand. The psalmist's complaint is poured out, like a libation, a drink offering. Spurgeon notes that we tell God our troubles not because God is ignorant. It can sound that way from our prayers—that our duty is to inform God of sad things of which God is unaware. Instead, prayer is for "our relief, not his information" (Spurgeon 1976: 654). The faint spirit of 142:3 is an opening for good news, a fertile disposition awaiting a seed, for only those with flagging spirits can come to sense another Spirit "at work in me" (Augustine 2004: 330). Alter notes that 142:3 is emphatic: "You, you know my path" (2007: 490). That emphasis on the way or path comes to fruition in Christ, who does not just know the way but *is* the Way (John 14:6).[4] I am struck with the self-pitying of 142:4—the psalmist feels utterly alone. Anyone conspired against may feel that. But this level of solitary misery seems unusual in scripture. The psalmist has a hint of reproach of God on his lips, aligning himself with the poor and lowly, demanding that God act (Hossfeld and Zenger 2011: 566). Dietrich Bonhoeffer worries about Christians applying such self-justifying imprecations to ourselves. The only one who can curse as though perfectly innocent is Christ—and he does not. So too we might say the only one who has ever been this utterly alone is Christ, abandoned by his friends, buried in a borrowed tomb. The hidden traps (142:3) actually caught him. No one is ever so alone as he.

And how did that turn out?

The psalm makes a turn with its fifth verse (142:5), proclaiming the Lord as his "portion." Here, as ever, the Bible is its own best commentator. When the land of Canaan was divided by lot into portions for each of the tribes, the Levites received no portion. The Lord is sufficient as their portion, providing for them in the offerings they as priests receive from others. They need no land, no claim,

---

3. T. S. Eliot, *The Sacred Wood: Essays on Poetry and Criticism* (London: Methuen, 1960), 125.

4. Eugene Peterson offers this observation with regard to his fellow evangelicals, who love John 14:6 but then seem to neglect the specific *way* Christ saves the world: personally, communally, on a small and intimate scale, not with entertainment or anonymity or via our lust for consumerism, but with the way of the cross. See Peterson, *The Jesus Way* (Grand Rapids: Eerdmans, 2011), esp. 1–18.

no private property of their own (Limburg 2000: 481, citing Num. 18:20; Deut. 10:8–9; Josh. 13:14). This quite material claim is often later spiritualized when we pray that the Lord is our "portion." Yet it is still a claim about possessions: God is greater.

The "maskil" of the superscription can frame the psalm either as elaborate poetry or as instruction (Limburg 2000: 480; Hossfeld and Zenger 2011: 565). There are many maskils earlier in the Psalter, but Ps. 142 is the lone maskil in the final third of the book. The historicizing link to David is also common earlier in the Psalter but has not appeared since Ps. 63. The content of the teaching piece here is prayer. David shows us how to pray in distress and reminds us that a creative God always has options on offer that are invisible to us in the dark. St. Augustine (2004: 327) offers here an image that delighted later medieval interpreters. Scripture should be ruminated on. Like a cow chews her cud, we swallow, then bring it back up, and chew some more. This is why, Augustine says (incorrectly), only ruminating animals are clean to eat in scripture: God wants us to ruminate on the law. Even, or especially, when we are in the dark awaiting deliverance. It is we who go in circles as we pray, and that for the good reason of our instruction.

St. Francis, according to his later biographer St. Bonaventure, died with Ps. 142 on his lips as his final prayer (Hossfeld and Zenger 2011: 568). With his followers gathered around him and his voice growing weak, "he, as best he could, broke out in this psalm: 'With my voice I cried to the Lord; With my voice I beseeched the Lord'; and as he finished it to the end. 'The just,' he said, 'will await me until you have rewarded me.'" Then, as Bonaventure writes, that "most holy soul was released from the flesh and absorbed into the abyss of the divine light."[5] One poor and lowly man, whose life is now a maskil, shows us that God permits the darkness only in order to bring about yet more light.

---

5. Francis of Assisi, *Early Documents*, ed. Regis J. Armstrong, J. A. Wayne Hellmann, and William J. Short (Hyde Park, NY: New City, 2000), 2:643–44.

PSALM 143

There have been great gains in shielding exegetes' eyes from traditional Christian interpretation so they can read the psalms more historically and literarily. And there have been losses. For example, an interpreter with only historical-critical lenses reading Ps. 143:10 likely would not catch a pneumatological reference: "Let your good spirit lead me on a level path." That may be no great loss in terms of discerning what the psalmist once meant. But for Christians gathered by the Spirit to be transformed into the body of Christ, it is a terrible loss indeed. It is God the Holy Spirit who sets us on the path of wisdom—not our own industry or aspiration. And God's Spirit is, simply, "good" altogether and the source of all goodness.

Now, this sort of reading may be wrong or even crazy or dangerous. But we don't know that without even considering it, do we?

Psalm 143 is the final of the seven great penitential psalms—ones the church has set aside to weigh the gravity of our brokenness and set our minds on the immense mercy of God. Yet its genre is not that of a straight lament as today's scholars classify these things; it is rather more "martial" than that, as Spurgeon puts it (143:11; Spurgeon 1976: 657). It does indeed have a kenotic shape, bending downward through 143:4, stretching back upward from 143:5–8, and then offering prayers heavenward to conclude (143:9–12). The church was wise to spy the shape of Christ's own kenosis here and call the psalm penitential.

The first verse's refrains "in *your* faithfulness" and "in *your* righteousness" are unusual, suggesting two poles of God's way with us, those of both mercy and justice.[1] God is ever both. Reformation-inspired interpreters see here God's own

---

1. Hossfeld and Zenger 2011: 572. John Chrysostom (1998: 305–17) builds his sermon on Ps. 143 on this same observation.

righteousness given as a gift to the undeserving—God hears because of God's own righteousness, for the ones praying have none.[2]

Psalm 143:2 has engendered most of the Christian commentary on this psalm, since St. Paul uses the verse to describe the hopeless sinfulness of humanity (Rom. 3:20; Gal. 2:16). Psalm 143:2's bleakness is especially stark in contrast to other psalms that positively beg for God's judgment, since it will show that the petitioner is righteous and his enemies worthy of condemnation (e.g., Pss. 7:8; 26:1–6, 11; Limburg 2000: 483). Paul's angle would seem to clash with 143:12—why summon God to destroy God's enemies if the psalmist is among them? Some have hypothesized that 143:2 could have been a petition to enter into a judicial arrangement of some sort so the psalmist might avoid being condemned for a crime for which he is imprisoned (Mays 1994: 433). Others, sounding like older Christian polemicists, speak of the failure of cultic institutions to acquit sins and look forward to another sort of salvation altogether.[3] Both readings seem tendentious. We might just say that 143:2 echoes the plain sense of many psalms (e.g., Pss. 14:3; 130:3) and much else in Israel's scripture (e.g., Job 4:17–21; 9:2; 15:14; 25:4), that human beings are in a plight from which we cannot save ourselves. None of us is entirely pure or righteous before God. Perhaps Paul is not nearly pessimistic enough. Psalm 143:2 recalls the "living being," Adam, that God makes in Gen. 2:7 (Hossfeld and Zenger 2011: 573). No "living thing" is righteous in 143:2. It is not only we human beings who are in trouble but every being that lives (Alter 2007: 492).

Modern theology has thrown up a good deal of resistance to the doctrine of original sin. St. Augustine at times makes it sound like a sort of biological contagion, inevitably passed on in the mechanics of the sex act, only avoided by Jesus because of his abnormal parental generation. There are missteps there (sin is *nearly* original, but God's original word is blessing—and sex, as Augustine says elsewhere, is a good gift of God that we misuse). The anthropology of Israel's scripture is indeed more textured and nuanced than some Christian exegetes have noticed. But passages like Ps. 143:2, picked up by Paul, show that the church has not been entirely tone deaf to scripture in our teaching about fallen humanity. It is no accident the church accentuates this strand of Israel's scripture in our teaching,

2. Mays (1994: 432–35) makes both these observations, citing not only New Testament uses of Ps. 143 but also similar Old Testament themes, as in Isa. 40–55, esp. 45:22–25.

3. Kraus (1993: 536): ancient institutions "of sacral law here suffer an incalculable decline and are at the point of vanishing (Heb. 8:13)," and a longed-for *justificatio impii* (justification of the impious) "announces itself here. The sacral ascertainment of the *tzedek* itself becomes doubtful and strives toward a final defeat" (537).

for sin is only emphasized as that which Christ has overcome—the shadow with which we block an unbearably great light.

Notice the psalm's kenotic progression in 143:3–4. Exegetes point out that the "crushing" of the psalmist's life marks this as one of the psalms about God's care for the poor (Hossfeld and Zenger 2011: 573). The "darkness" of those "long dead" (or, as the *Jewish Study Bible* translates more on point, those "eternally dead") suggests Sheol, the pit, the grave (Berlin and Brettler 2014: 1428). The psalm's downward progression has bottomed out, landing us in Holy Saturday.

And then, as so often in the psalms, there is a pivot toward praise. The psalmist remembers God's faithfulness, like Ps. 77 does at greater length. The psalmist stretches out hands (143:6). That is, acting out *the opposite* of being dead: praying (Berlin and Brettler 2014: 1428). The image of "parched land" is enormously passive (143:6). The land can do nothing to bring the rain. We at least can pray—as does the psalmist, whose spirit fails within. Far from an expression of despair, our own spirit's failure is a prerequisite for God to send us God's Spirit (143:10). The psalmist asks to hear of God's faithfulness in the morning—like soldiers in a siege who hope for good news on the morrow, or like sinners who wait for the sun to put away darkness (Alter 2007: 493; Augustine 2004: 356). The psalmist promises to flee not just from enemies but to God (apparently not all flight is cowardice!) (Augustine 2004: 357; Spurgeon 1976: 659).

This psalm also contains themes of wisdom, echoing the great Torah-teaching Pss. 1, 19, and 119. There are two ways—righteous and wicked—and those listening and praying along should take the righteous path (143:8, 10).[4] Yet perhaps unlike those other psalms, where the implication is that the righteous and wicked ways are clearly demarcated, here the psalmist needs help discerning which is which—hence the prayer for discernment, for deliverance, and for the Lord's Spirit. And, as many psalms pray, this one asks for revivification—for life in the midst of death (e.g., Pss. 30:3; 33:19; 41:3; 71:20; 138:7; Hossfeld and Zenger 2011: 576).

And the psalmist asks for God's own "good spirit," which Christians will want to render "Spirit." In biblical parlance, God's Spirit is just God's own self, all over again, discernible in his effects among us creatures.[5] Christians add the odd teaching we hold that the Spirit is another person within the triune life. The Spirit is the one who conforms the church to Christ to the glory of God the Father. And

---

4. Limburg 2000: 485. Like 143:5, Ps. 119 records regular promises to God that the psalmist will "meditate on your statutes" (e.g., 119:15, 23, 27, 48, 78, 148).

5. For more on the Spirit spoken of this way in the Old Testament, see Hag. 2:5 and Isa. 63:11–14 (Hossfeld and Zenger 2011: 576).

as this psalm makes clear, the Spirit does that by teaching us God's good ways, keeping us on God's good paths. Hossfeld (2011: 578) sees this Old Testament theology of the Spirit as the background of Paul's instructions to the Galatians, where he implores them to live not by the law but by the Spirit (Gal. 5:16–18). For this psalm, read according to the grammar of Christian doctrine, the Spirit is God within us, reviving us, transforming our hearts painfully from hearts of stone to those of flesh, "tearing us out" of our "demerits" and "engrafting" God's gifts into us, as Augustine (2004: 359) puts it. Sounds painful. As well it should. Nothing good ever has an easy time being born.

The final verse in Ps. 143 shows us how to be so torn from demerits and grafted into God's gifts. Even the psalmist seeks revenge. God's very word includes words of spite and hatred. It is easy for us to cluck our tongues at these from a safe distance. Those under duress, imprisonment, and death understand them far more readily. And precisely then it is important to transform those words into ones of grace and mercy rather than spite. The one who does this is, of course, God's own Holy Spirit, who transfigures us from those with no righteousness at all (143:2) to those overflowing with goodness, and who gives us eyes to see scripture's transformation from something ugly to something radiant.

PSALM 144

Pay special attention to how the Bible reads the Bible.

Here in Ps. 144, historians suggest, a later psalmist is picking up on and re-arranging the work of previous passages of scripture in a new context. Psalm 18 is another royal psalm that describes God's saving work in terms of natural wonders. Second Samuel 22 does much the same. Psalm 33 has a similar emphasis on the gift of being God's unique people. And Ps. 72 is a royal psalm that describes blessings for the king. Psalm 144 has rearranged these preexisting pieces with a purpose. It is not simply a military psalm (144:1). Martial elements are somewhat muted, and the combat seems to be against internal enemies and slanderers (144:8). The extravagant praise of the king in Ps. 72 has given way here to blessings not for the monarch but for the people (144:12–15). In fact, the royal psalm here is strained through the anthropology of passages in Job and Ps. 8 that insist on the transience of human life—all life, the monarch's included. It is not just one king whom God rescues. It is plural *kings*, perhaps even those beyond Israel (144:10). Scholars imagine that a latter-day monarch is picking up on biblical themes of God's deliverance of King David and applying them in a day of reduced monarchical power. To put this imagined king in less academic and more homiletical terms: God, you defeated David's enemies on the battlefield. Surely you can help Israel against these homegrown liars, can't you?[1]

As for the remix of the previously existing scriptures: only God creates ex nihilo. We only ever riff off of a melody that God begins.

1. I take these parallel and origin verses from Hossfeld and Zenger 2011: 581–90; Limburg 2000: 487–88 (he calls the psalm an act of "recycling"!); Harrelson 2003: 886–87.

The Bible gives us a model, then, for how to read the Bible. Previous passages of scripture are sung, memorized, beloved, and redeployed in new circumstances to shape a people after God's own heart. This is what those who are gathered in Christ have long done with the psalms. God already has bent the heavens and come down in the incarnation (144:4). Heaven was made to bow, and God brought heaven down with him, as Jonathan Edwards puts it (in Spurgeon 1976: 664). The psalmist then is "astonished beyond measure" at the love "by which [God] descends from his divinity" (Eusebius, *Proof of the Gospel* 6.9, in Wesselschmidt 2007: 406). How *now* do we, who make up this divine-and-human body of Christ, read these martial and royal words about putting away foreigners? Both Augustine and Chrysostom independently of one another see here a call to battle . . . against our sins. Reflecting on the call for military strength in Ps. 144:1, Chrysostom preaches, "There is, however, a worse war than this" (1998: 321). They didn't invent this move. Ephesians makes it too, where Paul writes that we battle not against flesh and blood but against "the rulers, against the authorities, against the cosmic powers of this present darkness" (6:12). The world is good, but we are not, and the fight to have our wills conform to what our baptism tells us we already are is a lifelong struggle.

Finally, this psalm has themes of antagonism against the "alien." This is a term that moves around a great deal in scripture. God's people Israel are commanded to love the alien and the foreigner in their midst, to feed them and look out for them and include them insofar as they can into God's covenant people. Yet still sometimes aliens are to be dominated (Isa. 49:23, where they "lick the dust of your feet"), sometimes they pay homage to Israel's God (Isa. 45:14, where they bring wealth as gifts of tribute), sometimes they bow to Israel's God (Isa. 45:22–23, quoted in Phil. 2:6, where "every knee shall bow"), and sometimes Israelites are commanded to separate themselves from foreigners even if that means dissolving marriages (Neh. 9:2) (Limburg 2000: 487; Mays 1994: 435–37). The New Testament picks up Old Testament promises that at the end of time even Gentiles would come to worship Israel's God as fulfilled in Pentecost and the birth of the church (Isa. 56:6). The church is a community forged in the womb of baptism, related through water rather than blood. And yet it is important to note the Bible's constant insistence that God chooses *one* people, Israel, to be God's favorite, God's beloved, God's bride, God's example to the world. In Christ, even we Gentiles get to be joined to God and God's people, made part of this beloved bride. It is very hard to hold together both God's mysterious choice of one people and God's blessing on all people. Disaster ensues if either is lost.

The psalm's opening verses are a warrior's prayer (144:1). But we already know from abundant evidence throughout the psalter and the tradition of the church that the letter of scripture often seeks to be read figurally. For Augustine (2004: 362), the fingers of 144:1 are an image of God's care for us down to the smallest digit, and of the specialization and unity necessary not only to bend a bow for battle but to be the church. For Augustine (366), discipleship is not a matter of one's own initiative; it is rather a matter of being trained by God to fight well. Spurgeon (1976: 662) speaks of other professions mentioned in scripture that require meticulous skill with fingers, such as metallurgy and weaving: God gives the gift behind every profession requiring whatever level of skill. These pieces of Christian midrash strike me as at least as interesting as the parallel cultural observation that King Thutmose III is depicted as learning archery from the Egyptian god Seth (Kraus 1993: 542). And then we can also demilitarize the image in the same way Jesus demilitarizes his own scripture: "Nothing so surely trounces the enemy than acting mercifully toward others," Augustine says. As soon as we forgive, the "fire of sin is extinguished in the flood of mercy" (Augustine 2004: 368).

The drums of war stop, and the psalm grows thoughtful, existential, musing on the brevity and vanity of life (143:3–4). Kings' monuments are usually meant to seem fixed, eternal—here the memory is not set in bronze or marble but in spiderweb. This is, as Alter (2007: 496) notes, a little odd for a victory psalm! But then the Bible is an odd book. Life's breathtaking brevity is noted here neither with Ps. 8's wonder nor with Job's truculence ("What are human beings, that you make so much of them . . . ?" 7:17–18), but with a sort of undoing of kingly legend (Harrelson 2003: 886). Our life is a shadow. God's is light itself. Chrysostom stops and tells a story about our language's inability to capture God. If someone claims to be measuring the sea in teacups, we wouldn't start calculating with him how many it would take. We would say he doesn't understand what sort of thing the sea is (Chrysostom 1998: 324). So it is with God, who is always beyond our measuring. There is an intermediary between God and us, however: the king. Most kings want us to remember their glorious deeds, one of Spurgeon's sources is right to point out. Israel's king remembers his unimportance (Joseph Hall, quoted in Spurgeon 1976: 663). The psalms couldn't say it better, though they often try (see Pss. 39:4–7; 49:12, 20; 90:5–6; 109:23; 146:3–4) (Berlin and Brettler 2014: 1429; Limburg 2000: 487).

Quickly the drums return as the Lord's saving work is remembered in terms of what we call natural disasters, one "tumbling" after another, earthquake and storm and volcano and smoke and flood (143:6–7).[2] Alter (2007: 497) points out that Hebrew is often more dramatic than our English; "crack lightning" in 144:6 is his translation for the onomatopoetic *broq baraq* in Hebrew. We may know "more" about creation than our biblical forebears did in terms of what causes such phenomenon scientifically. Yet our words still fail adequately to describe such wonders. And we do well to fear them still. Scripture imagines the inbreaking of God's reign in terms of the storm—Isa. 64:1 begs God to rend the heavens and come down. That passage is echoed in Jesus's baptismal scenes in the Gospels. Language of Christ's return and the arrival of the kingdom in full also draws on the language of natural wonders and meteorological terrors. And knowing how these are caused scientifically doesn't make them non-apocalyptic. The most terrifying, sandwich-board-crazy, "end is near" article I've ever seen has not an ounce of religion in it, but is rather about the coming earthquake along the Cascadia fault line that could one day destroy the Pacific Northwest of the United States and Vancouver Island and the Lower Mainland of British Columbia.[3] No word so hopeful as "repent" appears in it.

Psalm 144:7–8 gives us a glimpse of the source of the psalmist's irritation: "aliens" who have sworn an oath and not kept it. Their mistake, biblically speaking, was swearing an oath in the first place. The setting is either exilic, and the aliens are likely Babylonians, or postexilic, and they are those who have moved into the land as Judea was dragged away. Either way, they are not God's people and they are not keeping their word. The heart of the biblical tradition is that guests, foreigners, visitors are a blessing. They are angels; they are an obligation directly from God (Gen. 18:1–15; Heb. 13:2). And they, like everyone else, are also sinners. The breaking of one's word is a serious offense. Here the word "alien" might do best allegorically: St. John Chrysostom reads it as a reference to anyone who holds not to the truth; such a one is "more savage than the Scythian" (1998: 329).

Petitions end quickly, and the psalmist returns to praise, or a promise of praise once prayers are answered (144:9). And the anti-alien sentiment of 144:11 begs Chrysostom's question: How precisely do we treat the Scythian? The oppression of the alien and his cruel sword can be overwhelmed militarily, of course (144:1). Or they can be overwhelmed with reconciliation, since we, the ones praying, recognize ourselves also as enemies of God (143:2). The shape of biblical election is that God chooses Israel in order through Israel to bless all nations.

2. The tumbling image comes from Kraus (1993: 542).
3. Kathryn Schulz, "The Really Big One," *New Yorker*, July 20, 2015, http://www.newyorker.com /magazine/2015/07/20/the-really-big-one.

In the church, we recognize we are among the "all nations" streaming to Zion to worship Israel's God in Christ (Isa. 2:2–5; Gal. 3:27). Prayers against aliens then can become prayers for friendship. For we were once aliens, before being brought near in Christ (Eph. 2:13). And the answer to such prayers is indeed a reason for rejoicing, with a new song, on the ten-stringed lyre, as David often did and as this psalm remembers (144:9). Such instruments are for merrymaking between lovers, Augustine suggests (*Sermon* 33, in Wesselschmidt 2007: 406). And among all those who rejoice.

The psalm shifts radically in 144:12–15, opening a prayer for every sort of blessing imaginable. The psalm here shifts from singular to plural, the references to Ps. 18 are gone, and the note of lament is replaced with a nearly eschatological vision of *shalom*. The passage's desire for every good thing makes good literal sense: the victory of the king brings peace and so the blessings of prosperity (Alter 2007: 497). The blessings of the fruit of the ground and of the body and of cattle echo the promises of Deuteronomy for those who keep covenant with the Lord (Deut. 28:4–5). To those blessings are added a wall without breach and no scream in the streets (Ps. 144:14).[4] Limburg sees in the two parts of the psalm an expression of the two sorts of providential intervention that God undertakes in scripture: spectacular, nature-altering rescue (144:1–11) and ordinary, life-sustaining miracles of food, drink, child-bearing and child-rearing, and home (Limburg 2000: 488). Kraus sees here a prayer in the name and for the sake of a king by another later group trying to appeal to the king's God. In the name of David, a later gathered community prays to David's God. So too do those in Christ address God in a latter day and in *his* name (Kraus 1993: 544). Monks vowed to poverty, chastity, and obedience struggle a little with such material blessings. Chrysostom (1998: 330) points out that the psalmist has just prayed against every sort of vanity (144:3–4). Augustine (2004: 376–77) uses language from Jesus and the Song of Songs to speak of these blessings as indeed good, but not as good as God's eternal promises. I see here a prayer of blessing on the church. Christ, the son of David, is the one who prays this and all the psalms. He combats the enemy, directs us in what is important and what not, rends the heavens to come down, teaches us to rejoice, defeats every enemy, and prays for many offspring and every blessing on us, his own people and body. God is good for us. It can just take a long while, and a great deal of struggle (144:1–11!), to see that and how this is so.

---

4. Echoing Alter's (2007: 499) translation here.

PSALM 145

Human beings are praise-bearing creatures.[1] We become what we love. The psalms try to shape what we love away from ourselves alone, and those close to us, so that we love God and all of God's creation. They try to turn us inside out.

This psalm is unique. It is the only one with a superscription that dedicates what follows to "praise," *tehilah*. Yet the entire book of Psalms is called in Hebrew *tehilim*—that is, praises (Alter 2007: 500). This psalm is a sort of praise among the praises. It has a pride of place in Judaism, shaping other such prayers as the Kaddish, the prayer with which those who mourn praise God, and the Shemoneh Esreh, the central prayer in Jewish liturgy (Hossfeld and Zenger 2011: 604). The Talmud exults that the one who prays the *tehilah* of David three times a day "may be sure he is a child of the world to come" (Mays 1994: 437). This psalm appears in the Jewish prayer book more than any other (Van Harn and Strawn 2009: 149). Hossfeld describes Ps. 145 as a sort of *regula fidei* in Judaism—a means to discern whether an idea or practice is authentically Jewish (Hossfeld and Zenger 2011: 602). The psalm is a rule of praise.

Psalm 145 has, then, a similar place in Judaism to the Lord's Prayer among followers of Jesus. We are encouraged to say the Lord's Prayer regularly (rules for thrice-daily repetition turn up in ancient Christian literature and still in monastic practice). The psalm has, at its heart, the celebration of a king and his kingdom (145:11–13). And perhaps surprisingly for so specifically Jewish a prayer, it is, indeed, universalistic in scope. All people are called on to praise. All animals and

---

1. I take the language here from Hossfeld, who speak of the psalm's "universalism," that all people are "bearers of the praises of the name" (Hossfeld and Zenger 2011: 600). I add the Augustinian accent here.

inanimate objects too. The psalm, like Judaism in general, starts with one person praising. But it doesn't stop there. In the church, we see ourselves as the worldwide fulfillment of God's promise to cover the cosmos with Abraham's praise.

This psalm holds a singular place among the 150. It is the final acrostic psalm—each line begins with a letter of the Hebrew alphabet, showing that God will be praised from first to last, A to Z.[2] Such artistic limitations do not curtail freedom but rather enable it. It is the final psalm attributed to David. It is the last before the four hallelujah psalms that close the psalter. For all these lasts, these endings, Ps. 145 insists that the only enduring thing is praise of the Lord. This is an end that is unending. So too whatever in us that is praise lasts unendingly. Whatever is not comes to an end. Eventually.

With the psalm in mind, think for a moment about praise. Ask someone who praises God the reasons for their praise, and they will likely give you reasons for thanks—for children or job or friends. Those are good gifts indeed, but thanksgiving is slightly different from praise. When we praise, we offer God thanks for God's own sake, for God's beauty, not for anything God does for us. And we see this beauty resplendent throughout creation. God knows it is difficult for us to praise another being. So God gives the psalms to show us how to praise, and God gives us the entire choir of creation, whose praise is already in progress.

Augustine (2004: 379) puts the psalm's purpose boldly: here God praises himself, to give us creatures a pattern by which to praise him. Praise is joining in an inner-divine work already under way. We never start or finish it. Mays (1994: 437) describes Ps. 145 as the means by which David's praise continues unendingly. Those of us who see David as a sign of Christ are here taught how to pray like and with, or even *as*, Christ. Interpreters both ancient and modern see hints of what would become the Lord's Prayer, especially in 145:1's exaltation of the divine name (Chrysostom 1998: 333; Hossfeld and Zenger 2011: 602). That the Lord's Prayer would have Old Testament roots is not surprising—where else did Jesus learn how to pray other than from scripture? In its setting in the Psalter, it is an interesting counterpoint to Ps. 144, which lacks 145's many references to David's kingship. Psalm 145 suggests, then, Christ's divine nature, linked indissolubly to his human (Ps. 144).

The first verse here (145:1) forms an *inclusio* with the last (145:21), each calling for unending praise (Mays 1994: 437). The second (145:2) repeats the sentiment—trying to make even such hardheaded learners as us to understand that praise is

2. The others are Pss. 9; 10; 25; 34; 37; 111; 112; 119.

eternal. An anonymous rabbi said this of the practice of repeating the Shema thrice daily: "Out of repetition, sometimes a little magic is forced to rise" (quoted in Van Harn and Strawn 2009: 148). "Every day," the psalmist insists, not only on good days. Anyone can praise when fortune banks in our favor. The more difficult prayer is for praise to fill our mouths when we would rather spit out curses (Augustine 2004: 382). Preachers often encourage listeners to list their blessings, both material and spiritual, and notice they are "adrift in an indescribable ocean of blessings" as a result (Chrysostom 1998: 334). Interpreters often point out also that talk of a new king makes old kings nervous, as it should (145:11–13; in purportedly democratic countries we often miss this challenge to the legitimacy of our rulers—calling God our "president" doesn't do the same work). The grammar is significant also—talk *to* God and *about* God are intertwined inseparably. One early Christian adage along these lines was *lex orandi lex credenda*, the law of prayer is the law of belief, and vice versa.[3] We pray what we believe.

The next portion of the psalm, 145:4–9, show again this oscillation between the Lord's particular and affectionate care for Israel and his universal delight in all nations. God's marvelous works are woven into the entire created order for all to enjoy. God's wonders also take focal shape in his saving works on Israel's behalf. So we see the particular in 145:8–9's quotation of the "grace formula," as scholars call it, from Exod. 34:6–7. Only here it is shorn of some of its note of judgment—there is no mention of the third and fourth generation being punished for the guilty or the thousand generations of blessings for those who love. In scripture, God's acts are quite specific. Stories of the God of Israel are of particular people with specific names, geographies, and faces: God calls Abraham and Sarah, wrestles with Jacob, delivers Moses and Miriam, raises up David, sends prophets (too many to name!). And, here, God's goodness is "universal rather than national," Alter says (2007: 502), drawing up all things in praise. I would prefer not to set the two against each other. God's goodness is universal precisely by being national—God blesses the world *by* choosing Israel. God's praise starts with one person praising and extends to every atom of creation. God's blessings are always Israel-shaped—through the particular to get to the universal.

The mention of generations in Ps. 145:4 is significant. Israel's is a faith built on memory, from one generation to the next. Christianity, like Judaism before us, is a "democracy of the dead," in which folks in the cemetery get as much say as those

---

3. "The rule of prayer is the rule of belief," coined by St. Vincent of Lerins in the fifth century. The Latin adage tries to make clear that what we pray shows what we believe, that what we believe ought to shape what we pray. The two are not just inseparable—they are one.

walking around above ground.[4] Yet there may also be two kinds of generations here: the one we know now in history and another among the saints, where generations are not marked off by death, but among whom there is only life.[5] There is also, commentators often point out, an effusive rhetoric here. Any editor with a red-tipped pen would slash through 145:7's "they shall celebrate the fame of your abundant goodness." Surely "celebrate" is enough? With God it is not so. Spurgeon celebrates the excess: "Let them go on forever. They do not exaggerate; they cannot. You say they are enthusiastic, but they are not half up to the pitch yet; bid them become more excited and speak yet more fervently" (1976: 667). There is nothing of God that is not altogether mercy.

The next section, 145:10–13, opens with a sort of midway introduction in 145:10: all God's works shall praise. This choir has more voices than just us humans. Augustine calls creation "a supremely ordered elegance" (2004: 391). As ever in scripture, the things God has made will offer God praise (see also Ps. 19; Berlin and Brettler 2014: 1430). The things God has made are like the burning bush: they are full of the fiery presence of God, yet not destroyed.[6] Creation is not just to be praised for its own sake. It is also the context for the covenant. Many theologies of creation of late have taken stock of the crisis of ecocatastrophe. That is as it should be. Yet we don't praise creation because it's beautiful or in danger of being destroyed. We praise it because it's the theater of God's glory, the place where God works out his saving purposes in humanity, us included. To put it controversially, creation is not good for its own sake (neither is anything else).

Psalm 145:11–13 has a kind of backward acrostic—145:13 begins with *mem*, 145:12 with *lamed*, 145:11 with *kaph*. Read together you get *melek*, or king. Fanciful or not, these verses describe the kingdom of God, with four mentions (Hossfeld and Zenger 2011: 594). Jesus preached often about the kingdom, so we Christians associate it with him, but it is not original to him. It is in fact rooted in the Bible he learned while bouncing on Mary's knee, hearing her sing David's psalms. God's kingdom is glorious, powerful, everlasting—and worth talking about. I'm struck by how wordy this section of the psalm is—the very heavens cry out, so does the psalmist, so should we. Augustine (2004: 386) takes the strong verb in 145:7 in a happy translation as "belch forth." He elaborates: we eat and drink of God's mercy, like John reclining at the Lord's breast, and then belch out mercy,

4. It's G. K. Chesterton's famous language in *Orthodoxy* (New York: Barnes & Noble, 2007), 39.
5. Augustine 2004: 384. He goes on: "If we praise him in our chains now, how much more shall we praise him when we are crowned?"
6. One of Spurgeon's commentators makes the comparison (1976: 667).

with elaborate words, to others (John 13:23). This kingdom, as the creed says, will have no end. We bless earthly kingdoms with the wish that the monarch would live long (Berlin and Brettler 2014: 1431). There is one king undefined by death.

The last longish section of the psalm (145:13–21) does several things. It specifies God's care more precisely. The eternal king over all, praised by all, good to all, has special affection for those who are tottering and brought low (145:14). The Lord is near to those who call, fulfills the desire of those who fear, and watches over those who love him. Then in a sentiment many moderns find distasteful, God also promises to destroy the wicked (145:20). Perhaps our distaste for the latter explains our lack of delight in the former. As Flannery O'Connor says of our sentimental age, we have such a diluted sense of evil that we "forget the price of restoration."[7] A few specific applications here: Martin Luther takes the prayer of 145:15–16 as a model for Christians to say grace at table (see also Ps. 104:27–28). Augustine wonders at petitionary prayer—why does it feel so ineffective? He points to biblical prayers answered affirmatively (the devil's request to sift Peter in Luke 22:31) and not (Paul's against his thorn in 2 Cor. 12:8–10; Jesus's in Gethsemane in Matt. 26:36–46 and parallels). God's nonresponse to our cries could be like the physician ignoring the patient's pleas: the pain is for your good; it will hurt more eventually if I don't continue operating (Augustine 2004: 396). We see here the character of God's kingdom and the reason this psalm is so beloved in Judaism. It is a summary statement of the whole Psalter: the Lord is king over Israel and the Gentiles and all flesh (Van Harn and Strawn 2009: 364). We see the character of the kingdom that would be fleshed in Jesus: that this God "loves to reverse things" (Spurgeon 1976: 669). The psalm appears in the New Testament in slightly indirect ways when the faith is being proclaimed to outsiders (Acts 17:27), when it is being summarized for insiders (Phil. 4:5), and when it is being inhabited in the praises of Israel (Rev. 15:3; 16:5). The verse often drawn on for such brief and powerful summary is one that describes Israel's praise, Jesus's incarnation, and all creatures' deepest longing, acknowledged or not: "The LORD is near" (145:18).

---

7. O'Connor, *Mystery and Manners* (New York: FSG Classics, 1970), 48.

PSALM 146

"We are in the midst of the praises," Spurgeon writes. He imagines these final five psalms as mountain peaks, one after the other, each offering a more resplendent view than the former, keeping pilgrims hiking on despite exhaustion. These concluding peaks of the Psalter make good on the promise of Ps. 145:21, "My mouth will speak the praise of the LORD," from 146:1's individual solo to 150's exuberant chorus of every created being (Limburg 2000: 492).

There is a simple, two-part order to Ps. 146. The first offers wisdom to the hearer; the second describes the God of Israel. Psalm 146:5–6 presents the whole psalm, perhaps the whole of scripture, in short: our happiness is only in God, "who made heaven and earth, the sea, and all that is in them" (146:6; Hossfeld and Zenger 2011: 609). That line is not the only one in this psalm to find its way into an ecumenical creed. "His kingdom will have no end," as Nicaea proclaims, echoing 146:10.[1] Not bad for ten short verses. The psalm's two parts make complementary promises: one, princes in this world will fail to keep trust (146:3–4); two, the Lord will not (146:5–10). The first promise is a warning; the second, a consolation. The way the Lord rules is not only good news for the lowly (146:6–9). It is also unending, eternal, everlasting, and thus worthy of everyone's trust and praise (146:10).

The psalm repeats many other portions of the Psalter, a sort of "condensation of condensations," as Zenger says (Hossfeld and Zenger 2011: 609). One place frequently repeated is our earlier Pss. 103–104. This one also opens with "Praise the LORD, O my soul!" Modern theology has been hard on "soul" talk, fearing in

1. Among other places in scripture (e.g., Isa. 9:7 and Luke 1:33).

it a sort of empty Platonist or even gnostic promise of salvation without our body, community, or creation. But no one can accuse this psalm or this portion of the Psalter of body-denying or creation-ignoring or degrading "salvation." And yet Ps. 146 has a place for the soul. The language suggests something more substantial than merely one's "self" (modernity's obsession). As the psalm makes clear, our *nefesh* is the thing without which we are not, and the soul exists to praise God. While we praise God, we live. When we don't, we return to dust. Soul talk need not be body-denying—it can be body- and community-ennobling. All created things bespeak a generous and wise Creator. Admire them? Admire their Maker all the more. "Admire the edifice? Love the builder," Augustine advises (2004: 405).

"Do not put your trust in princes," the psalmist sagely admonishes, in one of scripture's least followed directives. Scripture's mistrust of monarchy is consistent and nearly uninterrupted. God tells the people they ought not to want a king, since a human king represents a rejection of God's own personal rule. Gideon refuses to rule over the people (Judg. 8:23). Samuel explains that having a king will go poorly, for "he will take" sons and daughters and lands and animals and crops (1 Sam. 8:11–18). Yet the Israelites want one, because other nations have one. Samuel, Kings, and Chronicles show how that fulfilled desire went. Scholars wonder whether the ruler referred to here is Ptolemaic or Seleucid or even the Jews' own Maccabeans (Hossfeld and Zenger 2011: 613). It hardly matters. Earthly rulers are no less mortal than the rest of us. Psalm 146 points out human rulers' impermanence, though of course depending on the severity of their incompetence or cruelty, their mortality can be a gift indeed! The reign of death does not just apply to people. It can refer to institutions as well—the "powers and principalities" about which St. Paul will make so much (Eph. 6:12).

The reign of death can also describe churchly power. Augustine (2004: 408) sees here his opponents the Donatists, who claimed that a sacrament worked only if the priest administering it was holy enough. What human being could be holy enough to be a channel of grace for the eternal God (146:10)? Anyone who will return to dust cannot be trusted to make us happy (146:4). Only Christ can give grace, and he has only unworthy ministers through whom to give it. Do not put your trust in princes, or in pastors, but in God alone. The salience of this advice will never cease during this age.

The second half of the psalm envisions YHWH's way of ruling in contrast to all other sorts of rule. And like the Sermon on the Mount, it starts with a beatitude. The only way to be happy is to have hope in the God of Jacob (146:5). And this God is characterized by the following actions: he executes justice for the oppressed, feeds the hungry, sets the oppressed free, opens the eyes of the blind, lifts up those bowed down, loves the righteous, watches over strangers, upholds widows and orphans, and ruins the wicked. This is almost a policy platform for the kingdom of God that Jesus would inaugurate. He physically embodies many of these characteristics of the Lord's rule directly, with his healings and teachings and feeding and liberating. We have here the deepest contrast imaginable between God's own way of ruling and the way of ruling of every other ruler. The latter are impermanent and impotent. The Lord's personal rule is forever, powerful, and dedicated to lifting up those crushed down. Adam fell, Augustine points out, but Christ voluntarily bends low, to lift him up. Augustine sees us, the church, in each of these characterizations of God: we are orphaned on our own, but in Christ are adopted. We are spouseless, and our bridegroom is away and we long for him. We are poor on our own, but in him made rich. We should strive even to be hungry: "beggars at the gate of his presence" (Augustine 2004: 416).

Some scholars argue that Ps. 146 tends in a universalistic direction rather than a particularistic one (Hossfeld and Zenger 2011: 614). The claim sits oddly with the hinge verse about the God of Jacob (146:5), but let's let it stand. Princes are not the only ones who return to the dust. All the rest of us do too. Jesus's kingdom is so directly described here that the Gospels could footnote each verse of the latter half of the psalm (146:7–9; cf. Luke 4:18–19). The people want a king. They finally get the only sort of king who can actually ennoble a people—put to death by the powers, reigning from a cross, an imperial seal over his tomb. That's the really surprising thing about this monarch: he is also laid down in the dust. His disciples thought he was the one to redeem Israel (Luke 24:21), but instead he turned out to be as impermanent as the rest. But a God who blew life into dust in the first place can do amazing things with dust. Augustine (2004: 411) reassures his listeners that God took the trouble to create them in the first place: Will God also not take the trouble to re-create us? There is hope here even for human rulers—those unhappy enough to be entrusted by the rest of us with the power to give order to civic or ecclesial life. There is no one but dust to do this work. But God can do amazing things with dust.

Spurgeon reports about a man who had some hope of salvation when he was a monk. When he became a bishop, he despaired a little. When named a cardinal and then elected pope, he despaired entirely![2] Be wary of the person who *wants* to rule. But the psalm's way of ruling, fleshed in Jesus, can be imitated and lived

2. The story is told of Pope Pius V (Spurgeon 1976: 673).

into by even us dust-creatures by the power of the Holy Spirit. This is no idealistic description of a reign that would be nice if it were ever this-worldly. It is how Jesus rules the cosmos now—and how we can rule in our small pockets of influence. It will not always work. We will lie in the dust too. But Jesus's way of ruling will be vindicated, ultimately and eternally.

Praise the Lord!

PSALM 147

The Psalter ends with a "cataract of praise" in the five psalms that "thunder" hallelujah.[1] And amidst that cacophony is the roar of this remarkable psalm about God's gentle restoration of Israel and rule over every particle of creation. Its final note is jarring: "He has not dealt thus with any other nation," over against our assumption that God should be as fair and impartial as we would be if we were God (147:20). No, God chooses a favorite, a beloved—Israel. And the Torah by which God governs Israel is the same as that by which he will renew the entire cosmos.

Perhaps because the Bible begins with God's creation of all things in Genesis, or perhaps because systematic theologies often start with creation, for whatever reason, we tend to start our reflection about God with the universal, the generic, with all creation and people. Then, if we can get over the "scandal of particularity," we might wander around to the election of Israel and the redemption wrought in Christ. This psalm begins precisely the other way. It speaks first of God's restoration of Israel after the exile (Ps. 147:2–3). Only then does it add, by the way, that God is the God of all creation (147:4–5). In its second half, it praises the security of a restored Jerusalem: God not only binds up wounds; God strengthens the walls against future wounds (147:13–14). And also, just in passing, God administers the change of seasons, feeds the smallest creature, and keeps the world spinning on its axis (147:15–18). God is whoever raised Israel from Egypt—and who also, it just so happens, creates the cosmos.

The psalm begins with the praise of praise itself (147:1). It is pleasant to praise (Mays 1994: 441). That's why we do it. Not to manipulate God into doing

1. Spurgeon's perfect language (1976: 676).

something we want. Not because God needs it. But because it's beautiful to do so. Praise is its own reward. Psalm 147 roots itself historically in the restoration of Israel. The exiles are gathered back in, their painful wounds tended, the scattered gathered, the walls restored and their bars strengthened, the people rededicated to the law (147:19) (Kraus 1993: 554, citing Neh. 12:27). It is well to pause and remember how surprising Israel's restoration is. Ancient peoples who were once defeated and carted off, their temple burned, are more likely to vanish than to be reconstituted. But as countless other texts in the Prophets and Psalms make clear, God worked surprisingly to bring about Babylon's vomiting up of Israel (Pss. 33; 104–105; Isa. 35; 40; Ezek. 34). These texts take on outsized importance in the New Testament. God always works surprisingly on behalf of the crushed. And the fact that God would work against Babylon and for Israel while far from home shows that God is ruler of all creation. Babylon, Assyria, Sumer—all speak of their gods as the ones who rule the stars, and in turn those stars rule over human fate. The psalmist defies them by saying the Lord of Israel actually rules the stars, counts them, and gives them names (147:4). It is YHWH who makes earth fertile, and no one else (147:8, 18). And while empires count soldiers and steeds and vassals, YHWH is unimpressed. Israel's God counts bandages for wounds, not horses (147:2–3, 10). This claim about the God of Israel's universal reign seems not a little unlikely. And yet how likely was it that Israel would be restored from Babylon? Yet there it is—a new wall, newly fortified, with Zion a joyful mother, her children feasting on choice wheat, all newly at peace (147:13–14). If that is so, unlikely as it once seemed, perhaps God does rule all things. Right in front of the psalmist's eyes are signs of the turning of the seasons (147:15–18). These don't even require faith to believe—just open eyes. Maybe just so God keeps covenant even when Israel forgets, and raises a people from the dead. It seems unlikely. And yet there is manifest evidence before our eyes. And so it is pleasant to praise.

Psalm 147 is theological in the proper sense (Van Harn and Strawn 2009: 368). It is about God, our *theos*. Human beings turn up in the song about as often as the raven and the horse. God's actions in history are extrapolated into participles (Mays 1994: 443). What God does among creatures is who God unendingly is: God did not just once bind up the brokenhearted or cast down the wicked—rather, God is the God who is constantly doing precisely those things.

God is also characterized here as transcendently and unimaginably powerful. God's "wisdom has no number," as Alter (2007: 505) translates 147:5. We can't even number the stars, some of which we can see. God can, and does, and even gives them names. We have no chance at numbering the wisdom of God, which we cannot see. St. Cyril of Jerusalem points out that a person cannot even number the raindrops on their roof in an hour (*Catechetical Lectures* 6.4, in Wesselschmidt 2007: 420). How much less can we number stars or divine wisdom? St. Augustine (2004: 426) is less impressed by the star-counting. It's not surprising that God can count the stars he made—he can count the hairs on our head, the grains of sand on the shore. Augustine is more impressed with God's counting—that is, personally calling—the saints by name. St. Paul in Phil. 2:15 tells the saints their shining will be like "stars." Both meanings can stand—we who stand in awe of nature can stand in greater awe that God raises up the brokenhearted into holiness. In other words, God's perfection is not distant and remote. It is unbearably intimate. The psalm has a kenotic shape. God's majesty is not removed from creation. It is as close as a mother bird to her baby. God gets close enough to the ice to melt it with divine breath (147:18). God's grandeur is that of a strong and tender nurse—binding those wounds of the brokenhearted tight for our healing (147:3).

There is a feistiness in this psalm, a bellicosity surprising for one so disdainful of warfare (147:10). Like other nature psalms (Pss. 33; 104; 105), this one seems to borrow heavily from the religions of Israel's neighbors. It is not Marduk who rides on the storm, distributing natural largesse and making earth fruitful (147:8, 18). It is YHWH of Israel. And he is not impressed with the thighs of soldiers or the strength of horses (147:10). God is keen, however, to feed the baby bird, whose helplessness and neediness are the perfect images for those who pray (147:9; cf. Luke 12:24). The psalm gives no hint that we eat by the sweat of our brow (Gen. 3:19). This is not creation cursed. It is creation in Edenic bloom, verdant and abundant.

As a preacher, my eye is drawn to the raven (147:9). Several commentators describe the raven as the centerpiece of this psalm's banquet (Limburg 2000: 496; Van Harn and Strawn 2009: 369). This bird has often taken on mythological interpretations in the history of Israel's and the church's preaching. For David Kimhi, medieval Jewish exegete, the mother raven abandons her young at birth because they are white and she's unsure of their patrimony! To call a woman a *Rabenmutter* is still a slander in Germany—a "raven mother" fails to attend to her child (Limburg 2000: 498). For Augustine (2004: 435), ravens cawing are orphaned Gentiles, needing taking in by a mother who will feed them. But for St. Gregory of Nazianzus, the raven represents "the whole feathered race" (*Letter* 101, in Wesselschmidt 2007: 420). The raven provides us human beings with very little by way of sustenance or companionship. God feeds the bird not for its usefulness but just because God made it and it is hungry. "Greatness is occupied with little things," Spurgeon says, and is not so taken up in grandeur as to neglect the particular or obscure (1976: 678). When Jesus draws attention to the raven, he likely has this verse in mind, as any reader of Israel's scripture would (Luke 12:24). Limburg thinks here of Edgar Allan Poe's "The Raven," with its refrain of "nevermore," and imagines a listener wondering if God will ever fail to love. The response, of course, is a hearty "nevermore" (Limburg 2000: 499). With the all-encompassing perspective of the psalm, we can say that all creation reflects its Creator. In an age of environmental devastation, where our machines' exhaust claims the role of melting snow that the psalm reserves for God (147:18), we must work anew to see God reflected in the tiniest creature and the farthest astronomical sign (147:4). The moment we think created things are all ours, we can use them up. But if we think there is more of God to adore in every creature, we have at least to pause and give thanks for the sacrifice of a creature's death—for its life is good. And when we see a raven, we pause and give thanks for the God who feeds it, and for Jesus who notices it, points it out as an example in his teaching, and then redeems it, and us, and all things.

This psalm is intricately put together. In one obvious way, it has two parts: 147:1–11 and 147:12–20. So obviously that the Septuagint treats it as two separate psalms. Yet as contemporary commentators point out, a three-part division is more apt (147:1–6, 7–11, and 12–20; Hossfeld and Zenger 2011: 622). Its third part begins with a joyous, secure, fruitful mother—the image of the distraught widow in Lam. 1 entirely restored. She is comforted, safe, no longer ruined (147:12–13). The city is entirely at peace, the prayer of Ps. 122:6 answered (147:14). The image of Israel's restoration is "idealized," as one commentator says (Berlin and Brettler 2014: 1432). The dangers and vicissitudes of history are over. Harm is undone, and even undoable. Mother Zion and her healthy children dine on the finest wheat (147:14). It is hard to resist discerning here christological and ecclesial images. Jerusalem is an image for the City of God in Christian imagination—here present in full. Augustine's hearers, perhaps more aware of the constant danger of destruction of their cities than we are (and more what we would describe as Pentecostal than any more starched and staid Protestantism), shout aloud at the description of Zion's peace (Augustine 2004: 464). Of course the image is idealized—and who without a peaceful city does not long for one? The mother in labor is charity, straining to deliver us saints, like Paul with his churches (147:13; Gal. 4:19; Rom. 5:5). We might imagine Mary here, delighting in adopted sisters and brothers of Jesus whom she labors to bear into faith. Finest wheat suggests the Eucharist. Call these interpretations fanciful if you wish—church is only there to stoke longing for a city that only God can bring. Perfect peace reigns only when corruptibility has put on incorruptibility (1 Cor. 15:50–54). Psalm 147 shows, with a divine agent and confident past-tense verbs, that that has begun in earnest.

The natural imagery in 147:15–18 is splendid as poetry and can be read as such. Yet again there are depths in a Christian imagination that have to be actively veiled, their exploration discouraged, for baptized hearers not to notice (perhaps this is why theologians and biblical scholars so often do mock Christian exegesis). The snow of 147:16, run through a Christian imagination, recalls Jesus's transfiguration, where he shines like snow. Augustine also thinks of God as a knitter, with us as the raw material: "God intends to make something. . . . He means to knit a garment out of them" (2004: 468). Ash is a sign of repentance. Bread crumbs are a sign of the Lord's Supper. And God's melting breath is a sign of the hardest heart of ice being one God can thaw—as God did with St. Paul. As the psalmist says to look no farther than restored Israel and the natural seasons to see God's faithfulness, Augustine (2004: 471) says to look no farther than the church: Christ has melted our hard individuality and resistance to make us edible, so that he can digest us with others into his body (1 Cor. 10:16–17). Most strikingly of all, modern commentators frequently see a hypostasized Word of God in these verses. The Word does as God wants swiftly, rules nature, bears the law. It appears alongside God's own breath as a fellow agent in creation, as in Ps. 33:6 (147:18). This is not mere imagery. The psalm is a treasure trove of trinitarian and christological and ecclesial language. We must learn anew from the psalm to see and to speak.

"He has not dealt thus with any other nation," the psalm concludes (147:20). The Word that feeds baby birds and governs the cosmos is given to Israel and Israel alone. God plays favorites. No—favorite. We are never given a reason for God's election of Israel other than God's own grace. This is among the deepest mysteries we have—why God chooses one people and not others. I have been in churches that recite this psalm in worship and seen faces contort as people realize what they have just sung before intoning the doxology. At least they're paying attention. Why Israel and not another nation? No idea.[2] But God lifts up the poor and casts down the arrogant (147:6). Christians have, most regrettably, managed to turn even this verse to anti-Jewish purposes: if God has done so much for Israel, they

2. Deuteronomy 7 offers a few clues—because the Lord loved Israel and made promises to its ancestors (7:8). I like the story in midrash, that God first offered the Torah to all nations, but only Israel promptly and joyfully accepted it. Scripture tends to disqualify would-be reasons—it is not because Israel is mightier or more numerous or better than others (Deut. 7:7). But when God chooses Abram, no clear reason is given (Gen. 12:1–4).

have no excuse not to recognize his Messiah (Chrysostom 1998: 360). We do better to let God's election remain mysterious—it does not include us Gentiles. We are only grafted into another faith by grace—it's not inherently our gospel, our book, our covenant, our good news, our God. The joyfully fulfilled mother of 147:12–13 has not only natural sons and daughters but also us adopted children (Rom. 8:15–17). How now will we treat our elder siblings in faith—the natural children whom our Christian forebears, we adoptees, have often mistreated?

PSALM 148

What is necessary to praise the Lord sufficiently? What sort of choir? What will they sing?

We cannot praise God with Ps. 148 without noticing the anthropocentrism of our usual worship. Not the anthropomorphism of the psalm, though that poetic device is obviously in place, but the anthropocentrism of our Sabbaths. Human beings are necessary to praise God, but not nearly sufficient. We need every creature under heaven to make adequate praise for God (148:7–13), and even then our choir is not nearly full enough. We also need every creature *above* the heavens—celestial bodies and angels and the waters above the firmament (148:1–6). Augustine (2004: 476) asks whether his congregation hears 148:7 and imagines a choir of dragons, formed up so that each can sing its part! Of course not, in one way; in another, yes, and a good deal more than dragons. Every creature we love or fear must praise. Every creature we cannot imagine but that exists only for praise, must praise (and, apparently, they also need reminding). Our language falls so flat—as Dante says, "How weak my words fall short of my conception, which is itself so far from what I say that 'weak' is much too weak a word to use."[1] Yet praise we must. The psalms are there for us to say, sing, inhabit, live. Then the pinnacle of creation—the reason for its existence—must also praise. That pinnacle is Israel, God's people, near to God's own heart (148:14).

The exuberant inclusion of nonhuman praisers may seem especially odd to people whose lives are distant from animals other than house pets. And it begs

---

1. Quoted in James Howell, *Introducing Christianity: Exploring the Bible, Faith, and Life* (Louisville: Westminster, 2009), 104.

the question of how our worship should join in praise with Ps. 148. St. Francis's feast day has become a popular one on which to bless animals. This can be a meaningless or sentimental gesture, more pagan than Christian. The saint himself had animals fed a double portion on Christmas. He would preach to birds and listen to crickets and scoop worms out of the way where they would be stepped on.[2] All creation praises—if we take time to listen. I have been struck at the response of sheer delight when having a donkey in worship for Palm Sunday; others have seen similar response from church and neighborhood for live Nativity scenes (the psalm appears just after Christmas in the Revised Common Lectionary). The point of course is not a "wow" (and actual smells and animal behavior can undo sentimentality quickly!). It is to say that creatures are only *there* in the first place to offer praise. Human creatures included. It takes this diversity of animal and plant and heavenly and human life to praise a God this creative and beautiful.

Psalm 148 is a "poetic reprise" of the Genesis creation story (Alter 2007: 509). We have the heavenly court, the celestial bodies, the waters above the heavens, the creeping things and cattle, the abundant fruit trees, and finally, human beings. Psalm 148 has three strophes for heavenly things—an important symbolic number for God (as in the threefold Trisagion of Isa. 6 and the three-part Aaronic blessing of Num. 6:24–26). Earthly things are represented by four strophes, signaling the entirety of the earth (four winds, four corners of the earth, four great rivers). The heart of the psalm (minus the introductory and concluding lines) has ten hallelujahs, suggesting wholeness, completeness, as in the ten creative words of Gen. 1 and the Ten Commandments given in Exod. 20:1–21 and Deut. 5:1–22. To re-add the opening and concluding lines gives us twelve hallelujahs, suggesting the twelve tribes of Israel and twelve months of the year.[3]

Modern interpreters often deride such numerological observations as fanciful. I have found it easy (and fun) to get a room laughing by piling them up, whether that room is full of church people or scholars. Yet Zenger is right to caution, "None of this is a game" (Hossfeld and Zenger 2011: 632). And poetry is not obviously our strong suit in contemporary North Atlantic cultures. The psalm describes the "skillfully planned order" that creation is (632). Actually, it does more than describe. The poetry of God is what launches this order into existence in the first place (148:5–6). This is not just ornate language. It is the

2. James Howell, "Commentary on Psalm 148," *Working Preacher*, December 30, 2012, http://www .workingpreacher.org/preaching.aspx?commentary_id=1519. He develops these ideas further in his *Conversations with St. Francis* (Nashville: Abingdon, 2008).

3. All these observations are from Hossfeld and Zenger (2011: 631).

Word through which all things came into being and by which they subsist from moment to moment. So in a way, those who would call it a "game" are right. It is disorienting to think that all that is rests on a foundation no more substantial than a word. The string suspending us in existence is thin indeed. And elaborately decorated at that.

The psalm presents a divine rationale for the study of the created order. The more the psalmist knows about things that exist, the better to be able to direct their praise as choirmaster. Scholars note that other cultures besides Israel order all they can observe into lists, all the better to praise the gods or entities who make or subdue them. For example, the Egyptians' *Onomasticon* gives the "beginning of the teaching" that Ptah created and Thoth wrote down, showing "heaven with its affairs, earth and what is in it" (Hossfeld and Zenger 2011: 632). In the history of Christianity, at times verses like 148:6 have been used to shut down scientific exploration—the sun and the stars *have* to move, earth *cannot* be in motion; look at the scriptures ("he fixed their bounds, which cannot be passed")! But the psalm ought to work in the other direction. Tell me *more* about the creeping things and the great trees and the weather; let's explore with greater detail the way the heavens actually work. As St. Augustine preached, God "wanted us to praise the Lord through our study" of the things God has made (2004: 484). If all of creation offers praise, it is praiseworthy to attend to its details. A teacher of mine used to say that if creation were in rightful submission to its Creator, every scientist peering through every microscope and every astronomer through every telescope would sing the doxology at every newly garnered piece of knowledge. I would add that more do than is popularly realized.[4] One day all will. Because every particle of creation already praises God.

When Karl Barth famously called creation "the context of the covenant," he surely had scripture like Ps. 148 in mind. This is not mere nature poetry. It is the lock for which God's redeeming work is the key—each fitting the other perfectly (148:14). The psalm's final verse has often been seen as an addendum shoehorning the poem into Israel's praise. Indeed, it doesn't fit the tight poetic composition of the preceding thirteen verses (Hossfeld and Zenger 2011: 632). It may be right historically that the final verse was appended as an afterthought. But theologically 148:14 makes a crucial point—Israel is the capstone of creation, the choirmaster who directs all other creatures in praise. Canonically the psalm fits perfectly here

4. For good recent explorations of the positive relationship between theology and science, see Roger Wagner and Andrew Briggs, *The Penultimate Curiosity: How Science Swims in the Slipstream of Ultimate Questions* (Oxford: Oxford University Press, 2016).

in the final hallel of the Psalter—with Israel ever as the jewel in each psalm's setting (Hossfeld and Zenger 2011: 638). In this psalm, the God who first said "Let there be" now says "Let them praise," and Israel is the people through whom God teaches the whole created order to do just that (Spurgeon 1976: 680; Mays 1994: 444–45). Zenger suggests the final verse was added as a redactor "tried to create an encouraging assurance for Israel in the face of national impotence," likely after the exile (Hossfeld and Zenger 2011: 634). The wording makes clear the interpreter thinks the redactor failed. And yet what can the God of Israel and Jesus do with impotence and failure (1 Cor. 1:18–31)?

What does it mean to instruct creatures to praise, when the only reason there *are* creatures at all is praise (148:2)? It would seem akin to instructing cars to drive or flowers to be beautiful or stars to shine. G. K. Chesterton's line always draws an appropriate laugh—angels can fly because they take themselves so lightly.[5] Yet there is nothing more serious than praise. Angels exist to praise—and so they show us that Ps. 148 is true.[6] All that is, exists only to praise. Milton and the traditions on which he builds suggest that some angels refuse to praise precisely because God became incarnate in a human being and not an angel. Angels are greater, less fickle, more powerful. Human beings are weak, change their minds, and ultimately sin and fall. It is hard to bow low to a God who bends so low as to take flesh and die for the undeserving. Some angels refuse, and so fall. Angels that continue to praise God remind us of the incarnation.[7]

Of course we moderns know "more" data than our ancient forebears about the heavenly bodies. We know better how many thousands of millions of stars there are, the great distance away from us each is. There are not waters above the heavens, such that rain can be dumped by opening the firmament like a window. Yet the "more" we know does not always lend to greater praise. Our forebears knew better than we that each increase in knowledge should draw more praise from our lips. Ancient peoples were astounded that land was suspended above the waters and did not cascade through. The stars are suspended in the sky and do not all fall and destroy us (Hossfeld and Zenger 2011: 635). The astonishment suggests proper knowledge. Wonder is the place from which praise, science, art, and any other sort of creativity comes.[8]

---

5. Chesterton, *Orthodoxy* (New York: Barnes & Noble, 2007), 112.
6. See "Between the Cherubim" in Williams, *On Christian Theology*; and the introduction to Williams, *Wrestling with Angels*.
7. Gary A. Anderson, *The Genesis of Perfection: Adam and Eve in Jewish and Christian Imagination* (Louisville: Westminster John Knox, 2007), 21–41.
8. So argue Wagner and Briggs, *Penultimate Curiosity*.

In 148:7–13, the listing of pairs suggests totality, entirety, wholeness—not just great mountains but even little hills, not just kings but old and young women, not just the great sea beasts but also the tiny creeping worm. The deep sea terrors of 148:7 are not destroyed in this vision. They are drawn up into Israel's praise (Hossfeld and Zenger 2011: 637). What would be the equivalent of things that evoke primal fear being invited to praise? (ISIS and earthquakes and cancer—praise the Lord?) The natural wonders listed can bring death as well as life, nuisance as well as wonder (Spurgeon 1976: 680). They should all praise. Fruit trees listed include the three most prevalent in the region and the scriptures—the fig, the olive, and the grapevine—with each playing a part in Israel's and the church's worship (148:9). The cedars are not only the stateliest of trees; they are also the raw material of the temple, as creation is the raw material for the covenant (148:9). Rulers are admonished three different times and ways in 148:13—apparently they need special encouragement (Spurgeon 1976: 680). Not just the celestial order and the earthly order but also the administration by which human beings govern one another should exult. And every kind of human imaginable—young and old, female and male—with all other differences national and ethnic washed away in baptism (Gal. 3:28; Col. 3:11). The horn of Israel is a sign of strength (148:14). As in the animal world, horns are stately, dignified, signs of power and authority. To shear horns is to take away power (Ps. 75:11). To raise them is to add to it (Limburg 2000: 500; Hossfeld and Zenger 2011: 638). And they are beautiful. The very existence of so much more beauty than is "necessary" is a sign of a God who is beauty itself.

The most important fact about this unimaginable diversity of things seen and unseen is that they are there. Their intricate order and diversity suggest a God who gives coherence to things, a God who determines there to be things rather than no thing. Their—our—existence praises. God makes them all through God's own word, which of course Christians take to be God's own self all over again, a Word to be made flesh (Ps. 148:5–6; John 1:14).

This praise is not uninterrupted at the moment. In the Septuagint, the psalm's superscription mentions the prophets Haggai and Zechariah, prophets of sorrow and exile. St. Augustine notes the link and remembers that our praises for now are "accompanied by groans" (2004: 476). The psalm promises joys on the other end of sorrow the same way Easter promises resurrection on the other end of death. This sort of praise won't be fully offered or heard or universally joined in until the last enemy is destroyed. Augustine (2004: 488–89) also notices the hinge between heavenly things (148:1–6) and earthly things (148:7–13) in this psalm. They are only divided so that in Christ God can unite them. We human beings, on our own, pass away and are constantly moved (148:6). But the Son of God took from us the means to die for us (our humanity) and gave to us the divinity he has from his Father. Ever the preacher, Augustine is constantly asking why someone should believe, as wonderful as all of this is. And he asks which is more reasonable to believe—that the eternal God could do something as unbecoming as die, or that we, who already exist, should exist unendingly? The former has already happened (that we don't recognize its scandal is a sign of how deeply Christendom still informs us). Augustine asks again: which is harder to do? To make all things out of nothing, or to make human beings into angels? The former has already happened, ergo . . .

Augustine is overlaying a grammar of kenosis and discipleship onto a psalm that, by itself, can seem rather static. For in Ps. 148 everything praises as itself. The lesson, many interpreters suggest, is that everything is in its place, given by God, and should not be moved (148:6). On the contrary, Augustine thinks one thing in creation is going to move a great deal indeed—from an avowed enemy of God to adopted daughterhood and sonship. Humanity, that is. And we see now precisely why Augustine has to read this way. On our own we would preach texts about atonement and growth in grace very seldom indeed. Atonement on Good Friday, or perhaps not even then, given our squeamishness about it and folks' absence in worship that day.[9] But once we are properly schooled in the God who is near us (148:14), we see that God everywhere, especially in the scriptures God has given us with which to search for and find him over and over again.

And while humans are being transfigured from more dim to more brilliant reflections of God, all creation, from the lowest thing to the highest, will come along with us.

---

9. So argues Fleming Rutledge in the introduction to *The Crucifixion: Understanding the Death of Jesus Christ* (Grand Rapids: Eerdmans, 2015).

PSALM 149

The notes of praise are uninterrupted in these final hallelujah psalms, except for some odd notes in the middle of Ps. 149. Suddenly the exultation is over the conquest of foreign kings, with talk of vengeance and two-edged swords and fetters of iron (149:6–8). For some, these verses are not just poison in themselves. They are a glimpse into a deeper rot in the heart of Israel itself: "The Jews intoxicate themselves on the glowing and oh, so unworldly dream that at some point they will conquer pagan tyrants." This false hope leaves them in "enmity with the whole world," and yet Israel is "unable to help itself" toward that end (Hermann Gunkel, quoted in Hossfeld and Zenger 2011: 646).

But we should look again and leave behind such a harsh judgment. This is a surprising sort of victory celebration. Those celebrating do so from their "couches," not an obvious place for military conquest (149:5). It is the meek, the "humble," whom the Lord lifts up (149:4). And the nobles and kings of the nations are not executed—they are bound—a key distinction. This is not a triumphal procession in which defeated rulers are mocked and executed. Rather, the leaders of the nations come to Zion to worship. Other scholars are as sure as Gunkel that a military conquest is here alluded to and intentionally deconstructed (Hossfeld and Zenger 2011: 643). These are not weapons of war by which Israel conquers. They are weapons of praise (149:1–4). A parallel for Zenger (651) is the servant song of Isa. 49:1–13, in which military language is also invoked (a "polished arrow") and then undone, undercut. YHWH's victory is through the Word, and the benefits of his saving work are for all people, not at their expense.

Psalm 149 occupies a key place in the Psalter. The penultimate psalm is like the second. Psalm 2 proclaims the coming of the Lord's anointed, who will smash foreign kings like pottery (2:9). The New Testament sees this messianic psalm as coming true in Jesus's ministry—where the only smashing is of our rebellion. Bellicose language can be turned to a variety of interpretations. The question then is what sort of intervention into history Israel's God promises and then makes good on. Certainly Ps. 149, like much of scripture, has been used to justify violent ends.[1] We have other texts that should hem us in against that sort of reading. This psalm, read aright, is among them.

The protagonists and beneficiaries of blessing in the psalm are "the faithful," the *Hasidim* in Hebrew, referred to in the psalm's opening, closing, and middle (149:1, 5, 9). The "faithful in glory" is the linguistic center of the psalm, with twenty-six Hebrew words before and twenty-six after (Limburg 2000: 502). In fact, the faithful are the key agents in the second half of the song, more so even than the Lord (Mays 1994: 446). What is the character of this faithful people? Well, clearly, they celebrate, and not just with their voices but with their whole bodies—with song and dance and exultation. They celebrate a king at a time when there is no king—the psalm seems clearly postexilic (Berlin and Brettler 2014: 1434). The note of a military victory seems not past tense but future.[2] It seems then to celebrate a victory that has not yet happened as though entirely assured. As the *Jewish Study Bible* puts it, God has already decreed the fate of the enemy, "even if it has not yet been fully enacted" (Berlin and Brettler 2014: 1434; cf. Alter 2007: 513).[3] The eschatology here is inaugurated. That is, the kingdom has begun and is celebrated as though present in full, though it is not yet, on strictly historical grounds. The psalm's placement in the canon says something further. Its penultimate place points forward to a coming victory in Ps. 150. And the universal song of praise with which the Psalter concludes is here focused on Israel as its means, its agent, its instrument for the restoration of all things (Hossfeld and Zenger 2011: 652).

"Sing to the LORD a new song," not one newly written, but one newly enacted (149:1). It is an eschatological song called for, as in Pss. 96:1 and 144:9, and Isa. 42:10 (Berlin and Brettler 2014: 1434). Zenger (2011: 647) goes so far as to call

---

1. James Mays gives the examples of this psalm encouraging the Maccabees' armed rebellion against Rome, inciting Catholic princes to arms during the Thirty Years' War, and sending peasants to arms under Thomas Müntzer in the War of the Peasants. Mays 1994: 449, drawing on Rowland E. Prothero, *Psalms in Human Life* (London: John Murray, 1903), 152–53.

2. We cannot tell where the victory is historically, so perhaps it is "intended for an eschatological future" (Alter 2007: 513).

3. Mays (1994: 448) calls the psalm "eschatological, almost apocalyptic," with a victory envisaged as in Mic. 4:13; Zech. 10:5; 12:6.

Ps. 149 a rereading of Pss. 96 and 98. These "YHWH is king" psalms imagine a display of God's glory before the nations, which abandon their gods as idols and recognize the Lord of Israel's cosmic sovereignty. That's a lot to garner from the one word "new"! Other Christian interpreters continue this trajectory. Spurgeon (1976: 683) notes that human beings never tire of making new complaints. Augustine (2004: 492) takes the word "new" as a sign of God's coming renewal of all things.

Israel is to be glad in its "Maker" (149:2). The word suggests God's creation of all things in Genesis, God's making of Israel's freedom in Exodus, and Israel's restoration after the exile (Hossfeld and Zenger 2011: 648). The Lord also remakes the souls of the singers. The instruments suggest not just jubilation. They also suggest worship in the temple (Berlin and Brettler 2014: 1434). Augustine sees a deeper mystery. A drum is skin stretched. A lyre is gut pulled tight. These suggest a sort of "crucifixion." This is not just something that happened to Jesus. It is, for Augustine, an image for each disciple's life, promised by Christ (Matt. 16:24) and exemplified by Paul, as "he stretched forward, Christ touched him, and the . . . truth rang out."[4] Augustine knows he's being "fanciful," as some denigrate such readings, or "playful," as others praise them. That's what preaching is—helping hearers recognize Christ in places that are first obscure, then illumined and delightful.

"The LORD takes pleasure in his people" (149:4). This is the reason God chooses Israel—out of sheer delight. It makes God happy to have a people. As Spurgeon says, God loves all people, as Jacob loves all his children. But Israel is God's Joseph (Spurgeon 1976: 683). The verbs are participles—they name what God is always doing. God chooses the poor and lowly and lifts them high, crowns and exalts them, and reveals his glory through them (149:4). *Yeshu'ah*, the term translated "victory" here, is elsewhere rendered "rescue." What the God of Israel is always doing was given a name, flesh, in Jesus (Matt. 1:21). And not in him alone. As Spurgeon puts it, God "makes his people meek and then makes them beautiful" (Spurgeon 1976: 683). Even meekness, lowliness, is God's action, not ours.

A couch is an odd place from which to praise (149:5). It is an even odder place from which to wield a two-edged sword (149:6). But it is a strange God who calls his elect to ponder his law even when they lie down (Deut. 6:7). These saints rest from their labors but not from their praises (Robert Bellarmine, quoted in Spurgeon 1976: 683).

4. Augustine 2004: 498. Paul uses crucifixion as an image for discipleship in Gal. 6:14; Phil. 3:10, and elsewhere.

The second part of the psalm seems simply a revenge fantasy to some. But we should look closer. The two-edged sword is an image for the scriptures in the New Testament (Heb. 4:12). Christ insists he comes bearing a sword, but then mandates that his disciples put physical swords aside (Luke 12:51; Matt. 26:52). The kings and nobles are bound—not slain. They are being brought to Zion to worship YHWH, as in Isa. 45:14. The prophets are full of oracles against the nations (Hossfeld and Zenger 2011: 651). These are not simply angry. They are pleas that God would make good on his promises to Israel before a watching world. Isaiah already is transforming this violent language into pacific language (Hossfeld and Zenger 2011: 651). Even the holy war traditions in Israel's scripture on which this imagery draws make for odd inspiration for any literalist bloodletting. In them God's people do nothing. They only stand still (Exod. 14:14). God alone fights. Here Israel joins in God's work only by its vocation to praise. Christianity didn't start the transfiguration of these verses from invitation to violence to insistence on peace—that was in motion long before us.[5] Augustine shows the depth of mystery. Paul is in physical irons, but the nobles and kings listening to him in Acts, like Festus and Agrippa, are becoming bound to the Word of God (Acts 25–26). The mystery goes deeper still in these irons. Folks turn to God first out of fear. But that fear becomes gold once we obey for love instead (Augustine 2004: 504). The mystery is thick indeed here. A text that seems on its face outrageous, undone by the New Testament, and not fit for Christian preaching actually shows the gospel—obscurely. Some kings and nobles give up their wealth and titles for the gospel. Others keep them, as though bound. Things are upside down with this gospel, backward rather than forward. That befits a God who saves by suffering, a lamb who defeats a lion, and a fisherman who saves an emperor rather than the reverse (Augustine 2004: 504).

This is a rare but happy place where a Christian patristic interpreter (Augustine) and a modern historical critic (Eric Zenger) and contemporary Jewish expositors (Alter; Berlin and Brettler) are in surprising agreement: Ps. 149 undoes violence rather than furthering it. God chooses the unlikely and crowns them with glory. The same reversal needs to happen in our lives and world as well.

---

5. Spurgeon: "We are not executioners of judgment but heralds of mercy" (1976: 694).

PSALM 150

Psalm 150 shows us how to make an end of things.

To be a creature is to have a beginning and an end. The praises of Israel begin with a choice of two ways, one of life and one of death, and with an admonition to be like a tree and not like chaff (Ps. 1). The praises of Israel end with a symphony, a crescendo, with every single thing that breathes praising the Lord. And also the things that don't breathe but do praise: rocks and trees, dirt and sky, angels and demons. Creation begins with study and discipline on the way to wisdom in the first psalm; here in Ps. 150 we conclude with jubilation in concert with every other creature with praise for our common Creator. This praise is not *for* any ulterior purpose. It is its own reward (Hossfeld and Zenger 2011: 657). "The end is music," Robert Jenson says.[1]

This closing psalm sets interpreters to musing about numbers. The verb "praise" appears ten times—a good biblical number, signifying both the ten times that Gen. 1 tells us "And God said" and the ten words of the Decalogue in Exod. 20. God's word of creation and liberation reaches its culmination here with jubilation (Hossfeld and Zenger 2011: 658). Seven instruments are named in Ps. 150— another biblical number signifying wholeness, completeness, a Sabbath of days for recreation and celebration (Hossfeld and Zenger 2011: 658). Augustine adds to that Old Testament Sabbath the number eight, from the day of the Lord's resurrection, to get fifteen, a factor of 150. One of his favorite numerological observations comes from the Lord's miraculous draft of 153 fishes in John 21. What does

---

1. This is the concluding word to the Lutheran theologian's magisterial *Systematic Theology* (New York: Oxford, 2001), 2:369.

153 signify? Well, fifty is one of the building blocks for this culminating psalm, 150. The final three is added via any number of means—the three persons of the Trinity, or the three days of Jesus's passion and resurrection, or the three ages of history (before the law, under the law, and under grace). Seven also signifies the gifts of the Holy Spirit, which, poured out on the church, allow it to keep God's law (ten). If you add up all the numbers between one and seventeen, what do you get? One hundred fifty-three (Augustine 2004: 508–10).

Could you have guessed that?!

This is a serious sort of playing. It adds nothing to our knowledge. It simply delights in what we already know and in all the things numbers can do and show. It piles on playful interpretations one after another, just as Ps. 150 does. It shows us that scripture is about more than disseminating information. Sometimes it plays, worships, shouts. Modern interpreters often frown in disapproval of such numerology. Then they proceed on their dreary way, as if interpretation has to be unrelentingly boring to be true. Ancient Jews and Christians alike, and some of their current-day heirs, know that numbers are nearly magical. So too is everything else that exists and is here called to praise.

The Lord is to be praised both in his sanctuary and in his firmament (150:1), on earth as in heaven (Hossfeld and Zenger 2011: 655). The sanctuary can be the temple where God dwells, and that sanctuary can also be a microcosm for the whole world (Berlin and Brettler 2014: 1435). The firmament is, of course, the expanse that shuts out the waters above us. More poetically, it is the order and structure God gives to everything in creation, to suspend creatures in existence and keep chaos from devouring us (Hossfeld and Zenger 2011: 659). The Lord is to be praised for his "mighty deeds"—that is, his creating and saving purposes for Israel (150:2). These are summarized often elsewhere in the psalms (e.g., Pss. 106; 145; 147) and are here just glanced at in passing (Mays 1994: 450). God's "surpassing greatness" is often a comparison to other kings and gods, and a sign of divine "inexhaustibility" and "ubiquity" (Hossfeld and Zenger 2011: 658). Modern interpreters often blanch at supposedly Platonic descriptions like "omniscient," "omnipotent," and "omnipresent," but in moments like this the Psalter is not far from them.

Now we have a litany of instruments (150:3–5). There are seven instruments listed—again signifying wholeness, completeness. Every instrument yet devised and those not yet devised is for praise of the God of Israel. In the local church, we may be through with the decades of the so-called worship wars, as if one sort of instrument is better than another for Israel's praise. This psalm suggests the only reason any instrument exists is the same as the reason any other creature exists—for praise. The first is the most important—the shofar, or ram's horn (150:3), which sounds at key moments in Israel: to announce a feast like the Jubilee or the Day of Atonement, to signal a battle cry, to announce a victory or a new king (Hossfeld and Zenger 2011: 659; Berlin and Brettler 2014: 1435). It is a sound deeply associated with temple worship—so even as universal as this psalm purports to be, its roots remain in Israel. Scholars wish we knew more about what sorts of instruments were used in what ways in Israel's worship (1 Chr. 15:16–28; 2 Chr. 5:12–14). There is some sign of instruments both sacred and profane here, instruments both of the royal court and of the shepherd or farmer at home (Hossfeld and Zenger 2011: 660). Many are deep in Israel's memory—as in Miriam's and the other women's celebration of the exodus (Exod. 15:20). Dance also recalls David's expenditure of all his might before the ark of the Lord (2 Sam. 6:5). And of course the individual instruments are open to any number of allegories. My favorite is Augustine's observation about the cymbals: A solo cymbal is musically useless. Cymbals can only play together, just as human beings are called to touch their neighbors with respect and love (Augustine 2004: 515).

The final call in Psalm 150—for everything that breathes to praise—is also a deep echo of Israel's long praise. YHWH blows breath into the first man in Genesis. Scripture often reminds us that if God revokes our breath, we return to the dust from which we came (Job 34:14–15). At the end, breath is the only difference between us and dirt (Limburg 2000: 505). And here breath is called to be used in the only creaturely occupation worth pursuing. God gave us breath with which to praise. And here all humanity is a priest, every creature the choir, all creation the temple—and all together expend every breath in endless jubilation offered to the one who thought it was all a good idea in the first place.

The end is music.

BIBLIOGRAPHY

Frequently cited works are listed here. Other works are documented in the footnotes.

Alter, Robert. 2007. *The Book of Psalms: A Translation with Commentary*. New York: W. W. Norton.

Augustine. 2003. *Expositions of the Psalms 99–120*. Vol. 5 of *Expositions of the Psalms*. Translated by Maria Boulding, OSB. Edited by John E. Rotelle, OSA. Works of Saint Augustine III/19. Hyde Park, NY: New City.

———. 2004. *Expositions of the Psalms 121–150*. Vol. 6 of *Expositions of the Psalms*. Translated by Maria Boulding, OSB. Edited by John E. Rotelle, OSA. Works of Saint Augustine III/20. Hyde Park, NY: New City.

Berlin, Adele, and Marc Zvi Brettler, eds. 2014. *The Jewish Study Bible*. 2nd ed. Oxford: Oxford University Press.

Brueggemann, Walter. 2014. *Psalms*. New Cambridge Bible Commentary. Cambridge: Cambridge University Press.

Chrysostom, John. 1998. *Commentary on the Psalms*. Vol. 2. Translated by Robert Charles Hill. Brookline, MA: Holy Cross Orthodox Press.

Harrelson, Walter, ed. 2003. *The New Interpreter's Study Bible*. Nashville: Abingdon.

Hossfeld, Frank-Lothar, and Eric Zenger. 2011. *Psalms 3: A Commentary on Psalms 101–150*. Translated by Linda Maloney. Hermeneia: A Critical and Historical Commentary on the Bible. Minneapolis: Fortress.

Kraus, Hans-Joachim. 1993. *Psalms 60–150: A Continental Commentary*. Translated by Hilton C. Oswald. Minneapolis: Fortress.

Limburg, James. 2000. *Psalms*. Westminster Bible Companion. Louisville: Westminster John Knox.

Luther, Martin. 1976. *Luther's Works: First Lectures on the Psalms II*. Edited by Hilton Oswald. St. Louis: Concordia.

Mays, James. 1994. *Psalms*. Interpretation: A Bible Commentary for Teaching and Preaching. Louisville: Westminster John Knox.

Spurgeon, Charles H. 1976. *The Treasury of David: Spurgeon's Classic Work on the Psalms Abridged in One Volume*. Abridged by David O. Fuller. Grand Rapids: Kregel. Formerly published as *Spurgeon on the Psalms* (1968).

Van Harn, Roger, and Brent A. Strawn. 2009. *Psalms for Preaching and Worship*. Grand Rapids: Eerdmans.

Wesselschmidt, Quentin F., ed. 2007. *Psalms 51–150*. Ancient Christian Commentary on Scripture. Old Testament 8. Edited by Thomas C. Oden. Downers Grove, IL: InterVarsity.

AUTHOR INDEX

SCRIPTURE AND
ANCIENT WRITINGS INDEX

40:6 21
40:19–20 104
40:31 17, 160
41:14 54
42:10 245
43:1–21 119
43:2 58
44:9–20 104
45:1 57
45:2 57
45:14 219, 247
45:22–23 219
45:22–25 215n2
45:23 94
48:20–21 42
49:1–13 244
49:8–12 56
49:23 160, 219
51:9–11 56
51:10 53n2, 58, 158
51:11 42
53:2 27
53:3 141
54:1 97
55:12 42
56:6 219
57:13 146
58 12
60:9 160
60:21 146
61 12
61:1 39
62:12 53n2
63:4 53n2
63:11–14 216n5
64:1 221
65:9 146
65:21–22 59

Jeremiah

1:16 37n3
4:12 37n3
5:3 121
10:1–16 104
10:12 181
10:13 176
10:24 121
11:15 151
11:20 194
12:3 194
15:15 194
23:5 167n4
29 38
29:4–9 188
29:14 147
30:11 121
30:21 77
31:9 20
31:18 121

31:34 19
32:17 161n2
32:33 121
32:41 189
33:11 54
33:15 167n4
45:5 161
51:15 181
51:16 176
51:34 143

Ezekiel

1:22 193
16:27 48
16:33–34 48
20:8 48
25:13 65
32:5–6 83
34 233
34:23 65
34:23–24 76
35:6 65
38:2 131

Hosea

2:19 178
3:1 178
10:14 185
11:1–7 20

Joel

3:1 147

Amos

2:14 196
3:5 144
4:1 205n4
5:11 59
5:12 205n4
5:19 196
5:24 3
8:4–6 205n4
9:1 196
9:6 28
9:11–12 65
9:13–15 147

Obadiah

1 65, 186

Jonah

3:4 70

Micah

2:1–5 146
4:13 245n3
5:2 164
6:8 3

Nahum

3:10 185

Habakkuk

2:18–19 104

Zephaniah

2:7 147

Haggai

2:5 216n5

Zechariah

3:1–2 72
10:5 245n3
12:6 245n3

Malachi

3:6 13
4:2 31, 135

New Testament

Matthew

1:1–17 78, 83
1:20–25 147
1:21 160, 246
5:3 205
5:4 148
5:5 146, 161
5:6 60
5:14–16 93
5:28 195
5:33–37 164
5:37 112
5:39 71
5:43–47 203
5:45 71, 96
7:23 191
8:11 55
10:42 30
11:30 114
13:24–30 26, 86
13:41 210
16:24 246
17 198
17:20 101
18:3 162
21:9 119, 124
21:41–45 77
21:42–43 123
22:44 76
22:46 77
23:37 9
24:35 13
25:31–46 146
26:24 69
26:28 160
26:36–46 227
26:52 247
27:51 123
28:2 57

28:19 33, 55
28:19–20 96

Mark

1:7 66
1:41 198
4:41 61, 134
8:23–24 149
11:9–10 119, 124
11:11 124
11:23 146
12:12 123
12:36 76
12:37 77
13:2 146
14:26 95, 112
15:33 208
15:38 124

Luke

1:33 228n1
1:46–55 36
1:55 38
2:19 63
2:41–52 97, 137
2:52 1
3:23–38 83
4:18 12
4:18–19 230
6:20 205
6:45 203
12:24 234, 235
12:51 247
13:31–35 137
15 20
15:8–10 135
19:38 119, 124
19:41–44 136
20:19 123
20:42–43 76
22:31 227
23:34 71
24:21 230
24:32 18
24:44 xxii
24:47 79

John

1 32, 151
1:14 190, 242
3:16 24
4:22 60
7:38 29
10:35–36 180
11:33 198
12:13 119, 124
13:1–17 66
13:18 69
13:23 227
14:6 56, 212

17:21 168
21 248

Acts (of the Apostles)

1:8 176n7
1:9 29, 165
2:30–32 167
2:31 107
2:33 78
4:11 123
5:31 78
7 43
7:46 167
7:55–56 78, 125
10:2 106, 173
10:13 143
10:22 106
13:16 106, 173
13:26 106
13:35 107
16:14 106, 173
16:26 57
17:27 227
18:7 106
25–26 247

Romans

1–3 205
1:16 115
1:16–17 49
1:23 45
2–3 111
2:1 45
3:4 108
3:13 202
3:20 215
3:31 127
4:5 71, 146
4:16 38
5:5 29, 235
6:1–4 47
6:6 208
7 208
7:25 202
8 24n6
8:15–17 173n3, 237
8:17 173
8:18–30 120
8:30 73
8:34 78
10:4 128
10:9 49
10:18 28
11 124
11:2 115
11:11–24 115
11:13–24 64

SUBJECT INDEX